Salt Spring

Salt Spring

The Story of
an Island

CHARLES KAHN

HARBOUR PUBLISHING

Harbour Publishing
P.O. Box 219
Madeira Park, BC V0N 2H0 Canada

Cover painting by Edward J. Hughes, RCA, *Ganges, Salt Spring Island* (1982),
courtesy Dominion Gallery, Montreal.
Design and page composition by Martin Nichols, Lionheart Graphics.
Maps by Mike Simpson.
Printed in Canada by Friesen Printers.
Passages from the following unpublished material have been reprinted with the per-
mission of the authors or copyright holders: "To Nora, Margaret, Edith, and Others"
by Leonard Tolson, "Our Life on Salt Spring Island, B.C." by Rev. E.F. Wilson, "Our
Tribal History" by Charles Horel, "Please Don't Come" by Reid Collins, and "537–653:
Vive la différence" by Shilo Zylbergold.
Photograph credits: BCARS—British Columbia Archives and Records Service; SSIA—
Salt Spring Island Archives.

Harbour Publishing acknowledges the financial support of the Government of Canada
through the Book Publishing Industry Development Program and the Province of
British Columbia through the British Columbia Arts Council for its publishing activities.

National Library of Canada Cataloguing in Publication Data

Kahn, Charles, 1945–
  Salt Spring

  Includes bibliographical references and index.
  ISBN 1-55017-262-X

  1. Saltspring Island (B.C.)—History. 2. Saltspring Island (B.C.)—Biography.
I. Title.
FC3845.S27K33 1998   971.1'28   C98-910677-2
F1089.S2K33 1998

THE CANADA COUNCIL | LE CONSEIL DES ARTS
FOR THE ARTS | DU CANADA
SINCE 1957 | DEPUIS 1957

This book is dedicated to Sue Mouat,
without whom this project would never
have happened, and to Salt Spring Island
residents—past, present, and future—
for whom this book was written.

Acknowledgements

In the late 1980s, members of the Salt Spring Island Historical Society, co-ordinated by Sue Mouat, set out to write segments of the history of Salt Spring Island. This committee conducted research for several years (funded in part by the New Horizons Program), recording their extensive findings in essays based on specific subject areas. This book owes much to the research and sub-sequent support of this committee: Gordon Brown, John Crofton, Mary Davidson, Tony Farr, Ivan Mouat, Sue Mouat, June Perry, Bob Rush, Mort Stratton, Bob Tolson, Peggy Tolson, Norman Wells, and Tom Wright.

In late 1996, I was offered the research material collected by the commit-tee and the licence to use it as I wished to shape a publishable history of Salt Spring. In addition to the work produced by the committee, I found a great deal of fascinating material in the Salt Spring Island Archives. Of special interest were the many tapes of interviews with old-timers. Archivist Mary Davidson was a strong resource and supportive throughout the project. Both she and Sue Mouat spent a great deal of time helping me find my way through the island's past.

I would like to thank BC historian Dr. Jean Barman of the University of British Columbia for her comments and suggestions on the draft manuscript and for sharing some of her own research on Salt Spring history and per-sonalities. I am also most appreciative of the material supplied by author Tom Koppel and the suggestions made by both him and Ruth Sandwell, who recently completed her doctoral dissertation on the early history of Salt Spring Island. Long-time islander John Bennett also helped me ensure that my descriptions of events that took place during his lifetime were accurate.

For the photos used in this book, I am particularly indebted to Dick Toynbee, who gave me permission to use a number of photos from his excel-lent book, *Snapshots of Early Salt Spring*. Also invaluable was the compre-hensive collection in the Salt Spring Island Archives. Numerous islanders were also good enough to share their family photos. Special thanks too to island photographer Derrick Lundy who allowed me to comb his superb col-lection of photos and reproduce several in this book. Thanks too to Mike Simpson and the Salt Spring Island Lions Club for the five maps prepared for this book.

In many ways, *Salt Spring: The Story of an Island* is a community effort. It has involved many islanders who were interested, willing, and available to talk about Salt Spring Island and the people who were part of its history. In addition to those already mentioned, the following islanders reviewed all or part of the manuscript and offered suggestions: Linda Adams, Bob Akerman, Chris Arnett, Malcolm Bond, Eric Booth, Arvid Chalmers, Brenda Cornwall, Denise Crofton, Hank Doerksen, Bill Goddu, Donald "Goodie" Goodman, Tom Gossett, Bill Henderson, May Henderson, Marc Holmes, Chuck Horel, Natalie Horel, Dan Jason, Mary Kitagawa, Bob Patterson, Linda Quiring, Gwen Ruckle, Lotus Ruckle, Hank Schubart, Maggie Schubart, Mike Steeves, John Stepaniuk, Mary Stepaniuk, Manson Toynbee, Tom Toynbee, Jacqueline Watson, Don Watt, Val Watt, Bob Weeden.

The following people provided information and encouragement along the way: Ruby Alton, Joan Angus, Bob Baker, Shelagh Ballard, Geoff Ballard, Margaret (Monk) Bapty, Robbie Beddis, Dorothy Beech, Cyril Beech, Ellen Bennett, Stephanie Bond, Jackie Booth, Kellie Booth, David Borrowman, Sharon Braun, Dorothea Brown, Juanita Brown, Bev Byron, Mike Byron, Reid Collins, Barry Cotton, Athol Cropper, Gordon Cudmore, Laura Cudmore, Fred Donaghy, Rodney Filtness, John Fulker, Ted Gear, Mike Gluss, Val Gyves, Nancy and Laurie Hedger, Tony Hedger, Bob Hele, Lillian Henn Muzychka, Florence Hepburn, Barb Hicks, Ray Hill, Helen Hinchliff, Michael Hobbs, Jean Hollings, Jean Holmes, Alice Hougen, Chuck Hougen, Dave Howell, Tony Hume, Anne Humphries, Lee Hurd, Joan Ingram, Lil Irwin, Eileen King, Norah Kropinski, Edward Lacy, Molly Lacy, Kathryn Landry, Evelyn Lee, Ron Lee, Marguerite Lee, Pat Lee, Robert McBride, Macgregor Macintosh, Martha Marcotte, Maria A. "Miep" Maslovat, Alison Maude, Bob Mikado, Sam Mikado, Mary Mollet, Helen Moorhouse, Neil Morie, Don Morrison, Shirley Morrison, Gillian Mouat, Kimiko Murakami, Richard Murakami, Rose Murakami, Irene Palmer, Greg Pauker, Elsy Perks, Penny Polden, Angie Preston, Lydia Purser, Frank Rainsford, Kathleen Rathwell, Patrick Reilly, Bernie Reynolds, Tony Richards, Arthur Rumsey, Louise Rumsey, Stan Sage, Bruce Sampson, Ken Sampson, Rocky Sampson, Dennis Seward, Donald Seymour, Don Simmons, Bob Simons, Marg Simons, Naidine Sims,

Ian Simson, Sheila Smith, Janice Spearing, Bob Spearing, Jim Spencer, June Stevens, Nancy Stevens, Bev Unger, Mike Verge, Jessie Wagg, Joan Walls, Ann Williams, Brian Wolfe-Milner, Louise Wolfe-Milner. There were also many others, far too numerous to list here, who volunteered suggestions and information or answered my telephone queries. I am also indebted to the many writers, often anonymous, whose articles in the Driftwood and other newspapers provided me with invaluable material.

This book has benefited greatly from the tireless work of Judy Norget, my own in-house editor, whose comments and suggestions on innumerable drafts of manuscript helped me develop a competent text. Harbour Publishing's editors Susan Mayse and Mary Schendlinger, and production manager Peter Robson also made a large contribution to the final product. Their professional care and concern was much appreciated.

Writing this book has been a rewarding experience. Along the way, I've met countless knowledgeable, interesting, amusing, and just plain nice islanders. All of them have been extremely generous with their time and patience in the face of my endless questions, and I apologize to anyone who I may have inadvertently missed in these acknowledgements.

Contents

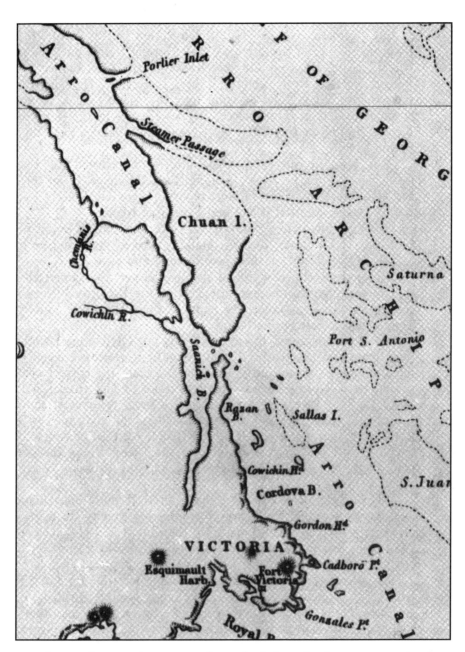

Part of a map showing Salt Spring as Chuan Island, drawn by Governor James Douglas to illustrate his "A Report of a Canoe Expedition Along the East Coast of Vancouver Island in 1852."

Introduction

Aboriginal peoples had several names for Salt Spring Island. The Cowichan called it Klaathem, which in their language means "salt." The Saanich called it ĆUÁN, which means "each end," referring to mountains at each end of the island.[1] Variations of this information have passed by word of mouth from generation to generation of Coast Salish people.

The first written mention of Salt Spring Island appeared in a letter written by Governor James Douglas in 1853, a year after he explored the east coast of Vancouver Island by canoe. Douglas believed that his discovery of salt springs on the island "would be of the greatest importance and become a wealth to the country."[2] His report was published with a map on which Salt Spring was labelled Chuan. The Cowichan had given this name, which means "facing the sea," to Mt. Tuam on the south end of the island. Over time Chuan became Tuan and eventually Tuam, which it remains today. Meanwhile, the salt springs were sufficiently intriguing for Captain Walter Colquhoun Grant (in 1849 the first settler to purchase land on Vancouver Island) to use the name Saltspring Island on a map included in his 1856 "Description of Vancouver Island."

Captain George Henry Richards, who charted much of the northwest coast between 1857 and 1863, renamed the island Admiral Island in honour of Rear-Admiral Robert Lambert Baynes, commander in chief of the Pacific station at Esquimalt between 1857 and 1860. Post-Richards maps showed the island as Admiral Island and Ganges Harbour as Admiralty Bay.

The salt springs captured the popular imagination, however, and the island became known locally as Salt Spring (two words) Island, in spite of Grant's 1856 one-word spelling. Saltspring (one word) became the island's official name when the Geographic Board of Canada adopted it in 1905, although Canada Post—with the support of many residents—still prefers it spelled as two words.

Perhaps the debate over the island's name planted the seeds of Salt Spring islanders' contentious natures. Throughout this story, you'll find accounts of islanders lining up on opposite sides of issues, and even on opposite sides of nonissues. Perhaps this can be explained by the kind of people attracted to island life—strong-willed (stubborn?), independent (perhaps isolationist?), often unconventional individualists whose opinions and beliefs cover every possible position on any idea or issue. Islanders find almost everything disputatious. Introduce an issue or express an opinion and you can expect lively debate.

Salt Spring Island covers about 182 square km and is about 27 km long and 14.4 km at its widest point. St. Mary Lake is by far the largest of the eleven named lakes on the island, and Bruce Peak at 709 m is the island's highest point.

The map of Salt Spring on the inside front cover of this book suggests the immense transportation and communications problems that early settlers faced on a mountainous island covered with old-growth forest and few roads. High ridges of uplands divide parts of the island from one another and the interior from the shoreline. Because of this geography, the early story of Salt Spring is largely the story of hard-working people in small isolated communities carving farms out of rugged terrain. It's no wonder that boats and water transportation were crucial to the early settlers and continue to be important to the island's well-being today.

Broadwell's Mountain (now Channel Ridge) cut off settlers at what is now Fernwood on the east, and even St. Mary Lake in the centre, from Vesuvius Bay on the west. The mountainous Cranberry and Mt. Maxwell area was effectively cut off from all other parts of the island and was thus one of the last areas to be settled. This upland region also separated the north and south ends, ensuring that each end of the island would develop in blissful ignorance of the other. The Fulford-Burgoyne Valley, stretching between Burgoyne Bay in the northwest and Fulford Harbour to the south, formed a large area of its own. It was cut off on the east from the Beaver Point community by the upland area around Reginald Hill and on the west from the Musgrave community by what was once termed Musgrave Mountain (now Mt. Sullivan, Mt. Bruce, Hope Hill, and Mt. Tuam).

Landings and, later, wharves developed at Fernwood, Vesuvius Bay, and ultimately Ganges Harbour in the north and at Burgoyne Bay, Fulford Harbour, Beaver Point, and Musgrave Landing in the south. Settlers visited the closest Vancouver Island port to receive their goods and mail and to ship their crops and livestock to the closest markets. For example, Vesuvius and

WHAT'S IN A NAME?

Names continue to plague the well-intentioned chronicler of Salt Spring history. Some problems are relatively minor, such as Walker Hook or Walker's Hook. Duck Bay is apparently a corruption of Dock Bay, and Stowell Lake developed from the name of an early settler named Stowe and the addition of two of the *l*'s that maps use to designate the word *lake*—Stowe L. became Stowel L., which then became Stowell L.

Salt Spring's community names can also be confusing. For example, in the past, Vesuvius and Central—called Vesuvius-Central in this book—often referred to the same geographic area. Similarly, the Fulford–Burgoyne Valley, which extends from Fulford Harbour to Burgoyne Bay, was referred to as both the Fulford Valley and the Burgoyne Valley.

Many names have changed over the years. For example, Ford Lake (named after Salt Spring pioneer Frederick Foord) started as Ford's but was changed first to Mollet's and then to Price's Lake before taking its current name. Stowell Lake was first Fisher's and then Emsley's. Roberts Lake was once Allen's. Blackburn Lake was first Conery's and then Brown's. Weston Lake was once Olsen's and later Stewart's. Maxwell Lake was once de Maines'. Tripp Road was once Mouat's. And Upper Ganges Road was once Bullock's. Bruce Peak was once the summit of Musgrave Mountain, and Baynes Peak is still the top of Mt. Maxwell.

Even the names of individuals can be problematic. In the past, some people had their names changed for them—with or without their approval—often because an immigration officer preferred an Anglicized name or thought that the new arrival would assimilate more easily with a simpler name. For example, Joseph King came to Salt Spring in the 1880s from Smyrna (now Izmir), Turkey, with another name, possibly Basilio, which was changed to King. John Stevens, the husband of King's stepdaughter, had the original Greek name Yjanaris, according to his gravestone. Sometimes writers have incorrectly identified islanders (e.g., Henry Bullock instead of Harry Bullock), and sometimes people changed their own names, as did William Patterson, who thought that his name looked better with two *t*'s (the English spelling) rather than the original Paterson (the Scottish version).

Fernwood residents relied on ships plying the routes between Victoria and Nanaimo, occasionally making the voyage to Nanaimo in their own vessels. The few residents who used Ganges Harbour relied on their own vessels to travel to Victoria. Settlers using landings at Beaver Point and Fulford Harbour travelled either to the Saanich Peninsula and then by land to Victoria or directly by sea to Victoria. Residents around Musgrave Landing intercepted ships travelling from Victoria to Nanaimo or travelled to the settlement on Cowichan Bay.

Salt Spring's communities developed independently, each with its own character and interests. To this day the character of south Salt Spring is distinctly (and proudly!) different from that of north Salt Spring, and this difference is a constant source of mostly good-natured discussion and banter.

The story of the island begins with the life of the Coast Salish people on Salt Spring's shores and continues through several periods of settlement by diverse peoples. People have always come to Salt Spring with their individual dreams. Many came to find a place where they could live free of the constraints that characterize most societies. This is still true today: almost every new islander arrives with a unique personal dream.

A WORD ABOUT SOURCES

This book is based on many primary and secondary sources: oral history accounts, government records, newspaper reports, ships' logs, unpublished postgraduate theses, and published histories. Quoted material is reprinted *almost* exactly as it first appeared; some misspellings and some punctuation have been tidied to make reading easier, where such oversights seemed accidental and changes do not distort the meaning of the original.

As much as possible, this history of Salt Spring is told in the words of islanders who were part of it. However, this does not ensure an unbiased account; it only means that the story told contains many biases in addition to the author's. Different people remember the same incident differently.

Admiralty chart, 1858–59, surveyed by Capt. G.H. Richards. BCARS CM/B892

1

In the Beginning: Aboriginal Salt Spring

ABORIGINAL SETTLEMENT

S alt Spring Island was originally claimed as Coast Salish territory, and still is.[1] Different Coast Salish nations have probably lived in the southern Gulf Islands for thousands of years. Those living permanently or seasonally on Salt Spring spoke two closely related versions of Coast Salish. Those in the south—including the Saanich, Songhees, and Sooke peoples—spoke the Lkungeneng (Straits) language. Those in the north—including the Cowichan, Chemainus, and Nanaimo peoples—spoke the Hul'qumi'num (Halkomelem) language.

Aboriginal people living around Salt Spring had a wealth of food sources. The sea provided them with almost unlimited supplies of herring and herring spawn, rock and ling cod, halibut, salmon, clams, mussels, oysters, crabs, sea urchins, ducks, sea otters, seals, and sea lions. The mouth of Fulford Harbour, near what is now the Tsawout Indian Reserve, was a particularly important herring fishery. On land, aboriginal people hunted deer and grouse, gathered berries of all kinds, and harvested the coveted roots of camas, wild carrots, and ferns.

Perhaps the most exciting events of the year for aboriginal people were duck hunts in the winter months. Fulford Harbour was a particularly good place for these hunts, as thousands of ducks flocked there to winter on the rich, sheltered estuary at the head of the harbour. Saanich men in canoes would glide into the harbour, surround the ducks, force them into a solid mass, then unleash a shower of arrows. The alarmed birds could escape only by diving under the canoes and swimming to safety. The hunters shot those trying to fly. After the kill, women who followed the hunters in their own canoes would gather the dead ducks.

Dave Elliott, Sr., an elder of the Tsartlip band, described another method of duck hunting in *Saltwater People*:

> Our people would use duck nets, they didn't shoot them. These duck nets were spread on top of the water and held up by floats. As the ducks were diving down for the herring spawn they would stick their head through a mesh and get caught. That's how our people took ducks at that time.

Aboriginal people valued the resources of the land rather than land for its own sake. Nevertheless, although never officially surveyed and registered, the territory of each group of aboriginal people was specifically defined and generally recognized and respected by other groups. Rivers, creeks, mountains, and other natural features indicated the borders of their lands. People who strayed outside their own group's area knew that they were invading

KEY DATES

3000–2000 BC	The oldest site of aboriginal habitation in the Gulf Islands is established between North and South Pender islands.
1800–200 BC	The earliest known aboriginal habitation on Salt Spring is established at Long Harbour.
1780	A smallpox epidemic dramatically reduces the aboriginal population.
1790–1850	Fierce intertribal wars take place between the Salish and Kwakiutl peoples.
1859	Nonaboriginal settlement of Salt Spring begins.
1877	The Tsawout Indian Reserve is established to the east of Fulford Harbour.

another group's space and that they might receive a hostile reception. Within their individual territories, aboriginal groups had ample space to feed, clothe, and house themselves, as well as to develop culturally. However, this did not prevent invasions from those seeking to expand their territories and increase their wealth at the expense of others. Elliott described conflicts:

> We used to fight with the northerners. They used to come down and attack our homes, our villages. Many serious wars were fought with the Haidas and the Kwagulths [Kwakiutl]. They used to take slaves when they would raid our villages. We also took slaves, if we took prisoners. This is the way it was before.

The territory of the Saanich included Salt Spring's southeastern shore and the islands east of Salt Spring and south of Active Pass, as far south as Orcas and San Juan islands. The Cowichan were dominant north of this area. The Saanich and Cowichan peoples shared the Fulford-Burgoyne Valley in Salt Spring's south end, with aboriginal people from the Saanich Peninsula on Vancouver Island claiming the valley east of Fulford Creek and those from Cowichan Bay controlling the valley west of the creek. Salish people in the 1940s told anthropologist Wayne Suttles that there was one village on the south shore and another on the north shore of Fulford Harbour.[2]

The depth of more than 130 registered midden sites on Salt Spring makes it clear that aboriginal people were visiting and living on the island for centuries before European contact. An archaeological dig in Long Harbour in 1987–88 discovered evidence of two periods of settlement. The older period dates from 2200 to 3800 years ago.[3] However, more extensive archaeological work elsewhere in the Gulf Islands suggests that aboriginal habitation predates that. For example, a site between North and South Pender islands is thought to be between 4000 and 5000 years old, and the shell middens at Montague Harbour on Galiano Island and at Helen Point on Mayne Island are estimated to be at least 3500 years old. As well, the Penelakut claim that their village on Kuper Island "has been continuously occupied (except for seasonal resource-procurement migrations elsewhere) for hundreds, if not thousands, of years. This is borne out by genealogies and by the archaeological evidence at Penelakut Spit [on Kuper Island]."[4]

Work on the 1974 archaeological dig on the property of Ray and Beth Hill at the end of Churchill Road. Photo by Ray Hill

THE BUSINESS OF CLAMMING

The island's many clam middens are the most visible evidence of aboriginal presence on Salt Spring. Rev. E.F. Wilson, writing about the island in 1895 (*Salt Spring Island, British Columbia, 1895*), felt that the middens proved that aboriginal people had been visiting Salt Spring for thousands of years:

> Twenty years or so ago it was no strange thing during the months of May or June to see the shores of Ganges Harbour swarming with Indians—500 or more in number—their long, curiously shaped canoes drawn up on the beach, the object of their visit being to dig, roast, and preserve the clam-fish. That these visits must have been made to the same spot for centuries past is evidenced by

the great depth of the clam-shell soil, three, four, and even in places as much as seven feet in depth, with trees 200 years old or more growing in it.

Wilson described how clams were processed and used as articles of trade:

> Along the shore, ... they would dig the "clams," getting them up out of the wet sand and shingle with a piece of scrap iron or a "hardak" stick made hard in the fire. Then they would make a number of holes in the beach, each from a yard to a yard and a half wide and about 18 inches deep. In these holes they would place wood and kindle fires, then throw rocks in and make them hot. On the heated rocks they would empty the clams they had dug, bushels and bushels of them, and cover them all up with mats and bags. When the mats were removed the shells were all open and the clams partly cooked. Then came the operation of "scaling clams"—scooping them out of the shell. Long, slender sticks were then procured, and the clams being threaded on them, the sticks were bent into a hoop and hung up before the fire for the fish to brown. Then they looked very tempting and were ready for market. What the Indians did not require for home use they sold or traded to the Indians of the interior.

According to Wilson, the aboriginal people also caught enormous quantities of herring, herring spawn, and smelt, some of which they traded with aboriginal people from the Interior of BC. A favourite spot for all of this harvesting was the spit sheltering Walter Bay to the south of Ganges.

This is one of three petroglyphs that Gordon Cudmore found at low-tide mark during the construction of his log dump in 1963. Authors Beth and Ray Hill suggested that these petroglyphs stood on the seaward side of a now-submerged village site in Fulford Harbour. This petroglyph is now in Drummond Park.

The Long Harbour dig found evidence of post holes at its greatest depth—the oldest period of settlement—but not at higher, more recent, levels. These post holes indicate bighouse construction rather than temporary seasonal shelters. Artifacts found in Fulford Harbour included ceremonial bowls, more likely created in a permanent settlement than brought by summer visitors.

When Anglican bishop George Hills visited Ganges Harbour in 1860, he recorded in his diary, "We pulled up to the head of the harbour & walked up a winding trail through a deserted Indian village to a log hut."[5] Was this village the remains of a permanent settlement? We really don't know. A 1974 archaeological excavation near Ganges Harbour unearthed twenty-two burials of an estimated thirty-two individuals, dating from about 1700 to 2400 years ago.[6] Wayne Suttles quoted a Saanich man as saying in about 1950 that his grandfather had a plank house (a bighouse) at or near the head of Ganges Harbour. Dave Elliott, Sr., reported that elders told him that the original Saanich winter village site was on a sand spit on the west side of Ganges Harbour (probably the spit on the outside of Walter Bay). They called it SYOWT ("place of caution").

Maps of Salt Spring archaeological sites show most sites near Ganges Harbour, Long Harbour, and Fulford Harbour. Any permanent aboriginal villages on Salt Spring would most likely have been in these three locations. An aboriginal informant told Suttles that, early in the nineteenth century, a Salish man gathered the people from Fulford Harbour, Ganges Harbour, Active Pass, Pender Island, and Stuart Island and formed a new village in Saanichton Bay on Saanich Peninsula. This seems to confirm that Ganges Harbour and Fulford Harbour were permanent settlement sites before the building of Victoria in 1843.

It is not clear why people abandoned these villages. One possible explanation is that a smallpox epidemic spread by infected Europeans in 1769 killed so many aboriginal people that not enough remained to maintain villages.[7] Cowichan people gave another explanation to anthropologist David Rozen in 1972. They suggested that the most exposed Gulf Island settlements had been abandoned because of fierce wars between the Salish and Kwakiutl. These wars from about 1790 to 1850 led to many deaths, kidnappings, and enslavements. Elliott supported this theory in explaining why the Lummi, a Coast Salish people, moved south:

> The Lummis now in the mouth of the Nooksack River in Bellingham Bay are the brothers of the Saanich people. They originated right here in what is now Shoal Harbour. That is the home of the Lummis and the reason they moved away is because they were right on the path of the Haidas and the Kwagulths [Kwakiutl] as they made their way up and down the Coast making war on other people. . . .
>
> The Lummis got so tired of being attacked all the time, they got tired of being on guard, they got tired of having to have a trained army always on the alert, and just expecting to be raided at any time, especially at night, especially during the summer weather

when the Haidas and the Kwagulths came down.... That's why they moved away.

In *Saltwater People*, Elliott also described permanent and summer communities:

> From December and through January our people did not travel. Our people came home in the fall as the bad weather began to set in. They came in from their territory to the Saanich Peninsula. The Saanich Peninsula was their home. They went out to work in their territory to hunt, gather, to fish and do whatever they had to do to get things ready again.

TREATIES AND RESERVES

Neither the British government nor the Hudson's Bay Company (HBC) made much effort to obtain title to the land from the Salish people before the first settlers arrived in 1859, although James Douglas, a chief factor of the HBC, did negotiate a few treaties involving Coast Salish lands on Vancouver Island, paying for them with trade goods. He assured the aboriginal peoples that "they would not be disturbed in the possession of their Village sites and enclosed fields, which are of small extent, and to carry on their fisheries with the same freedom as when they were the sole occupants of the country."[8]

Elliott wrote that aboriginal people often did not understand the treaties they signed:

> Douglas invited all the head people into Victoria. When they got there, all these piles of blankets plus other goods were on the ground. They told them these bundles of blankets were for them plus about $200 but it was in pounds and shillings.
>
> They saw these bundles of blankets and goods and they were asked to put X's on this paper. Our people didn't know what the X's were for.... One after another, they were asked to put crosses on the paper and they didn't know what the paper said.

Aboriginal people received small compensation for their land and then found themselves confined on reserves. In *Wisdom of the Elders*, Ruth Kirk

SMALLPOX!

In March 1862, a miner from San Francisco brought smallpox to Victoria. The virus spread quickly, especially among aboriginal people. Anthropologist Wilson Duff estimated that twenty thousand aboriginal people (one-third of the total coastal aboriginal population) died of smallpox between 1862 and 1865. Tsartlip elder Dave Elliott, Sr., described what happened:

> We didn't know of diseases like the ones brought to us by the Europeans. It wasn't the settlers who brought them, it was the explorers who brought V.D. and measles. Influenza and smallpox came up with the miners. Smallpox cut our population down to almost nothing....
>
> The Indians came down to Victoria because they could buy guns and ammunition, the foods that they were getting used to and so on. While they were here smallpox broke out in 1862. There were 10,000 Indians camped around Ogden Point, along Dallas Road....
>
> When smallpox broke out in the Indian camp the city authorities gave orders to set fire to the camps. Can you imagine that? People already sick and dying and somebody comes and sets fire to your shelter. They ordered the Indian camps burned down. They set fire to the camps.... Those people had to leave. They spread out into those islands some of them and headed for home, wherever they came from and they died all along the way. Wherever they stopped they spread the disease. They died by the thousands.

quoted an aboriginal informant: "We had a really big territory and we used every bit, season by season. But then white people put us on one little spot [in this case the present village site]."

The small, 43-acre (17 ha) Indian reserve on the eastern side of Fulford Harbour was established in 1877. Earl Claxton, Sr., of the Tsartlip band said that elder Baptiste Jimmy told him in a mid-1930s interview that there were once two bighouses on this reserve. For many years a likeable Coast Salish man, Charlie Zalt Zalt, lived there with his wife. Bea Hamilton told their story in *Salt Spring Island*:

> For some years Charlie had been planning to have a great potlatch. For this he needed wealth and he sold fish to the C.P.R. boats as they docked at Beaver Point wharf. . . .
>
> He had several fine canoes lined up in the Big House on the Reserve, and he was getting lots of Indian blankets in to give away as gifts at the Potlatch. . . . After the Potlatch, Charlie would have qualified to become a Great Chief himself, the greatest ambition

ACCORDING TO "NEEDS"

In 1873, the federal government recommended that aboriginal people receive land (Indian reserves) according to "needs," which the government defined as 80 acres (32 ha) per family of five. At the time, according to Ruth Kirk in *Wisdom of the Elders*, the British Columbia government suggested that 20 acres (8 ha) were enough for aboriginals. Although the size of the Salt Spring reserve suggests that only two aboriginal people were living on Salt Spring at that time, contemporary accounts report the visits of many more. According to the Indian Act, the title to reserve land is held by the Crown on behalf of the band, and the land cannot be sold.

of an Indian. The Indian and his wife went out as usual in their canoe on a fishing or visiting trip—and vanished mysteriously. The canoe was picked up later on the beach at Portland Island and the opinion was that the pair had been robbed and murdered for they always carried the bulk of their fortune with them—most Indians used to, we are told. The sum of three hundred dollars was found in their camp.[9]

Nobody lives on the reserve today.

Salish canoes like the one shown here were an invaluable means of transportation for aboriginal people and Salt Spring settlers alike. BCARS A-05373

2
Land for Five Shillings

GETTING SETTLERS ON THE LAND

When the United States seized California from Mexico in 1848, Hudson's Bay Company (HBC) chief factor James Douglas realized that Britain had to populate its colonies quickly and economically or lose them to American expansion. Britain gave HBC, already established on Vancouver Island, jurisdiction over Vancouver Island and the neighbouring islands from 1849 to 1859. In return for exclusive trading rights, the HBC was to encourage settlement in the colony, paying all civil and military costs through the sale of land and natural resources. Only British subjects from Great Britain, Ireland, or the Dominions were allowed to settle in the colony.

On Vancouver Island, the HBC was much more interested in making money than in establishing settlements. By 1853, the colony had only 450 nonaboriginal inhabitants, 300 of them in Fort Victoria and most of the rest in Nanaimo where the HBC was mining coal. Almost all were employees or retired employees of the HBC or its subsidiary, the Puget's Sound Agricultural Company. Meanwhile, the population of the Oregon Territory to the south had grown to more than 13,000.

In 1858, about 30,000 men, mainly Americans, passed through Victoria on their way to the gold fields of the Fraser and the Thompson rivers. When gold finds failed to live up to their expectations—often within a few months of their arrival—most would-be miners returned to the coast. Many continued

---

KEY DATES

1846 The Treaty of Washington with the United States limits Britain's sovereignty to Vancouver Island and the mainland north of the 49th parallel.

1849 Britain grants the Hudson's Bay Company (HBC) jurisdiction over the colony of Vancouver Island with the proviso that it develop an agricultural colony.

1851 HBC chief factor James Douglas is appointed Governor of Vancouver Island.

1858 The gold rush along the Fraser and Thompson rivers begins.

On August 2, Britain creates the mainland colony of British Columbia from New Caledonia (an early name for much of mainland BC).

Britain resumes full control of the colony of Vancouver Island.

1859 The first settlers come to Salt Spring.

---

south to the United States where inexpensive land was available, but others either chose to stay on Vancouver Island or could not afford to travel farther. Some asked the government for land on which to settle.

The official price for land was set at £1 (about $5) per acre. Settlers had to make a down payment of 25 percent of the total cost of their land and pay the balance plus 5 percent interest within four years. Failing this, the land would revert to the government, and the purchaser would lose his entire investment. Land on Vancouver Island was then considered expensive, especially as equivalent or better land was available for a quarter of the price in the United States. Also, Americans could pre-empt unsurveyed land by claiming a plot, using and living on it, and paying for it only after it was surveyed.

The large unemployed population in Victoria threatened the colony's security. And since few could afford the expensive land in the Vancouver Island colony, settlement was progressing slowly, which only increased the threat of an American incursion on British land. As well, Victoria merchants were pressing for the establishment of a farming community that would support their businesses. The gold rush had brought boom times to Victoria, but by 1859 it was suffering from a depression.

THE PIG WAR

The 1846 Treaty of Washington endangered good relations between Britain and the United States by leaving in doubt the ownership of Bellevue Island (now San Juan Island). Both nations claimed it. The Hudson's Bay Company had a sheep farm on the island, and American miners returning from the gold fields had settled nearby. In 1859, a miner shot an HBC pig that he had often found rooting in his potato field. This led to a confrontation that threatened to involve both Britain and the United States. Had full-scale hostilities broken out, the British would have been greatly outnumbered and the battle might have spread to Vancouver Island where, once again, the Americans outnumbered the British. A compromise solution to the "pig war" was reached just in time: the United States established a post on the south end of San Juan Island and the British established a post on the north end. Ownership of the island was finally settled by international arbitration in 1872, when Kaiser Wilhelm I of Germany awarded the island to the United States.

Indigent would-be settlers on Vancouver Island began to draw up petitions and hold public meetings in Victoria calling for cheaper or even free land. On June 13, 1859, the *British Colonist* in Victoria suggested that "public lands ought to be open to pre-emption . . . on condition of actual residence and the cultivation of a certain number of acres with improvements, and a reasonable period allowed to pay for the land." The colonial government soon decided to make land available at affordable prices.

Joseph Despard Pemberton, the colonial surveyor, responded to the public pressure for farmland by creating several rural districts on Vancouver Island. In July 1859, he reported that about 80,000 acres (32,000 ha) in the Cowichan and Nanaimo districts had been subdivided into hundred-acre lots at a cost to the government of only about one-third of a cent per acre. He told Governor James Douglas that much of the land was not worth £1 per acre and should be sold more cheaply. (He proposed 4 shillings and 2 pence—a little over $1—per acre.) However, the best that Douglas was prepared to offer at this time was a slightly lower down payment.

John Copland, a young Scottish lawyer, represented a group of men who wanted land in the Cowichan district. Since the Cowichan land had already been claimed, the government offered the group unsurveyed lands in the Chemainus district, which included Salt Spring Island. Thirty members of the group chartered the *Nanaimo Packet* on July 18, 1859, and set out to explore the district. The delegates liked what they saw and, as a result of their report, 241 people applied for land, 29 on Salt Spring.

It seems that the government's attitude toward the price of land had moderated somewhat. In an 1859 letter to Copland, surveyor Pemberton agreed that the original twenty-nine pre-emptors could settle on Salt Spring's unsurveyed lands without paying "an immediate instalment," as the government required, because they had no money.

Pemberton added that the settlers would have pre-emption rights over land on which they made improvements. He was prepared to delay surveying indefinitely, which would give settlers time to accumulate money. As in the United States, settlers would have to pay for the land only after it was surveyed. At this time, Salt Spring and Chemainus were the only places in what is now British Columbia where land could be pre-empted, although in 1860 the government proclaimed new land regulations allowing prospective settlers to stake up to 160 acres (65 ha) anywhere on the mainland, other than in a town or aboriginal settlement.

The pre-emption scheme, a government program to help poor prospective settlers, came with strings attached. Pemberton outlined rules regarding the pre-emption of land in a letter to Douglas:

- The price of the land would not exceed 5 shillings ($1.25) an acre.

- Single men could pre-empt a maximum of 100 acres, but married men were allowed to pre-empt 200 acres.

- Settlers wishing to register the land they wanted to pre-empt could do so for a fee of 10 shillings ($2.50), provided that the land did not already belong to someone else.

JOHN COPLAND:
THE POOR MAN'S CHAMPION?

Lawyer John Copland was born in Scotland in about 1822, studied law at the University of Edinburgh, and in 1852 went to spend six years in Australia. In a 1990 newspaper account, T.W. Paterson described Copland as strongly built and argumentative, and his wife as "a little Englishwoman of quick, nervous action, black snappy eyes, and a tongue once described by a victim as able to cut both ways like a knife." They arrived in Victoria in 1859, undoubtedly equal to the raw frontier society they met.

Copland's rebellious antigovernment stance quickly allied him with others in Victoria, led by *British Colonist* editor Amor de Cosmos, who opposed the authoritarian rule of Governor Douglas and the inequitable influence of the HBC. Perhaps this is why Copland fought so hard to obtain cheap land for poor would-be settlers, including many Australians. Or perhaps he wanted a share in the potential profits of land ownership on Salt Spring.

Although Copland pre-empted land on Salt Spring, he was never listed as a resident and by 1861 he had sold his land. Meanwhile, in the 1860 elections he fruitlessly attempted to represent Salt Spring in the colony's House of Assembly. In 1862, he won a seat on Victoria's first city council. Copland eventually returned to Australia.

- If two settlers claimed the same piece of land, priority would be given to the one who had registered his claim.

- Pre-emptors had to occupy their land within fifteen days of registering their claims. If they left their land for three months, their registration would be cancelled and they would have to reregister. (This proved a major problem for settlers who wanted to earn money to pay for their land by, for example, working in Victoria.)

- Pre-emptors could transfer their claims from one piece of land to another simply by registering again and paying another 10-shilling fee.

- Payment would not be required until after a government land survey was completed, and this would not be done until a majority of the registered claimants requested it, ideally within two years.

- Pre-emptors were prohibited from occupying aboriginal lands.

- The government reserved the right to expropriate land for public use.

Pemberton may have suspected that some pre-emptors were Victoria speculators. To prevent land speculation, he added two more conditions to the pre-emption of land:

- Settlers who left their land gave up all right to it.

- Settlers could not sell their land without a licence from the government to do so.

Women could not pre-empt land unless they were widowed with dependent children. Only men pre-empted land on Salt Spring.[1]

Not everyone who pre-empted land actually settled on it. Some were land speculators who never intended to move to Salt Spring; others went on to the Cariboo gold fields; still others changed their minds. Some came immediately; others took their time. The first ship to Salt Spring on July 27, 1859, carried only seventeen of the first group of twenty-nine pre-emptors.

By the end of 1859, 117 people had permission to settle on the island before surveying and without making a down payment. However, fewer than half of these people actually occupied their land before 1860. Many unsurveyed property boundaries were disputed for years. In fact, more than a decade later surveyor Ashdown Green reported that extensive acreage identified by settlers did not exist and that many boundary conflicts would have to be resolved at a later date. Pre-emptors eventually paid a dollar per acre for their land.

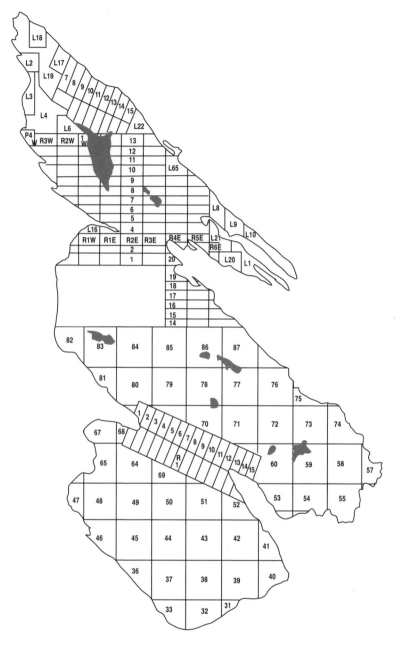

Salt Spring was surveyed in ranges (R) from east to west and in numbered sections as shown here. Beggsville (Fernwood) and the Fulford-Burgoyne Valley were the only exceptions to the strict grid pattern imposed by the government, perhaps because they were both settled very early.

Staying on the Land

Many settlers found it difficult to abide by the 1860 pre-emption condition that prevented them from leaving their land for more than a three-month period. James Shaw wrote to J.D. Pemberton:

Victoria, May 15, 1861
Surveyor general

Sir

I beg to inform you I have taken possession of lot six in a valley running east & west on Salt Spring Island right opposite Maple Bay on December 26, 1859, improvements built a house ft. 21 by 16 and cleared some land and planted potatoes and other improvements to the value $200.

My neighbours all left for the mines in 1860. I remained on the claim four weeks after they left but found it unconvenient and unprotected from Indians so I left 'til some of my neighbours returned from the mines. I was on the claim on the 26 of August 1860 and found the tools and house the same as I left them.

I got an accident. I injured one of my hands and was not able to visit my claim until March 18, 1861. I found a man in charge for Lewis Buchard. I told the man in charge not to make any improvements. I was the first settler on the claim. I have visited the claim since but did not see Lewis Buchard. Sir I hope you will give me possession of my claim. You will oblige.

Your obedient servant
James Shaw

Because Shaw had been away for more than three months without government permission, he lost his claim to the land. Often a claim jumper could take advantage of improvements an original pre-emptor had made and obtain an improvement certificate from the government, putting him a step closer to taking title. As Ruth Sandwell points out, "the pre-emption system involved a three-stage form of land 'ownership'—staking a claim, obtaining a certificate of improvement, and finally paying for the land."

At the time of the 1860 Cariboo gold rush, the government allowed restless pre-emptors to leave their land for a six-month period to try their luck at the gold fields and perhaps earn money to pay for their land. On their return, some people found that others had settled on their land in their absence. Later, the Vancouver Island Land Proclamation of 1862 allowed pre-emptors to leave their land if they appointed someone other than another pre-emptor in their place to take care of it. Nevertheless, other pre-emptors always seemed to watch who left the island, and claim jumping was common. The only way a settler could prevent it was to stay on the land until it was registered in his name.

Jonathan Begg, one of the original settlers on Salt Spring, described early land distribution:

> I found the land system in such a deplorable condition that no one out of employment of the H.B.Coy could procure an acre of the public domain. I saw that justice and reform was necessary, so I commenced a movement which has since changed the whole land system of the colony. I got up a public meeting in one of the principal hotels where strong resolutions accompanied by an urgent petition to the governor and local legislature was carried. A deputation of the most respectable citizens was chosen to wait upon the governor &c. So the movement went until the H.B.

governor and council had to submit to the popular demand. The result is we have been allowed to pre-empt for 2 or 3 years the public land to the extent of 200 acres each with the prospect of being able to obtain them at about $1.25 per acre, as by that time they will be in the hands of the local legislature who are pledged to a man to reduce them to the above figure.[2]

Jonathan Begg, John Copland, and the government all may have played a role in changes to land policy that led to the settlement of Salt Spring in 1859.

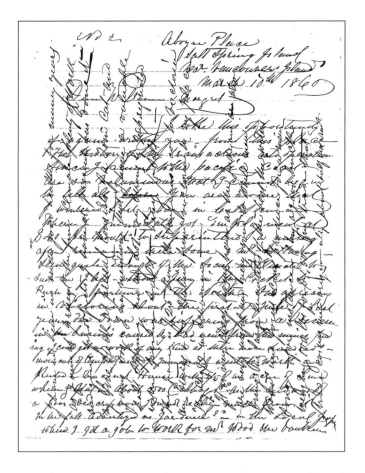

To save paper and postage in 1860, Jonathan Begg wrote his correspondence the usual way, then turned the sheet ninety degrees and wrote another message across the first one. The result looked like code and must have been a nightmare to read. SSIA

Eking Out a Living
1859–1872

THE INITIAL CAST OF CHARACTERS

The first settlers pre-empted land in the northern part of Salt Spring Island, possibly because it was most easily reached by steamers travelling between Victoria and Nanaimo. Passengers had to land by rowboat near Vesuvius Bay on the west and near Beggsville on the east, as there were no landings. Most of these pre-emptors claimed the fertile land in the Vesuvius Bay-Central Settlement and around Ganges Harbour. Small communities quickly developed in Vesuvius-Central,[1] Beggsville, and eventually Ganges Harbour.

The Vesuvius-Central area was settled mainly by two groups: Blacks, mostly from California, and Portuguese. Thirteen Black settlers arrived in 1859, and several others joined them the next year (see chapter 4). The Portuguese—John Norton, Delarvo Norton, Estalon José Bittancourt, and Manoel Antoine Bittancourt—also arrived around 1860.

On the northeast slope above Trincomali Channel, in Begg's Settlement or Beggsville, lived ambitious Jonathan Begg, former Hudson's Bay Company (HBC) employee Henry Sampson (see chapter 5), and schooner captain Edward Walker. Farther south, just west of Walker Hook, lay Edward Mallandaine's property. James McFadden, another former HBC employee, pre-empted land north of Sampson's in 1861.

John Patton Booth, who later became deeply involved in Salt Spring's political life, had land along both sides of Booth Canal. Another major would-be pre-emptor was John Ducie Cusheon, who claimed 1000 acres

KEY DATES

1859 Jonathan Begg opens his store and post office at Beggsville (now Fernwood).

The Saltspring Island Stone Company operates on the west side of Salt Spring just south of Southey Point.

1860 About seventy landowners live on the island.

1864 One hundred acres are set aside for public use at Central Settlement, where the first school is erected; John Craven Jones is the unpaid teacher.

There are five hundred head of cattle on the island.

1866 The colonies of British Columbia and Vancouver Island are united on November 19.

Dr. James Hogg, the first doctor to live on Salt Spring, is killed on his pre-emption.

1869 John Maxwell and James Lunney donate land for a permanent wharf at Burgoyne Bay.

1871 British Columbia becomes a province of Canada. The population of Salt Spring is estimated at ninety-one people.

1872 A new government wharf is built at Vesuvius Bay.

(400 ha) between Ganges Harbour and Cusheon Lake. Both men came in 1860; Booth spent the rest of his life on the island, but Cusheon quickly moved on.

The first arrivals cannily ferreted out the best farmland in this mountainous and heavily forested island, which was crossed only by deer tracks and the trails of aboriginal peoples. In 1860, two Irishmen, John Maxwell (see chapter 5) and his partner, James Lunney, established a cattle ranch at the foot of Mt. Maxwell, in the almost flat west end of the Fulford-Burgoyne Valley. The valley had easy access to Fulford Harbour at one end and to Burgoyne Bay at the other. The next year, they imported one hundred Texas longhorns from Oregon. The cattle had to swim to the beach in Burgoyne Bay from the boat that brought them to the island. About the same time, Theodore Trage (see chapter 6) pre-empted land east of Reginald Hill and eventually established an orchard.

In 1860, Norwegian-born John Sparrow settled in the Fulford-Burgoyne

A LOT OF TROUBLE FOR NOTHING

One of the most unusual pre-emption stories is that of John Ducie Cusheon, a Victoria businessman. Cusheon's name appears in the second list of pre-emptors in 1859. In a letter dated August 27, 1861, to colonial surveyor Joseph D. Pemberton, Cusheon claimed that he had acquired the pre-emptions of four other settlers in the first group of pre-emptors—Samuel Francis Stephens, Joseph Frontin, William Adams, and James Stephens—just one month after they registered their pre-emptions. Cusheon now asked Pemberton to record in his name 1000 acres (400 ha) of land, including his own 200. He planned to raise cattle and other stock.

Cusheon wrote that he had already spent $3000 to clear and fence the land, erect buildings, and clear about 5 km of road to Ganges Harbour, using the labour of sixteen men over four months. Cusheon said that he wished to buy the land from the government; Governor Douglas had told him that land could be purchased for about $1.25 per acre. But the government could not sell unsurveyed land, and if Salt Spring land were surveyed at this time, every other pre-emptor would have to pay for his land immediately, which was impossible. Cusheon was permitted to buy only his 200 acres (80 ha) and he left the same year for the gold rush in the Cariboo. Only his name remained—in Cusheon Creek, Cusheon Cove, Cusheon Lake Road, and Cusheon Lake.

Valley east of John Maxwell and played an increasingly energetic role in the quickly developing valley community. Nearby was Joseph Akerman, a market gardener from England who had settled first in Victoria, growing produce on the site of today's provincial legislature. In 1862, Akerman chose land straddling Fulford Creek about midway up the valley. In the same year,

Frederick Foord chose the pretty basin above Fulford Creek surrounding the lake that now bears his name.

In 1864, Michael Gyves pre-empted land among giant cedars just north of Akerman. He had originally emigrated from Ireland to New York where his brother lived. Unable to find work there, he joined the US Army and was posted to San Juan Island during the British and American dispute over the island's ownership. After his discharge, he moved north, trying his luck in the Cariboo gold rush before returning to Victoria. There he met John Maxwell, who encouraged him to settle on Salt Spring and find a house-keeper and wife. He soon met his life partner—Ṯuwa'H Wiye, later known as Mary Ann "Granny" Gyves—the daughter of a Cowichan chieftain. Gyves produced cedar shakes from his fine pre-emption, rowing them to markets in Sidney and Victoria.

Other south-end communities were settled later. When Henry Ruckle arrived in 1872 (see chapter 6), there were already several cabins in the

Michael Gyves pre-empted land in 1864 and made his living by cutting cedar shakes. Courtesy Val Gyves

Ṯuwa'H Wiye (Mary Ann "Granny" Gyves), daughter of a Cowichan chieftain and common-law wife of Michael Gyves. Courtesy Val Gyves

Beaver Point area, probably built by men of Hawaiian descent. Also in 1872, William Lumley was among the first to settle in the south-end community of Isabella Point. He later married a daughter of a Hawaiian-born settler. (For more about the Hawaiians, see chapter 7.)

Almost all the early settlers were single men. A few, such as Theodore Trage and Henry Spikerman or John Maxwell and James Lunney, arrived together and worked as partners. Others undoubtedly helped each other as much as possible in an isolated community where distances between homesteads were relatively great and unmanageable without roads. Several took aboriginal wives, usually without traditional religious or civil ceremonies, and had large families, who were a great help on the farms. Descendants of many of these pioneers still live on the island.

GETTING ON AND OFF THE ROCK

Transportation and communication, among Salt Spring settlements and between them and their Victoria and Nanaimo markets and suppliers, posed a major challenge. At first, each island settlement traded with its closest centre: the south end with Victoria and the north end with Nanaimo.

Settlers brought sailing vessels with them, and some, such as E.J. Bittancourt, provided a transport service for their fellow islanders. Most people, however, relied on the traditional Salish canoe to get around, sometimes with Salish paddlers. It was the Salish who had taken the Akerman family and their belongings 11 km from the Saanich Peninsula to the mouth of Fulford Creek in the early 1860s. In the next decade, pioneer author Margaret (Shaw) Walter of Galiano Island, and later Salt Spring, recorded how her neighbour, Elizabeth Griffiths of Salt Spring, managed to collect her mail:

> There was no post office near us in those days, so she had our mail matter collected along with their own when it arrived at Vesuvius Bay, then the only port of call and

distributing centre for steamers on the northern half of
Salt Spring Island; and sent it over to Galiano—perhaps
once a month, by a special Indian, "Capt." Peatson he
called himself [Peatson's aboriginal name was Hul-ka-
lalkstun], brother to Capt. Verygood, in whose largest
canoe Mrs. Griffiths made her business trips to Victoria
or Nanaimo as the case might be. These two brothers
were rather outstanding natives.... When his [Capt.
Peatson's] little canoe reached there—about a four-mile
journey, he would shout for one of my brothers to come
and help him. It was generally next day before he left.

Sloops and schooners such as the *Nanaimo Packet* that passed Salt
Spring en route between Victoria and Nanaimo were unable to load
directly without landings or wharves. So at first, weather permit-
ting, crewmen would whistle for canoes to come alongside to pick
up or deliver mail, passengers, or freight. Sailing schooners arrived
unpredictably in these early days and couldn't be depended on. All
settlers needed access to a canoe, skiff, raft, or dugout to reach ships
or travel to Vancouver Island.

Vessels en route to Victoria or Nanaimo sailed past both sides of
Salt Spring. In a letter to his sister and brother-in-law dated March
10, 1860, Jonathan Begg in Beggsville wrote: "Schooners pass to
Victoria by my place from Nanaimo about 3 times a week, and we
have a weekly mail. I am Post Master...." Sylvia Stark remembered
arriving in 1860 on a sailing vessel that dropped passengers and
freight on the northwest side of the island.

The first landing was probably built at Vesuvius Bay. From 1864
to 1866, the SS *Fideliter* regularly stopped there with mail on its run
from Victoria to Nanaimo. (A new government wharf was built at
Vesuvius Bay in 1872.) Meanwhile, in the south end, Maxwell and
Lunney donated 3 acres (1.2 ha) to establish a wharf at Burgoyne
Bay in 1869.

A rough road from the St. Mary Lake area to Vesuvius Bay was probably the first on the island. But the farmers at Beggsville were still isolated. In 1865, Edward Mallandaine and Jonathan Begg requested that the *Fideliter* call at Beggsville as well as Vesuvius Bay, since travel across the mountain from Beggsville to Vesuvius Bay was extremely difficult and hauling produce was almost impossible. The Vancouver Coal Company, which owned the ship, refused. Company officials instead suggested that Beggsville settlers cut a road through to the quarry north of Vesuvius Bay. Louis Stark, who had industriously put roads through his own property and volunteered his labour to put connecting roads through other people's land, pleaded with the chief commissioner of land and works: "A sentral [sic] road is all that we ask for and let us make little roads and pigtrails to come to it by our own labour." Although every male Salt Spring landowner over age eighteen was supposed to devote six days a year to building roads, most early pre-emptors were either absentee landowners or too poor to donate the time. Resources for road building were not available until British Columbia joined Canada in 1871.

HOW THEY FARED

The first settlers on Salt Spring had enormous problems to overcome. They found most of the land heavily forested. There were no roads, no wharves, no regular transportation to and from the island, no stores, no mail service and nobody to ask or hire for help. Most pioneers were poor and had chosen Salt Spring mainly because they could pre-empt land and pay for it years later. They lacked farming experience, money, and the equipment necessary to hack homes and farms out of the forest. Many had minimal food and clothing, and all had to worry about cougars (which they called "panthers"), wolves, and bears. They also faced the hostility of some aboriginal people who saw them as trespassers (see chapter 5).

The settlers' first task was to clear land and build shelters. They began by clearing plots large enough to build their cabins out of the way of falling trees. Clearing land was a long, labour-intensive process, and the settlers had to burn almost everything they cleared. Marie Wallace, a daughter of Louis and Sylvia Stark (see chapter 4), who were freed slaves who arrived via California, remembered the process:

> Dad and the boys worked hard with axe, saw, and auger, working the hard way, but they soon cleared the logs from around the house. They felled trees, bored holes on both sides of the tree, kindled a fire in the holes. The holes measured rail length. When they burned through, they were split in rail lengths for fencing. They cut and dried the wild meadow grass for the cattle in winter time. But they soon raised a big field of tame grass around the house.

Wood was saved only for houses, barns, and snake fences. A pall of smoke must have drifted over Salt Spring for generations, since this slash-and-burn method of clearing the forest was legal until the mid-1920s.

Early dwellings were primitive at best. Elizabeth Griffiths, the daughter of Mr. and Mrs. Thomas Henry Lineker, who settled in Ganges Harbour in 1859, said her family's first home in gold-rush Victoria was made of hastily sewn-together HBC blankets. On Salt Spring, the family occupied a log cabin with an earth floor; their only source of light was a wick dipped in oil. Elizabeth and her brother dug clams and netted herring, often their only food for days at a time.[2] Jonathan Begg "erected a cabin—14 x 17—it is a log one and covered with shakes on poles, being altogether more open than a house that would freeze to death a cow in winter in Canada [probably southeastern Ontario], with nothing but a small fireplace and mud floor, yet so beautiful is the climate that I have passed the winter in it very comfortably."[3] Louis and Sylvia Stark arrived in 1860 to find:

> an unfinished log cabin [started by a settler who had changed his mind] surrounded by trees and thick underbrush. It was anything but encouraging. It called for work, in which she [Sylvia] would have to take part. . . . They hung a quilt up for a door, and the neighbors came and helped Mr. Stark to put a roof on the house

Settlers used a stoneboat, a wooden sleigh pulled by an ox or a horse, to remove stones from their fields or to transport other objects. In this photo, Joe Nightingale, who settled in the Fulford-Burgoyne Valley in the 1880s, moves a sack of feed. SSIA

to keep out the rain. Sylvia...found it hard to get used to their wild surroundings. It was so lonely, being located in an isolated place quite a distance from the settlement.

Once settlers had cleared an area of trees, they could farm among the stumps, which they would remove over many years. Their first crop was usually potatoes or peas, which they could plant even when stumps prevented ploughing or the farmer could not yet afford oxen and a plough. Until the 1880s, there were no horses on the island, but every farmer who could afford it bought a yoke of sturdy, placid oxen, much preferred to horses. Marie Wallace described her parents' early farming experience:

There were no tractors. [Louis] Stark made a homemade tractor. Finding a V-shaped body of a tree, he put a coulter in the end and spikes along the sides. They called it a drag. Hitched to a pair of oxen, it proved effective in tearing out roots and cultivating the ground.

Stark was reared on a fruit farm in Kentucky. He grafted and planted fruit trees among the stumps. His plan was to have the fruit trees coming on while the stumps decayed. In time they would be easy to dig out.

They soon had enough land cleared to plant grain for their own use. They kept chickens, turkeys, and pigs. The bears caught some of their pigs, the young ones, and the turkeys ran wild. When they wanted turkey, they had to shoot them from the trees.

Begg's store became a nucleus for the northern community. Begg, with seemingly boundless energy, functioned as a one-man chamber of commerce. Less than two months after his arrival on the island, he wrote a letter to the *New Westminster Times*, which was printed and distributed in Victoria:

> Salt Spring Island,
> Sept. 19, 1859.

> Sir: It would be a great boon to the settlers of this Island if arrangements could be made for the establishment of a branch post office here, as under present circumstances we are put to the inconvenience and expense of going to Victoria, a fact which to a beginner is a matter of vital importance. I may observe that it will entail no expense upon the expenses of this Colony, as the packet which carries the mail to Nanaimo, calls at this island weekly.

> I am, Sir, your ob't. serv't.,
> J. BEGG.

Just a few days later, on Saturday, September 24, 1859, the same newspaper featured Begg's unabashed boosterism:

> SALT SPRING ISLAND.—From Mr. J. Begg, one of the first, and most respectable of the settlers, on Salt Spring Island, we are rejoiced to hear a most satisfactory account of the prospects of their happy little community. The settlement of the land is progressing

favorably, and considering all circumstances, rapidly. Cabins are being built, ground being cleared, and other difficulties disappearing before the energetic labourers who have undertaken the task of pioneers.... The salt springs of this Island will probably some day prove of great value—some parties have boiled down the water from these springs, and from 5 quarts of water obtained one quart of pure excellent salt. There are extensive free-stone deposits in many parts of the Island, the value of which can hardly be too much appreciated.

EXPENSIVE LETTERS!

Until 1860, mail from the Vancouver Island colony was delivered courtesy of the Hudson's Bay Company on ships bound for San Francisco, Panama, and Europe. The postal rate to a foreign destination was the US rate for that destination plus 5 cents. A half-ounce (14 g) letter to Australia cost 48 cents and one to Britain 34 cents; in 1858, a letter to the United States via California cost 33 cents. At this time, as Begg wrote in his letters to his sister and her husband, a pound of turnips cost a cent, a pound of butter 50 cents, a buck $1 to $1.50, and a 10- to 20-pound salmon 12 1/2 cents. And many colonists eventually paid only a dollar per acre for their land! So people thought carefully before mailing letters.

In 1860, the main post offices in the colony of Vancouver Island were in Victoria and Nanaimo. Three years later, unlicensed ships were offered a tax break for carrying mail to Nanaimo, Salt Spring, Comox, and Cowichan. At this time, the licensed steamer *Emily Harris* was carrying most of the mail between Nanaimo and Victoria at no charge. Even in 1865, however, mail to Britain from Vancouver Island was still being delivered via the United States.

Statistics for these early days can only be approximate, as the sources vary so greatly in their estimates. According to Begg, the population of Salt Spring Island was 50 in March 1860.[4] On August 23 of the same year, the *British Colonist* recorded the number of landholders as almost 70. An 1865 history of the area states that Salt Spring was "inhabited by 70 or 80 settlers," which would suggest little increase between 1860 and 1865 (if all these figures are correct).[5] Still another estimate in 1866—this time by a visiting minister— gave the population of the north end of the island alone at "17 couples, 22 single men, and 42 children." Although he did not visit the south end, its population was estimated at about 15 to make a total of 113 for the whole island.[6]

Many settlers had large crops of barley, oats, and potatoes and were raising cattle, pigs, and other animals for the Victoria market. The Salt Spring Island Agricultural Association was formed in 1860. The *British Colonist* estimated that there were more than five hundred head of cattle on the island in 1864, and in 1868 island farmers began to participate in the annual exhibitions of the brand new Cowichan, Salt Spring, and Chemainus Agricultural Society.

When George Hills, the Anglican bishop from Victoria, visited Salt Spring in September 1860, he found a thriving community:

> The plots are laid out in oblongs of 200 acres each. In the whole island some 8000 acres are taken up. . . . Although hardly a year has elapsed, yet much has been cleared. A log barn has been built upon each. Some three or four acres have been brought under cultivation in each lot. Garden produce of all sorts is to be seen. Cabbages, potatoes, beetroot, onions, tomatoes, peas, cucumbers, watermelons, carrots, etc., & wheat & oats, [also] pigs, poultry & calves.
>
> The soil is good generally, a light kind, some very good black loam, a great deal of this latter principally in the valleys. I should say there is no better land in British Columbia that I have seen, nor in Vancouver Island. There is considerable wood to be cleared, but extensive open ground [is] covered with fern. The timber is not heavy or thick. There is good water from wells. Grouse are to be had. Deer in abundance & good. Fish plentiful. Miss Lineker today was at the water's edge raking in smelts. We

had some for dinner & capital they were. In winter wild fowl are abundant. Mr. Lineker told me he could come down & shoot as many as he wanted whenever he liked. The settlers complain of the hawks, the chicken hawks who pounce upon the chickens at the very door of the house.

Single white women were few in the colony. In the diary of his 1860 visit to Salt Spring, Bishop Hills noted: "There are sixteen settlers [in the northeast part of the island], mostly young men. Nearly all are living with Indian women." Among the first settlers who took aboriginal women as common-law wives were Henry Sampson, John Maxwell, Theodore Trage, and Michael Gyves. According to Margaret Walter, whose family settled on Galiano Island in the late 1870s, the HBC encouraged former employees "to take a Native woman and settle down."[7] Several apparently followed this advice on Salt Spring. Mrs. Walter wrote with great respect of the aboriginal wives:

> These native wives...adapted themselves in a surprising degree to the white man's ways—learning also to speak English more or less. One thing seemed curious in this direction. The mother often spoke to the children in her own tongue but the youngsters invariably answered in English—at least those we knew did. And, while these wives might be docile, this did not mean subservient. Should conditions become too uncomfortable there was always the tribal reserve to fall back on, and hubby had to choose between seeking them out there or having his domestic arrangements put out of gear. This used to amuse my mother, who thought they were more independent in various ways than their white sisters. But such disagreements seemed to happen seldom and the union was as a rule kept loyally on both sides. As time went on they might be moved, or persuaded to marry legally, and one of such events we knew of, took place when the father and mother were married, and their grandchild christened on the same day.

The Anglican Church, which opposed mixed marriages, arranged for the importation of single, unemployed young women from Britain as potential wives for unmarried colonists. In September 1862, sixty-two women arrived in Victoria aboard the first bride ship. They were described in one article in the *British Colonist* as "60 select bundles of crinoline" and in a later report as "mostly cleanly, well-built, pretty looking young women—ages varying from fourteen to an uncertain figure; a few are young widows who have seen better days. Most appear to have been well raised and generally they seem a superior lot to the women usually met on emigrant vessels." In honour of their arrival, businesses in Victoria closed and prospective suitors eagerly rowed out to the boat. The women were described as future governesses or servants, but everyone knew they were really destined to marry settlers. Another thirty-six women arrived in January 1863 aboard the *Robert Lowe*.[8] Joseph Akerman was one of the eager young men greeting this ship, and he was rewarded when Martha Clay agreed to become his wife. The Akermans raised eight children: Fanny, Joseph Jonathan, Tilly, Martha, George Edward (Ted), Jim, Tom and Bill.

Salt Spring's small population ensured that families would increasingly intermarry. Akerman's son George Edward (Ted) and Mike Gyves's daughter Ellen's marriage, for example, united two Fulford-Burgoyne Valley pioneer families. Some original families have multiple connections.

Most services were difficult or impossible to obtain in Salt Spring's pioneer society. The community was fortunate that a recently retired English physician, Dr. James Hogg—who had come to Canada with his daughter, the future Mrs. J.D. Cusheon—took over the Lineker pre-emption in the early 1860s. Hogg was reported to be "peculiar in some way but trustworthy professionally."[9] According to Marie Wallace, for example, Hogg successfully treated Louis Stark's severe reaction to a smallpox vaccination, reducing the swelling of his arm with cold compresses made of mud from the bottom of a spring. Unfortunately, Hogg died in 1866 not long after upbraiding an aboriginal man named Willie for stealing produce from his garden. The September 17 *British Colonist* reported, "an inquest was held by the Cowichan Magistrate, and a verdict returned of death from natural causes." The settlers suspected but couldn't prove his murder.

Outlaws, aboriginal and otherwise, also preyed on relatively helpless homesteaders. There was no law enforcement until 1872, when Henry Sampson was appointed as the first constable.

Wild animals—cougars, bears, and wolves—threatened lives and required a close watch on poultry, livestock, and children. Until islanders learned to cope with the wild environment, they had many frightening experiences.

THE CZAR OF SALT SPRING

Salt Spring has always had its share of eccentrics, but the "Czar of Salt Spring Island" must have been one of the oddest. The May 6, 1861 issue of the *British Colonist* reported that a man named Rowe gave himself that title:

> Rowe, the crazy surveyor, is said to have taken up residence on this pleasant little island, built him a hut, and declares himself czar of the whole concern—Vancouver Island included. He carries two revolvers and a double-barrelled shotgun, and threatens with bodily injury everybody who presumes to approach his habitation. Whenever opportunity offers, he issues proclamations commanding his "faithful subjects" to perform all sorts of ridiculous services. He is considered a great nuisance by the settlers, who talk of sending him to Victoria to be cared for.

Apparently, Rowe would often pretend to have been attacked by aboriginal people in the early morning hours. His cries for help and shots from his revolvers disturbed everyone within earshot. They responded several times to these "emergencies" before learning to ignore them. When Rowe began making whips with which to torment his subjects, islanders gave him a wide berth and ultimately ignored him. In October 1861, according to the *British Colonist*, they were saved from Rowe's histrionics when he was murdered in Saanich for his guns and blankets by Cowichan people.

Margaret Walter recounted two of Martha Akerman's encounters with cougars:

> She told of one evening taking poultry from their fowl house to another, some distance away. Her husband was also carrying some, and on the other side of the fence dividing what was probably a field from the road or trail where they were walking, a panther kept pace with them and the squawking hens in their hands. This got on his wife's nerves and she cried out, "Joseph, if this beast follows us any longer I will drop the fowls," but her husband's only reply was, "Don't drop the fowls."
>
> Another experience must have given her a great shock. While busy at some gardening work near the home when her husband was elsewhere, she laid her baby girl on the ground while she went on with her task. Happening to lift her eyes later on she saw a panther walking down between the rows toward her little daughter. With no weapon at hand she ran screaming toward it and it must have been fairly close for she spoke of lifting her foot as if to thrust it away. Whether it was the movement, however, or the sound of what would be frantic screaming, the animal turned back and left them. She said little about her feelings in the matter, but her quiet remark,"I did not sleep much that night," told its own story.

Winter greatly magnified all problems in the isolated farms and spread-out communities. The winter of 1861–62, the first for many settlers, was especially fierce, with ice, snow, and extremely low temperatures. Settlers lost more than a hundred head of cattle and ran short of food and firewood. The winter was equally hard on wildlife, poultry, and other livestock. Desperately hungry wolves and cougars attacked domestic stock and even humans. Mail delivery and other communication with larger communities on Vancouver Island halted for weeks. In May 1862, the *British Colonist* reported that one-third of the settlers had left the island. Those who remained learned from their experience and managed better in the following, almost equally bad, winter.

From the outset, homesteaders had to look beyond their lonely pre-emptions to the outside world for both their supplies and their markets. No one

Willis, the oldest child of Louis and Sylvia Stark, had a lifelong reputation as a great cougar hunter. Photo by Jessie Bond, SSIA

was entirely self-sufficient. In addition to some hardware, hand tools, coal oil, flour, seeds, shoes, blankets, seed potatoes, and the almost indispensable oxen, even some staples such as flour, sugar, tea, oatmeal, and salt had to come from Victoria or Nanaimo. Begg's store supplied some of these goods, but residents in the roadless south end of the island travelled by boat to Victoria or Nanaimo for their supplies. Fortunately for Salt Spring farmers, the expanding cities also provided almost unlimited markets for their surplus produce.

SURVIVING IN AN ISLAND WILDERNESS

Most farmers had modest harvests of small fruits (Salt Spring's famous orchards were not yet producing) and vegetables, and sometimes raised chickens and pigs. John Maxwell, who shipped about twenty head of cattle a month to Victoria, was far and away the island's largest exporter of food. Others like Theodore Trage, who rowed his strawberries and other small fruits to Victoria, were more typical.

Jonathan Begg was an active and ambitious merchant. Soon after he arrived in 1859, he started his Salt Spring Island Store and quickly renamed it more grandiosely "The Balmoral Store." It included a post office, probably unofficial at that time. The Balmoral Nursery soon followed, selling flowers, ornamental shrubs, and fruit trees. According to Salt Spring author Bea Hamilton, Begg allowed no spitting in his store or swearing when women were present, enforcing this policy with vicious swipes of his broom. He often accepted produce and game in exchange for goods. Begg also served as returning officer in the 1860 elections, a road commissioner, and a director of the Salt Spring Island Agricultural Association.

Begg sold out and left the island in December 1863. No one knows why he sold or where he went, perhaps back to his native Scotland or to join his sister and brother-in-law in the United States. Richard Brinn and Thomas Griffiths took over the nursery. On June 7, 1864, the British Colonist reported that the nursery "may safely be set down as the largest in the whole colony of Vancouver Island." Decades later the James Brothers Seed Company would operate from the same favoured location.

Industry flourished early on the island. In 1859, five men (Henry Elliot, William Senior, John Lee, Robert Leech, and E. Williams), who subsequently left for the Cariboo gold rush, started the Saltspring Island Stone Company, which operated for about a year just south of Southey Point. In 1860, Bishop Hills described another business operated by "four Germans... occupied in cutting shingles for roofing & staves for salmon casks from the cedar." A few years later, Michael Gyves was cutting cedar shakes from the huge 2-metre-diameter trees that had attracted him to his pre-emption in the Fulford-Burgoyne Valley.

Organized religion soon arrived on Salt Spring. In 1860, Anglican Bishop George Hills celebrated church services in settlers' homes. Rev. Ebenezer Robson, a Methodist missionary from Nanaimo, preached in a Black settler's home on February 21, 1861. About sixteen months later, Robson gave a service in a log cabin at Central, built at his suggestion as a schoolhouse. William Robinson, a Black settler, offered a Sunday school class for children in the same building. Also in 1862, Rev. R.L. Lowe of the Church of England (known as the Anglican church today in Canada) began to visit Salt Spring. His first services were held in private homes.

In 1865, Ebenezer Robson began monthly Methodist services in the Central Settlement schoolhouse. The Church of England followed suit in 1869, when Rev. W.S. Reece of Maple Bay began monthly visits to the island. Early ministers, all of whom lived on Vancouver Island, often faced dangerous and uncomfortable travel to and from Salt Spring, as Robson's diary suggests:

> Left early and paddled against a strong wind till about 10 1/2 a.m. when we rounded the southerly point and hoisted sail. After about 2 hours sailing we came to an Indian house on Salt Spring Island and as our canoe was not sufficiently large to endure the gale we hired an Indian with a large canoe and took ours in tow. As soon as we had started from shore the wind, which was very strong, carried the canoe forward with such speed that it became unmanageable—the Indians could not keep it to its course and instead of running up the channel we ran across and were obliged to come to under the shelter of an island. After a short rest we started again. The wind was blowing in a gale, the Indian in charge of the canoe became terrified, his squaw began crying, the sail was carried away from the mast, and finally the owner of the canoe refused absolutely to go further. This was about 8 p.m. so we went on shore in the cove of an island and camped for the

night. I supped on boiled herring & potatoes and lay down to sleep on a wet mat and covered myself with a shawl during the night the rain frequently awoke me by pattering down on my head.

Education was another need of early Salt Spring residents. John Craven Jones, a Black schoolteacher with a first-class teaching degree from Oberlin College, Ohio, taught Salt Spring's youth, possibly as early as 1861.[10] He offered classes in the log cabin in Central Settlement. He served both the Beggsville and Vesuvius-Central settlements without pay until the 1869 creation of Salt Spring Island School District, when he was given an annual salary of $500.

In a remarkably short time, a pattern of life and community emerged on Salt Spring. On August 7, 1865, the *Nanaimo Gazette*'s correspondent described the island in glowing terms:

> Having recently visited Salt Spring Island, you may be glad to hear that the settlers there on the whole, so far as I could ascertain, are well satisfied with their prospects this year, and are all diligently employed in adding to their improvements and in preparing for the in-gathering of the harvest, which bids fair to exceed in quantity and quality that of any previous year....
>
> ... Let me add that, if any one wants to rusticate for a few days he could not enjoy himself better than by spending them amongst the hardy pioneers of Salt Spring Island.

In 1871, Rev. W.S. Reece estimated that ninety-one people lived on Salt Spring.

4

The Black Community

WHY THEY CAME

Many of Salt Spring Island's first settlers were Blacks who came from San Francisco. Some were former slaves or children of slaves, but all were free citizens of the United States when they immigrated to British Columbia. They included merchants, miners, farmers, and teachers, among others. All shared a desire to escape discriminatory California law and to live fully as free citizens. Like many settlers, they had little money. The offer of free land drew them to an island wilderness.

Around 1960, in her nineties, Marie Wallace, a daughter of one of these families, recorded her mother's (Sylvia Stark's) account of the emigration:

> The coloured people in California were becoming alarmed over general agitation under southern pressure to make California a slave state. In 1852, the federal government had passed a law permitting the return of fugitive slaves fleeing to northern states to be returned to their owners in the South. . . . Furthermore the state legislature had taken what appeared to be the first steps against the coloured race. The effect was to deprive them of the ability to protect their property from spoliation by the white man. By these acts coloured people were disqualified from giving evidence against a white person. . . .
>
> The emancipation of the slaves in the United States was a burning political question. The Negro people were dissatisfied with the

KEY DATES

1858 Blacks from San Francisco send a delegation to Governor Douglas to inquire about the prospects of emigrating to Vancouver Island. After a favourable reception, about six hundred people move north.

1859 Thirteen Blacks, with and without families, pre-empt land on Salt Spring Island.

1861 John Craven Jones begins teaching school at Central Settlement.

1868 William Robinson and Giles Curtis are murdered in their cabins within eight months of each other.

1869 Abraham Copeland is elected to Salt Spring's first school board.

1873 John Craven Jones and Henry W. Robinson are elected to Salt Spring's seven-member council.

1875 Louis Stark moves to the Nanaimo area.

laws of the country. They met at San Francisco to discuss how best they could improve their hard lot.

A committee was sent to B.C. to interview the government. Governor Douglas received them and extended them a cordial welcome to establish themselves on British soil. As a result of this favourable report by the committee, fully 600 coloured people came to B.C. . . .

Sylvia Stark remembered that a delegation of coloured people called on Governor Douglas requesting permission to form a colony of coloured people on Salt Spring Island about that time, but he refused, saying it would be to the best interest of all to have a mixed settlement.

Most of the sixty-five-member delegation soon settled in Victoria, but one delegate returned to San Francisco to report glowingly on the delegation's findings. The Blacks to whom he reported decided that their best course was to emigrate to Vancouver Island.

Mifflin Wistar Gibbs, a businessman born in Philadelphia, was one of the Blacks who came to the colony of Vancouver Island from California. He trained as a lawyer in Victoria, became a member of Victoria's city council in the 1860s, and was Salt Spring's delegate to the 1868 Yale Convention, which decided that British Columbia would join the Canadian Confederation. Gibbs recalled:

> We had no complaint as to business patronage in the State of California, but there was ever present that spectre of oath denial and disfranchisement; the disheartening consciousness that while our existence was tolerated, we were powerless to appeal to law for the protection of life or property when assailed. British Columbia offered and gave protection to both, and equality of political privileges. I cannot describe with what joy we hailed the opportunity to enjoy that liberty under the "British lion" denied us beneath the pinions of the American Eagle.[1]

Gibbs returned to the United States in 1869, however. The Blacks who stayed settled throughout what is now British Columbia. A small community developed at the north end of Salt Spring, including four of the first twenty-nine pre-emptors in 1859: Armstead Buckner, Fielding Spotts, William Isaacs, and E.A. Booth. Buckner, born in Virginia, pre-empted land occupied today by the Salt Spring Golf and Country Club. Spotts eventually settled on the Saanich Peninsula and may never have taken up his pre-emption on Salt Spring.

Before the year ended, several other Blacks arrived, including Abraham Copeland, who chose land on the west side of St. Mary Lake where part of Tripp Road is today; William Harrison, Copeland's son-in-law, who pre-empted to the south of the lake; William Robinson, who settled on the north side; Hiram Whims, who established an upland farm on the ridge between Fernwood and St. Mary Lake; the Jones brothers—John Craven, William, and Elias—who took land on the gentle slope leading

An early photo of sisters Marie Wallace and Louise Wiley, daughters of Louis and Sylvia Stark, c. 1885. A portrait sitting was considered a solemn occasion. BCARS F-01893

down toward the west side of Ganges Harbour; Levi Davis; and William Isaacs. Daniel Fredison, a Black from Hawaii, rounded out the 1859 arrivals, settling on land that is still a large farm on Mansell Road.

There were no women in the original group of Black settlers. Most men sent for their families only after they were settled. Among those arriving in 1860 were Giles Curtis, B. Franklin Wall, and Louis and Sylvia Stark, who first pre-empted north of Vesuvius. Another Black, G.H. Anderson, pre-empted land to the south of John C. Jones's land on the west side of Ganges Harbour.

Most of the Blacks settled near each other in the north end of the island. When Methodist missionary Ebenezer Robson visited in February 1861, he noted in his diary:

> There are in the settlement 21 houses on the same number of claims. Four of the houses are inhabited by white people and the remainder by coloured people. I preached in the house of a coloured man in the evening to about 20 persons all coloured except three and one of them is married to a coloured man.[2]

How many Blacks actually settled on Salt Spring is a matter of conjecture. Some Blacks, like other early settlers, pre-empted land on paper but never physically took up their pre-emptions. Ethnographer Charles Irby calculated that there were only six Black families on Salt Spring when the Starks arrived in 1860. Irby wrote that the Black population had risen substantially by Robson's 1861 visit:

> There were 15 family names of blacks on Saltspring Island in 1861, including two Robinsons, at four different locations. Seven were located south and southeast of St. Mary Lake at Central Settlement, four at Vesuvius Bay, three were about two miles north of Vesuvius Bay, and one was at Ganges Harbor (Admiral Bay). . . . The important feature is that they were dispersed, which stifled island communication and economic cohesiveness.[3]

Some of these people stayed on Salt Spring, but most did not. Many, like Mifflin Gibbs, eventually drifted back to the United States after the Civil War, when the climate for Blacks changed. Those who remained on Salt Spring or elsewhere in Canada thrived, however. Whether well educated, especially

RACIAL PREJUDICE ON SALT SPRING?

Most early settlers were probably too busy establishing themselves to be able to spend much time worrying about racial differences. And they were unlikely to refuse a neighbour's help just because he was a Black. Many believe that little racial prejudice existed in these early days, but Rev. Ebenezer Robson recorded one instance in his diary:

> Mrs. Lenniker [sic] says Mr. L. nor herself will come to any meeting when the colored people associate with the white. Poor woman—she says some people might do it but she has been brought up so that she cannot—was the daughter of a church of England clergyman.

Widespread intermarriage among settlers of different ethnic backgrounds ensured little prejudice among people born on the island. Still, many British who settled on the island after the 1880s socialized largely among themselves and retained social customs that excluded others. In a letter dated March 6, 1947, islander John A. Caldwell wrote:

> All of them [Blacks] are highly respected for their coop-eration, honesty, and integrity. For fifty-five years we have lived among them. I, and later my children, attended school with them. They worked for us and we worked with them on government projects, agricultural shows, politics, school board, etc. and have nothing but the best to say for them.
>
> We feel that given equal opportunity there would be no coloured problem. Our Coloured Folks here realize there is intolerance among all classes and creeds and they consider the source and accept it philosophically. In fact, a few of them welcome a certain amount of it as bringing out their latent strength.

skilled, or just plain ambitious, they took advantage of the available opportunities to have a good life in a country freer than the one they had left.

Among the most successful Blacks were the three Jones brothers, who had been born in Raleigh, North Carolina, where their father had tried unsuccessfully to set up a school for Black children after purchasing his freedom from slavery. When whites burned his school for the third time, Jones moved his family to Ohio. All four of his sons graduated from Oberlin College, and three emigrated to Canada, initially to Salt Spring.

William and Elias Jones stayed on Salt Spring only briefly, however, and left for the Cariboo gold rush in 1861. William became one of Barkerville's first dentists and a mining investor and spent the rest of his life in the Cariboo. Elias eventually returned to Oberlin.

John Craven Jones, Salt Spring's first schoolteacher, initially taught three days a week in the log-cabin school at Central Settlement and walked to Begg's Settlement where he taught another three days in a shed on the southeast corner of Fernwood Road and North End Road. Jones was reportedly sniped at and occasionally beaten, reputedly by aboriginal people, as he travelled from one school to the other. Jones received no pay for his work until 1869 when he was officially appointed schoolteacher at a monthly salary of about $40. Early settlers were probably overjoyed to have a qualified teacher for their children, but a school inspector was critical in a June 1872 report:

> ... The 28th was examination day, but there were only three pupils in attendance, 2 girls and a boy. The boy was working in Latin Grammar, having become such a proficient in English Grammar and Geography that these two subjects were dropped a year ago and Latin substituted! So the teacher reported. An examination in these branches and Arithmetic did not by any means establish the fact of former proficiency. Teacher's time comparatively wasted by itinerating between Middle and Northern Settlements. Circumstances do not warrant it as none of the children are more than three miles from the school house and the road is improving year by year. There are 25 children of school age in the two settlements above referred to, of whom 7 reside in the northern settlement and 16 in the middle settlement.[4]

In the mid-1870s, John Craven Jones returned to Oberlin. He married in

1882 at age fifty-one and moved to Tarboro, North Carolina, where he taught for another twenty-five years. He died in 1911 at the age of eighty.

Several Black pioneers took part in local government on Salt Spring. Copeland was elected to the first three-member school board, which made John Jones's position as teacher official. Then, when Salt Spring was incorporated in 1873, Jones and Henry W. Robinson, another Black, served on the seven-member council. The election of Gibbs of Victoria as Salt Spring's representative to the Yale Convention may reflect the political influence and involvement of Blacks on Salt Spring.

THE STARK STORY

The Starks are the best known of the Black families that came to Salt Spring. In 1860, Louis and Sylvia Stark, both former slaves from the United States, settled north of Vesuvius Bay and ten years later moved to the northeast shore of Ganges Harbour opposite Goat Island. The arrival of the Starks is colourfully described in daughter Marie Wallace's notes of her mother's memories:

> It was a bright day in 1860 when the Starks moved to Saltspring Island.... They came to the northwest side of the island in a sailing vessel. The cattle [15 dairy cows] were lowered into the water with strong ropes, where they swam to land and took the trail leading up to their home, lowing as they went on without anyone to guide them.
>
> The passengers clambered down the side of the ship on rope ladders, and into two Indian canoes, manned by two Indians, a man and his wife. A Hudson Bay Co. man landed with them. Mr. Macaulay, the Hudson Bay agent, offered to stay with Mrs. Stark and the two children while Mr. Stark went down to the settlement to get conveyance to haul their baggage.

In his diary, Rev. Ebenezer Robson noted the progress of the Starks' home building and Louis's land clearing (described in chapter 3) on his 1861 Salt Spring trip:

> They with their children 3 in number are living on their own farm. It is good land & they only pay $1 per acre for it. Mr. Stark

FROM SLAVERY TO FREEDOM

Sylvia Stark's parents, Howard and Hannah Estes, were slaves in Clay County, Missouri, where Sylvia was born in 1839. About ten years later, Estes managed to buy his family's freedom, and on April 1, 1851, the Estes family began an eventful six-month overland trip to California. There Sylvia met and married Louis Stark in the mid-1850s. In 1858, the Estes family and the Starks decided to migrate to British Columbia. While Louis Stark and Jackson Estes drove fifty head of cattle overland, Sylvia Stark, her parents, and her two children travelled on the steamer *Brother Jonathan*. They all met in Steilacoom, Washington Territory, and continued to Victoria together. Sylvia's parents bought a farm in Saanich and Stark preempted land on Salt Spring.

has about 30 head of cattle. He sowed one quart of wheat near his house last winter and reaped 180 qts. in the summer. . . . His turnips of which he has a large quantity are beautiful and large—Also cabbages etc. etc. His wife who was converted about 2 months ago filled my sacks with good things—4 lbs. fine fresh butter, 2 qt. bottles new milk. Mr. Stark gave me some of his large turnips.

Sylvia Stark looked to religion to help her cope with life in a rough environment. Her husband Louis was unsympathetic, however, and Sylvia would pray secretly by herself in the woods.

Marie Wallace recorded several of her mother's frightening encounters with aboriginal people:

One evening five Indians came to the Stark cabin on the mountainside. . . . The three children were asleep, the youngest a baby in the cradle. They walked right into the house and began to examine everything in the house. They even counted the blankets on the bed, and talked among themselves. Then one of the men took a gun from over the mantle where Stark kept several guns ready loaded and began to examine it. Stark shouted to him to be careful as the gun was loaded and grabbed the muzzle turning it away. . . . Sylvia was praying silently. . . . In the scuffle, Stark held onto the gun, turning the muzzle upward. Suddenly there was a terrific blast, the bullet going through the roof. Immediately to the surprise of the Starks, the Indians left quickly. It is quite evident they were afraid of Stark, who was known to be a good marksman, and he was not afraid of them.

*

An Indian going by the name of Willie had made an attempt on Stark's life, but the latter had seen the gunsight glistening in the sun. The gun was pointing towards him in the man's hands. Instantly Stark shouted to him, calling him by name. The man was afraid when he saw that he was detected. He knew if he missed Stark, Stark wouldn't miss him. He was trembling when Stark came up to him. After that Stark was very careful. He always took his dog with him when he went into the woods.

*

One day, a Native stole into the house silently in his moccasin feet. They always came in without knocking. He asked in Chinook, "*Kah mika man?*" ("Where is your man?") Sylvia answered in Chinook, "*Wake syah.*" ("Not far away.") The dog . . . was lying asleep on the floor. But when the man spoke, the dog jumped up and would have caught the man by the throat, when Sylvia prevented him, though with some difficulty. That stopped the prowling.

Despite these episodes, the Starks generally had good relations with their aboriginal visitors. Marie Wallace wrote:

But as a rule the Indians were quite friendly. They sold their commodities, salmon and all kinds of seafood, and berries in their season. They needed the *chickamin* (money, in Chinook). There was one man whose name was Verygood, Captain Verygood. So named, he gained the respect of all who knew him. W.O. Stark [Marie's brother Willis] learned from him something about the customs of the early Natives.

In 1868, William Robinson, a Black neighbour of the Starks, was shot in the back while sitting in his own cabin. Robinson, a mild-mannered man who taught Sunday school, was about to leave Salt Spring to return to his wife in the United States. Eight months later, Giles Curtis, a Black friend of Howard Estes who had come to help on the Starks' farm, was also murdered in his cabin. Curtis was not only shot but had his throat slashed with a butcher knife. In both cases, everything worthwhile was stolen from the cabins. And both murders were blamed on aboriginal people (see chapter 5).

The murders of his closest neighbours so unnerved Louis Stark that he moved his pre-emption to a safer location called Fruitvale, opposite Goat Island (possibly so named because Stark grazed his goats there) along the eastern shore of Ganges Harbour. Stark, who unlike many of the other Black settlers was nearly illiterate, explained the situation to land agent Joseph Trutch in 1869:

> Mr. Trutch land agent dear Sir I Beg leave to inform you that I have ben oblige to move my famerly from my claim as the indiens is daingers I cannot get any man to live on the place Since cirtice was killd for this caus I have commencts improving a peace of land on the n.e. Side of gaingers harber and Joind on the South east end of david overtons claim thir is forty or fifty acurs of this land near to other Settlers which I would be veary thankfull if you will record this to me and take one hundred acures from my old claim and record to me one hundred ondly untill I can get a man on it[5]

The Black community in the north end of the island began to disperse. In about 1875, Louis Stark moved again, this time to the Cranberry district near Nanaimo. Sylvia didn't move with him, preferring to remain on Salt Spring with her oldest son, Willis, who took care of the Stark holdings. Willis died in 1943 at the age of eighty-seven. All the other Stark children moved away from Salt Spring.

Louis Stark's attempts to find peace in his old age near Nanaimo were thwarted. A rich coal seam was discovered deep under his property, and people interested in mining it offered to buy the land. Louis refused to sell in spite of threats against his life. In 1895, he was found dead at the foot of a cliff. The family firmly believed that Stark had been murdered. Louis's youngest daughter, Louise, inherited everything he had. His will stipulated that his wife, Sylvia, was to receive only "1 dollar in lieu of dower because she has some years since without cause left my bed and board. Consequently she is not entitled to my property."[6] Sylvia died in 1944 at about 105, one year after her son Willis.

Sylvia Stark, over ninety years old, c. 1930, holding a bowl of apples. Marie Wallace, one of Sylvia's daughters, is in the background. SSIA

MOVING ON

Most of Salt Spring's Black population settled in the north end of the island, but at least two moved to the south end. For some time, Hiram Whims's son, William, and his wife Emily (Sampson) had continued to farm the land Hiram pre-empted not far from the present Fernwood dock. However, in 1880, William bought fifty acres from John Sparrow in the Fulford-Burgoyne Valley, where he lived in his later years. Jim Anderson, another descendant of early Black settlers, first owned a cabin near Walker Hook and then, during the 1930s and 1940s, lived on Isabella Point Road.

Many Blacks returned to the United States, although others simply moved away from Salt Spring. Among those who left the island were Abraham Copeland and his family, who sold their 153 acres (61 ha) on St. Mary Lake to Thomas and Jane Mouat in 1885, and Levi Davis and his wife, who sold their property in 1895 to John T. Collins and moved back to Kentucky. In that year Rev. E.F. Wilson, who himself had bought Armstead Buckner's property a year earlier, estimated that of a total population of 450 people, 40 were "coloured," about the same number as there were in 1862. A few left British Columbia but returned in later life:

> Ernest, John and Edward Harrison, children of the son of 1865, attended Oberlin College, Ohio. Then John and Ernest returned to Salt Spring using their knowledge for the betterment of the island. Later Ernest moved to Victoria, taught athletics in the Y.M.C.A. there and is proud of the many coaches of today practicing his teachings. He sang in the choir, was returning officer at his precinct elections, and between times did a little boxing. John, on the island, built up a show place on his farm . . . on St. Mary's Lake. He was active in the church, sang in the choir, was a board member. . . [and] for many years was Treasurer of the Agricultural Association.[7]

In 1998, only a few descendants of the original Black settlers lived on Salt Spring, and they represented only two families—the Starks and the Whimses.

Charles Appleby lived on Salt Spring at the beginning of the twentieth century. Though he was considered deranged, he seemed to have some extrasensory powers. One day in 1911, he became very upset and claimed that the Iroquois, *the steamer then serving the Gulf Islands, had sunk. People tried to calm him, but his story proved true. Twenty-one people died that day when the* Iroquois *sank off Sidney. SSIA*

5

Government, Law, and Disorder

BUT WHERE DO WE VOTE?

T he first settlers had barely arrived when they experienced their first local election. On December 20, 1859, a cross-section of pre-emptors signed a notice in the *British Colonist* nominating Victoria lawyer John Copland to represent Salt Spring Island. The pre-emptors included Edward Mallandaine, publisher of British Columbia's first business directory; schooner captain Edward Walker; businessman John Ducie Cusheon; and farmer Fielding Spotts. Copland, who earlier that year had represented the legal interests of would-be settlers, was a logical choice. Amor de Cosmos, the owner-editor of the *British Colonist*, supported Copland, but the pro-government camp strongly opposed him for his open criticism of James Douglas's government.

Other problems faced Copland. Only non-resident Salt Spring landholders in Victoria knew that they had to register to be eligible to vote. On remote Salt Spring, residents were unaware of this requirement. The register was re-opened after de Cosmos protested, but Copland claimed that this was only after the voters' lists had already been posted. The lively debate culminated in the *British Colonist*'s championing of Copland in an editorial on January 5, 1860:

> If any other man than a resident there had a claim to be elected by that constituency it is Mr. Copland. But for his efforts in

Key dates

1860 J.J. Southgate, a resident of Vancouver Island and a supporter of the Douglas government, is elected to represent Salt Spring in the colony's legislative assembly.

About fifty Cowichan attack a party of fourteen Bella Bella in Ganges Harbour.

1861 A group of Haida rob Jonathan Begg's store in Beggsville (Fernwood).

1862 Frederick Marks and his daughter, Caroline Harvey, are murdered on Saturna Island.

1863 Two settlers, Bill Brady and John Henley, are attacked by a small group of Cowichan at Bedwell Harbour, Pender Island.

Major John Peter Mouat Biggs of Chemainus is appointed justice of the peace for Chemainus and Salt Spring.

1869 Tshuanahusset of the Halalt nation is convicted of William Robinson's murder.

1872 Henry Sampson is appointed constable of Salt Spring.

chartering a vessel to explore the island, getting a pre-emptive system established and securing the franchise to the settlers, there would have been no Salt Spring Island.

The government appointed Jonathan Begg as returning officer and called the election for January 13, though Copland claimed that he had been given a date of January 20. The government apparently did little to inform Salt Spring voters of any election date. Communication was difficult in a scattered community without post office, community centre, or school. The election notice was posted in a central place, but it was just an uninhabited shack deep in the woods.

The election results were a foregone conclusion. Attorney General George Hunter Cary congratulated the government candidate, J.J. Southgate, even before the election, and only one of the settlers who had nominated Copland, Edward Mallandaine, was able to vote. In a letter to his sister and brother-in-law, Jonathan Begg summarized the election a few months later:

Artist Edward Mallandaine's impression of the 1860 polling booth on Salt Spring, proba-
bly Begg's store. As it turned out, the voting activity might have been even quieter than
that shown here. BCARS 1279

We had an election of legislative assembly men and Salt Springs
etc sent a member. I was appointed returning officer on the occasion. The members had to be worth $1500 so we had to appoint
a man from Victoria as no settler could qualify. The member is
elected for three years. By that time we hope to be represented by
a local man.

Islanders protested the procedure that made Southgate their official representative in Victoria.

Before the next election three years later, Salt Spring settlers requested a
revised list of qualified voters, but without regular postal service, few voters
realized that they had to add their names to the list, which this time was
posted at the uninhabited farm of J.D. Cusheon. No one went to what was a
very inconvenient location for the two main pockets of settlers in the island's
north and south ends, and the voters' list stayed the same. Victoria residents—first solicitor G.E. Dennes and later merchant J.T. Pidwell—also won
the 1863 and 1866 elections.

ROBBERY, RUSTLING, AND MANSLAUGHTER

On-island law enforcement was a pressing need for Salt Spring settlers. Isolated on scattered homesteads, they were at the mercy of any passing marauder or thief.

The aboriginal population was blamed for most robbery and violence, though the evidence was often circumstantial. Aboriginal people resented newcomers settling on their land and they made their resentment known. Marie Wallace recalled:

> That was the time the local Natives themselves were quite hostile. They held meetings with much Skookum pow-wow—Chinook strong talk—as they saw their beaches and hunting grounds usurped by the incoming settlers and the sight of carcases of animals lying on the beaches, their hides taken and the meat left to spoil. When an Indian came to one of such, he made a clucking noise with his tongue which indicated disgust. It only served as fuel to an already heated situation.

Some aboriginal people travelling the coast to Fort Victoria helped themselves to settlers' produce—they considered food common property—and a few stole goods. Sniping was also frequent, and settlers covered their windows at night to avoid being shot. Fearful of further violence, even full-scale war with the far larger aboriginal population, they hesitated to fire back. Skeletons discovered later suggest that settlers sometimes secretly killed and buried aboriginal "troublemakers." Officially, they avoided violence and appealed to British authorities in Victoria to defend them by enforcing the laws.

Aboriginal hostility caused some trouble, but outlaws—both aboriginal and white—caused more. Since aboriginals far outnumbered white settlers in the early days, aboriginal outlaws were probably involved in more incidents than white ones. In some cases whites were responsible for inciting trouble by selling aboriginal people whiskey or by encouraging them to steal. Also, many rough characters lived in these turbulent times, with some slipping back and forth between the colony and the United States.

Historians have access to few unbiased accounts of 150 years ago and must often rely on the newspapers of the day. For example, much has been

A SOMETIMES CO-OPERATIVE SOCIETY

Despite occasional problems, most relations were apparently positive between Gulf Islands settlers and aboriginal people, who often helped and learned from each other. In another letter to his relatives, Jonathan Begg wrote, "It is very cheap living here as the Indians who are very useful and very good to white men bring us large quantities of the best the waters, woods, and forest can produce for a mere song." Many settlers took aboriginal common-law wives, and it may have been this widespread intermarriage that made the early settlement on Salt Spring possible.

Historians Ruth Sandwell and John Lutz discovered little evidence of racial tension after 1864. In a website titled "Who Killed William Robinson?" they commented: "A close look at published memoirs and letters suggests that relationships between natives and non-natives were much more cordial than historians, or newspapers, or court records, suggest. Goods, services and even medical help were exchanged on a regular basis. The most convincing evidence of the closeness of aboriginal–non-aboriginal relations, however, comes from the 1881 census that indicates that 45% of the marriages and 57% of the children were of mixed race. The majority of inter-racial unions were between aboriginal women and non-aboriginal men."

made of the July 1860 "massacre of Admiralty Bay," also known as the "Ganges Harbour battle" (Admiralty Bay was the original name for Ganges Harbour). No whites were involved in the conflict between two aboriginal groups—Cowichan and Haida (or Bella Bella, depending on which account of the "battle" you read)—but its ferocity left Salt Spring settlers feeling extremely vulnerable.

At least two contemporary accounts survive: a letter from Thomas Henry

Lineker to Governor James Douglas on July 9, 1860, and Marie Wallace's notes, recorded many years later, of Sylvia Stark's quite different description of what appeared to be the same incident. Later histories and accounts embellished the story greatly with either unsubstantiated additions or imaginative—and not necessarily accurate—description. As writer Eric Roberts suggests, "The story, like certain types of cheese, improves with age." Lineker, one of the few witnesses, wrote immediately following the incident, and his account is considered the most accurate:

> . . . On the 4th of July last, at noon, a canoe with nine men, two boys, and three women of the "Bella Bella" tribe came in here with a person named McCauley who had business with some of the settlers. While he was talking to me, the Cowichans numbering some fifty, who were encamped here (& who on the arrival of the Bella Bellas manifested an unfriendly spirit, but afterwards appeared friendly), commenced firing, a general fight ensued which lasted about an hour, and ended in the Cowichans killing eight of the others, and carrying off the women and boys as prisoners, the fight occurred so close to my house, that I sent my wife and family into the woods for safety. During the night one of the Bella Bellas came to me, wounded. I pointed out a trail which would lead him to the Northern part of the island, hoping he might get away. I felt I could not give him shelter without being compromised in this murderous affair. Two men have just arrived here from the other side of the Island, who inform me that a week since some Northern Indians took two of another tribe out of their boat and cut their heads off.
>
> The Indians have all left here, probably anticipating an attack, in such an event we should be anything but safe, especially should they in any way molest the Settlers. We number here twenty-six men, scattered over about two miles square. Considering their defenceless position the Settlers trust that Your Excellency will deem it expedient to afford them such protection as you in your wisdom may think necessary.[1]

Aboriginal people also looked to the British for protection. The southwest coast peoples hoped that superior British technology would protect them

WHO WAS MCCAULEY?

Sylvia Stark identified McCauley (sometimes spelled "Macaulay" or "McCawley") as a Hudson's Bay Company agent (see chapter 4), while Thomas Henry Lineker said that he accompanied the northerners on unspecified "business with some of the settlers." It's difficult to know who this man was, but we can speculate!

In *Homesteads and Snug Harbours*, writer Peter Murray identified him as John McCawley, a renegade who preyed on aboriginal people and settlers alike:

> McCawley was an Englishman who came to Vancouver Island via Hawaii, San Francisco and New Westminster. He was said to have fled Hawaii to avoid embezzlement charges, and had left San Francisco in a similar hurry. In New Westminster he had been charged with assault but was acquitted. McCawley was described as "a ladies' man," tall, slim, blue-eyed and handsome with a carefully curled and waxed moustache.

In his *British Columbia Coast Names: Their Origin and History*, John Walbran also describes a man named Macaulay:

> ...A white man named Macaulay, who had been illicitly supplying intoxicants to the surveying camps, was made a prisoner by the *Plumper's* officers, and the *Active* conveyed him to Esquimalt. On the way Macaulay showed the crew of the *Active* a large quantity of gold dust which he had received in trade from the Fraser river Indians. The crew on arrival at San Francisco the following winter spread the news, and the rush to the Fraser river of 1858 was the result.

Perhaps Macaulay sold alcohol illegally and started the Fraser River gold rush. Perhaps he really was an employee of the HBC profiting from illegal private arrangements. Perhaps his greed for the furs that the northern aboriginal people were supposed to be carrying caused their deaths. Perhaps he was also involved in cattle rustling on Salt Spring. Or perhaps these occurrences involved different men with similar names: Macauley, McCauley, McCawley. We may never know for sure, because no historical record mentions him. All we have are tantalizing bits and pieces of information.

from raiding northerners. And the northwest coast peoples occasionally sought the protection of British gunboats as they made their way home after trading in Victoria.

Salt Spring settlers hoped for a resident justice of the peace, but Governor Douglas did not agree:

> The latter [the settlers] though greatly alarmed suffered no molestation whatever from the Victorious Tribe, who, before leaving the settlement expressed the deepest regret for the affray, pleading in extenuation that they could not control their feelings, and begging that their conduct might not be represented to this government in an unfavourable light.[2]

Hostility was continual between southern and northern aboriginal peoples (see chapter 1). Although battles rarely involved settlers, the warfare of the aboriginal nations frayed everyone's nerves. The government attempted to negotiate treaties, but many Cowichan and Chemainus bands declined. They considered the land being settled by white people theirs and they outnumbered the better armed intruders. Jonathan Begg's September 24, 1859, report in the *New Westminster Times* showed the settlers' concern:

> We have to urge upon the Government the necessity of some immediate measures being adopted to settle the Indian claims, if they exist, upon these Islands, as the settlers are subjected to constant annoyance and insult from these claimants, more especially by the "Penalichar tribe," [the Penelakut band on Kuper Island] who boldly tell the settlers that the Island is theirs, and that Gov. Douglas has "cap-swallowed" it, which, in the elegant Chinook jargon, we believe, means stolen it. This subject deserves immediate attention.

The British authorities were well aware of their delicate position—incautious actions could easily trigger large-scale war and bloodshed—and they were patient, although usually stern, in enforcing their laws.

Douglas decided not to appoint a resident justice of the peace because "none of the resident settlers..., having either the status or intelligence to serve the public with advantage in the capacity of local justices, no appointment was simply for that reason made." Douglas saw no reason to spend £500 ($2500) per year for a regular stipendiary magistrate for Salt Spring and felt that a justice of the peace alone could not have prevented the aboriginal skirmish. Douglas believed that a white man's interference could actually have provoked an attack on the settlers. He did, however, agree to appoint a justice of the peace if a suitable person were available.

In May 1861, another incident involving aboriginal people alarmed the settlers. Haida from the Queen Charlotte Islands arrived in about thirty canoes and camped near Beggsville. They first stole goods from a house belonging to Edward Mallandaine and then discovered Jonathan Begg's store, where they reportedly stole "flour, potatoes, turnips, and a flag."[3] When Henry Sampson, Begg's neighbour, tried to stop them, they threatened his life, and he was forced to retreat. The Haida left early the next morning.

As it turned out, these Haida had also stolen goods from Victoria and from the schooner *Laurel* and other vessels. The government sent one of its two gunboats, the *Forward*, under Lieutenant Charles R. Robson, in pursuit. Jonathan Begg and Henry Sampson were on board to identify the stolen goods. The *Forward* eventually found the Haida camping at Willow Point on Vancouver Island. When the Haida refused to return the stolen goods, Robson had his men fire on the encampment, and in the ensuing exchange of fire four Haida and one crewman of the *Forward* were killed. Robson took five Haida chiefs prisoner and recovered the stolen property.[4]

An inquiry found that the Haida had had some provocation, at least for their assault on the *Laurel*, whose crew had sold them whiskey diluted with salt water. The government, learning of the greed and dishonesty of the ship's crew, released the Haida chiefs.

Nevertheless, the authorities felt that it was important to punish "wrong-doers" to preclude further lawlessness. Lieutenant Robson wrote to his superior:

> I am fully aware that I have incurred a grave responsibility in having taken so decisive a part; but after mature deliberation I came to the conclusion that acts of this sort, partaking more of the nature of a piratical foray than anything hitherto attempted, must, for the safety of the settlers and small craft navigating these inland waters, be met by prompt and decisive action, and I am equally of [the] opinion that whether there be sufficient evidence or not to convict the actual perpetrators, the moral effect of the lesson they have received will operate in a most salutary manner upon the Northern Indians for the future.[5]

Aboriginal people were blamed for several attacks in late 1862 and early 1863 on islands near Salt Spring. In April 1863, a German settler, Frederick Marks, and his fifteen-year-old married daughter, Caroline Harvey, were taking shelter from a storm on Saturna Island, when they were attacked and killed. The body of Marks was never found, but his daughter's was found several months later. It was generally believed that the culprits were from the Lamalcha (or Lamalchi) band from Kuper Island.[6] Four Lamalchi were eventually hanged for the murders of Marks and Harvey.

In a second incident two days later, a small group of Cowichan visited William Brady and John Henley, who were camped at Pender Island's Bedwell Harbour. The Cowichan returned that night and shot through the men's tent, fatally wounding Brady. Although wounded himself, Henley managed to beat off the attackers. Brady died three days later, and Henley took the news to Victoria.

In response, the gunboats *Forward* and *Grappler*, the paddle sloop *Devastation*, and the corvette *Cameleon* searched the coast for the murderers. On April 20, 1863, the *Forward* approached the aboriginal village at

Lamalchi Bay on the southwest side of Kuper Island and opened fire on the village. The Lamalchi returned fire from shore, killing a British seaman. The British found no suspects, but eventually destroyed the Lamalchi village and hanged three Cowichan for the murder of Brady and the *Forward's* seaman.[7]

THE LAMALCHI VERSION

British Columbia history tends to come to us straight from British sources. However, there are two sides to every story. The aboriginal version of the Kuper Island bombardment in 1863 was told and retold by generations of Tsartlip elders and finally recorded by Dave Elliott, Sr., in *Saltwater People*:

> There was an Indian village at the south end of Kuper island, <u>WLEMÁŁĆE</u>. Something happened out on those islands, some people were murdered, some people were killed and robbed and somebody in the village of <u>WLEMÁŁĆE</u> got blamed for it. The authorities at the time decided to teach the Indians a lesson. They sent up a Man-of-War from Victoria, . . . cannons sticking out all over it. . . .
>
> They sent a man ashore and they told him to tell those Indians they have to give this man up who was blamed for the murders out on the island. His name was TIOȻ. They went ashore and they spoke to the Indians and they told them, "We're here to get this man, this man was responsible for those murders out on those islands." They said to this naval officer, "We can't give him up because he's not here, he hasn't been here for a long time and we don't know where he is." But the officer insisted anyway, "You either give that man up or we're going to blow your village all to pieces. There will be nothing left

of it." They still said, "How can we give this man up if he's not here?"

The naval officer returned to the ship with its guns already trained on the village. They fired volley after volley after volley on that defenceless village. These people had never done a thing to them. When they were finished shelling that village it was flattened to the ground. There was nothing left, there wasn't a house left standing. . . . Since then there's never been a village. There's still no village there today.

These events finally led Governor Douglas to appoint a justice of the peace for Salt Spring. On May 12, 1863, he chose John Peter Mouat Biggs of Chemainus, a retired major from the British Indian army. Biggs fitted Douglas's criteria for a justice of the peace, since he was both educated and wealthy. Salt Spring islanders, who justifiably felt that their justice of the peace should live on their island, were not pleased.

Every spring brought complaints from Salt Spring farmers, who claimed that aboriginal people stole their produce as they moved from Victoria to their home villages. On March 12, 1864, the *British Colonist* reported that a farmer named Hollins had had his turnip crop cleaned out in one night. According to the report, a large group of Cowichan was living on Salt Spring and had "become very troublesome to the settlers by their thieving propensities." Were they also stealing cattle from John Maxwell and James Lunney's Burgoyne Bay ranch?

On March 27, 1867, John Maxwell, whose cattle on his Fulford-Burgoyne Valley ranch had become highly marketable, wrote to the *British Colonist* complaining that for five years he had suffered cattle rustling. He claimed to have lost five cows in one month alone. Maxwell was bitter about the lack of support from the Victoria government and threatened to take personal

RANCHER JOHN MAXWELL

John Maxwell.
Courtesy Barbara Lyngard

John Maxwell was born in Ireland in 1835. As a young man of twenty-five, he arrived on Salt Spring with his countryman James Lunney. They pre-empted 350 acres (142 ha) and gradually added to them until the ranch reached 1000 acres (400 ha). The two men had previously struck it rich in the Fraser River gold fields. On Salt Spring, they built a cabin at the foot of what is now Mt. Maxwell, cleared and fenced their land, planted an orchard, and seeded grass to provide feed for the one hundred Texas longhorns they had imported from Oregon.

Maxwell's aboriginal wife, Mary, was only about fourteen when the couple's first child was born in 1865. The Maxwells went on to have a total of five sons and two daughters. Of John and Mary Maxwell's children, John died at a young age; James went missing during World War I; David married Clara Trage and continued to live on Salt Spring; Samuel, Mary, and Elisa moved to San Francisco; and Dick lived his whole life on Salt Spring with his wife, Emily. In addition to farming, John Maxwell earned money working on the roads. He was also a strong member of the community. In 1869, Maxwell and Lunney donated 3 acres (1.2 ha) for a wharf in Burgoyne Bay, south Salt Spring's first wharf. From 1883 to 1900, when it closed, the Burgoyne Bay Post Office was in the Maxwell house, run by one or another of the Maxwell children.

action. At this point history and legend intertwine.

According to the story, Maxwell and Lunney took stock of their situation. From tracks, they deduced that forty to eighty aboriginal people led by a white man (identified as such because he wore shoes) were regularly climbing to the peak of Mt. Maxwell to plan their attacks. The ranchers could call on only a dozen men, including hired hands and neighbours.

The cattle were ready for market, and the rustlers were due to appear at any time. The men in Maxwell's party waited on the mountain slope for several nights. His instructions were not to shoot until he gave the signal and then only over the heads of the rustlers. Maxwell wanted above all to avoid reprisals from an adversary that vastly outnumbered his own force.

Just when it seemed that the men would have to return to their farms without having achieved their goal, the rustlers appeared. What followed was in keeping with the best western movies. Maxwell's men held their fire until the signal. Then, running from tree to tree, they fired over the heads of the marauders, suggesting by their actions that they were a small army of men. The would-be rustlers took to their heels, escaping in canoes that they had left in Burgoyne Bay.

There was indeed a white leader. He apparently tumbled into the last canoe in a desperate attempt to escape, but one of his aboriginal partners suspected a trap and quickly knifed him to death. Some contemporaries identified him as the same man connected with the Ganges Harbour Battle—McCauley.

This sequence of lawlessness ended in 1868 with the murders of two Black settlers, William Robinson and Giles Curtis, eight months apart (see chapter 4). The settlers abhorred these murders; both men were quiet, law-abiding, helpful to others, respected, and well liked. Islanders increased their pressure on the government for a resident police officer. In April 1869, the new justice of the peace, John Morley, arrested an aboriginal man named Tshuanahusset, of the Halalt nation, for Robinson's murder. It appeared that the man was a scapegoat, however, as no real evidence or motivation indicated his guilt.

Despite the protests of both settlers and aboriginal people, Tshuanahusset was tried, convicted on circumstantial evidence and the word of another aboriginal man who evidently disliked him, and executed for the murders. A letter to the British Colonist on June 5, 1869, expressed a thoughtful reaction to this possible travesty of justice:

I am afraid that we are, as a community, too careless about the lives of the Indians, and yet it seems to me that we ought to be more particular about an Indian than a white man on trial for his life, for the latter hears and understands all that is brought against him, and has an opportunity to explain away things that might otherwise tell against him, while an Indian understands very little that is said, and is in consequence unable to prompt his Counsel on matters that would favor his case.

Only in 1872, one year after the colony of British Columbia had joined the Canadian Confederation, was a resident constable, Henry Sampson, finally appointed to police Salt Spring.

Tshuanahusset of the Halalt nation, who was executed for the murders of William Robinson and Giles Curtis.
BCARS F-8822

Salt Spring's First Constable: Henry Sampson

English-born Henry Sampson joined the Hudson's Bay Company at nineteen as a carpenter at newly built Fort Rupert in the colony of Vancouver Island. In 1852, when the coal ran out in Fort Rupert, Henry was transferred to Nanaimo. At the end of his five-year contract, he worked on his own. By 1856, he was married to an aboriginal woman and had children in school.

In 1858, Sampson went to southern Vancouver Island, where he had heard cheap land was available for homesteading. He was one of the twenty-nine potential settlers who inspected Salt Spring in 1859 and one of the first seventeen homesteaders.

Henry Sampson. SSIA

In 1866, Henry turned in his wife, Mary Ann Sampson, for poisoning a neighbour, William McFadden, with the help of McFadden's daughter. The daughter was acquitted, but Mrs. Sampson was convicted. The sentence was eventually overturned, but Mrs. Sampson left Salt Spring with another man. Henry began living with Lucy Peatson, the daughter of Captain Peatson, the aboriginal man who provided boat service to Gulf Islands settlers for many years. Lucy was only eighteen when she met Henry. Two years later, she gave birth to the first of the couple's fourteen children. On February 4, 1905, Henry and Lucy were finally married in a ceremony conducted by Rev. E.F. Wilson. A number of Sampson descendants still live on Salt Spring and on nearby Vancouver Island.

Lucy Sampson.
Courtesy Dick Toynbee

Henry became constable of Salt Spring in 1872. His knowledge of several coastal aboriginal languages and of aboriginal people in general, which he had gained in his work for the HBC, stood him in good stead as a constable. His equipment consisted of only a musket, handcuffs, and a canoe.

The first jail on the island was located at Central Settlement, opposite the log schoolhouse. It was a small wooden structure with wooden bars covering the windows and a large padlock on the door. The jailhouse was probably seldom used, however, as it was too far from Henry Sampson's farm near Fernwood to let him care for prisoners, who were likely held in a lockup on Henry's own property.

6

A Troubled Adolescence

1873–1883

POLITICS, LOCAL GOVERNMENT, AND MORE POLITICS

When British Columbia entered Confederation in 1871, a new twenty-five-seat British Columbia legislature was created, and Salt Spring Island resident John Patton Booth won a seat. With the colony's debt eliminated as a result of Confederation, politicians were in an enviable position of spending money without worrying about existing debts. Booth, like other ambitious Salt Spring settlers, wanted more public services. When asked about Salt Spring's immediate needs, he asked the provincial secretary for a thousand dollars to build roads to connect the scattered island settlements and another thousand dollars to build two new schools.

Some residents saw this as just a beginning and believed the services they wanted would come only through local government. In September 1872, they asked the government to issue letters patent to incorporate the island. This was granted almost immediately, with the announcement appearing in the *Government Gazette* of January 4, 1873. Thus began ten years of bickering among Salt Spring residents, who tended to split on north-south lines, those in the north generally supporting incorporation and those in the south opposing it.

Municipal elections for the new Corporation of the Township of Salt

KEY DATES

1873	Salt Spring Island is incorporated and becomes a municipality.
	Burgoyne Bay School District is formed.
1874	Salt Spring's first post office is established.
1874–75	The first land survey of Salt Spring is conducted.
1880	The Burgoyne Bay Post Office opens.
1881	The population of Salt Spring reaches 258.
1883	The municipality of Salt Spring is dissolved by the legislative assembly.

Spring Island were held within ten days of the official announcement, and the first council meeting took place on January 30, 1873. The seven members were Thomas Caradoc Parry (warden), Henry W. Robinson (clerk), Charles McDonald (collector), Frederick Foord (treasurer), Joseph Akerman (assessor), Jacob Crook Crane, and John Craven Jones.

Few of the generally independent, self-sufficient south Salt Spring residents supported incorporation, which to them meant only higher taxes. Many wanted roads to get their crops to market but were otherwise content to be left alone. Edwin Pimbury and his brothers led an anti-incorporation faction, which soon asked the legislative assembly to dissolve the municipality.

Rising debt and taxes, blamed on salaries for council members, were apparently the chief complaints. (Salt Spring residents have always vigorously resisted tax increases.) Residents also felt that councillors were profiting at the expense of other settlers and that the municipality should be divided into wards. Edwin Pimbury complained to the lieutenant governor in January 1874 that councillors were violating the Municipal Act of 1872. Theodore Trage, Henry Spikerman, William Walsh, Michael Gyves, John Cairns, and John Maxwell—all south-end residents—signed documents supporting Pimbury.

Pimbury's letter was referred to the attorney general, who advised the protesters to take the matter to the Supreme Court of British Columbia, which they could not afford. The question of incorporation simmered until 1881. In the meantime, John Booth lost the 1875 election and Edwin Pimbury replaced him in the provincial legislature, which probably reflected the general opposition to Salt Spring's incorporation.

JOHN PATTON BOOTH

John Patton Booth was born in the Orkney Islands in 1838, came to Canada at four, and arrived in Victoria when he was twenty-one. Booth pre-empted 200 acres (80 ha) straddling what is now Booth Canal. There he lived until he married Elizabeth Griffiths, who ran

the extensive Fernwood nursery and orchard that her late husband had purchased from Jonathan Begg. After the marriage, Booth sold his own land to Arthur Walter and moved to the Fernwood farm.

Booth's name seems connected with every Salt Spring public organization of the day. He was an officer of the Salt Spring Island Agricultural Association, a road commissioner, one of three elected members of the first school board, reeve of the Township of Salt Spring Island, and one of two representatives from the constituency of Cowichan in the first provincial legislature.

John Patton Booth's large and impressive funeral at St. Mark's Church in 1902 was attended by Premier James Dunsmuir and thirty other members of the legislature. BCARS A-1092

Booth lost two subsequent provincial elections but won again in 1890 in the new North Victoria constituency, which included most of the Gulf Islands. He held the seat until his death in 1902. At the time of his death, Booth was Speaker of the British Columbia legislature.

The By-laws of 1873 for the Township of Salt Spring Island

Salt Spring's 1873 by-laws included reference to:

I. *Road committees.* To inspect and report to the council on road requirements and costs with a pay scale that ranged from $2.25 per day for a road overseer to $4.00 per day for a man and team.

II. *Bulls.* To protect farmers' cows from unsanctioned unions, no bull was allowed to run free during April, May, and June of each year. Transgressions would cost a bull's owner $5.00 for each offence.

III. *Licences.* A licence was required to sell "goods, wares, merchandise or vending Liquors."

IV. *Public places.* The following "public places" for posting of public notices were identified: Burgoyne Bay School House, Burgoyne Bay Wharf, Central School House, Vesuvius Bay Wharf, and Begg's Settlement School House.

The incorporation fight ended after the 1881 municipal elections. Nineteen settlers from the south end paid $100 to sue the council clerk and returning officer—Henry W. Robinson—and his two associates—Charles Horel and Henry Rogers—for malpractice during the election. None of the defendants appeared in court, and the suit was not contested. The election was disallowed, and Robinson was charged with the costs. Ironically, there were no opposing candidates in a second election, most settlers refused to vote, and the existing council continued to serve.

The nineteen settlers went a step further a month later, when they petitioned the lieutenant governor to take action against Robinson and the justice of the peace, Frederick Foord. They charged that these men had run the council almost alone, had concealed the council's financial dealings from taxpayers, and had committed many irregularities—including common assault—during the election. Foord denied all the charges, accused the petitioners of perjury and not attending council meetings, and claimed they simply wanted to avoid taxation. The government did nothing at this time.

In 1882, John Booth was charged with retaining his position of reeve without election (perhaps unfairly, since there had been no opposition in the election) and for being a "puppet" of the councillors. Opponents to the municipal government objected to having a government that they had refused to support but that had continued to function nonetheless.

By now, everyone was thoroughly sick of incorporation. Even Booth was ready to end it, and wrote to Premier William Smithe:

> There seems to be an impression among some of the people here that you are going to wind the whole thing up and do away with it altogether. Should you have any such intentions and can see your way clear to do so, I do not think any one will object, providing the government take charge of and keep in order our wharves and roads. Our two wharves are in a dangerous condition at present, and if not attended to before long will probably fall. . . . Please give the matter your serious consideration as soon as possible because if we have to start things running again there is no time to lose.[1]

On May 12, 1883, the provincial legislature passed an act to cancel the letters patent establishing a municipality on Salt Spring. The island's first experience with self-government had failed, largely because of the councillors' insensitivity to opposition and the islanders' reluctance to give power to a higher authority, especially over taxation. Salt Spring has often considered re-incorporating, but islanders' inability to agree has prevented it.

BUILDING COMMUNITIES

By 1872, there were two communities in north Salt Spring—at Fernwood (Beggsville) and Vesuvius-Central—and one in the south, in the Fulford-

Burgoyne Valley. Settlement soon speeded up throughout the island. The population almost tripled from an estimated 91 in 1871 to 258 a decade later, when 65 percent of the residents were women and children under fourteen. There were 148 people in 39 families in the south end and 110 people in 32 families in the north end.[2]

The Beaver Point area began to develop into a recognizable community. Two Germans, Theodore Trage and Henry Spikerman, had shared 640 acres (256 ha) in the Beaver Point area since their arrival around 1860. A third German, Henry Meinerstorf, was living farther north on the west side of what is now Ruckle Park until at least the mid-1870s. A number of other settlers had come and gone, including several immigrants of Hawaiian descent (see chapter 7).

A QUIETLY SUCCESSFUL FARMER

Theodore Trage was born in Germany in 1834. He arrived in New York twenty years later and may have reached Salt Spring as early as 1860. He and his partner, Henry Spikerman, each pre-empted land between Reginald Hill and Beaver Point. Like many early settlers, Trage lived with an aboriginal woman, Susannah George, with whom he had four children—Adolph, Emma, Clara, and Bertha.

Susannah and Theodore Trage. Courtesy Barbara Lyngard

Trage was a horticulture graduate of the University of Heidelberg. He and Spikerman quickly developed the largest orchard on the island, with 1800 trees on about 20 acres (80 ha). The rest of the 839-acre (335 ha) farm was eventually used to graze sheep. In the early days, Trage rowed his strawberries and other small fruits to market in Victoria. Between 1898 and 1902, the farm shipped 1800–2400 boxes of apples each year. On Trage's death in 1902, the farm passed to his son.

Like many early settlers, Trage was civic minded. Although his name is absent from the first voters' lists, in 1874 he was one of those who registered his opposition to the incorporation of Salt Spring. In 1885, he and Spikerman donated 40 acres (16 ha) (the land was registered in Spikerman's name) for a new school at Beaver Point. (Trage's daughter Bertha later became one of the school's first teachers.) Eventually, this land formed Beaver Point Park, adjacent to Ruckle Provincial Park, and contained both Beaver Point School and Beaver Point Hall. Trage was also a founding member of the Salt Spring Island Fruit Growers' Association in 1896 and remained actively involved in it until his death.

Settlement at Beaver Point had a major boost in 1872 when Henry Ruckle, now one of Salt Spring's best-known pioneers, pre-empted land on the island. Ruckle was born in 1835 in Ireland of German parents. He emigrated to Ontario, then to California, before coming to Salt Spring. Ruckle immediately hired Japanese labourers to help him clear his land. (Japanese men were often contracted by Canadian organizations in cities like Victoria, and afterward had to return to Japan.) Ruckle cooked for his workers and built himself a cabin to live in. Only a year later, Ruckle informed the government that he had built a house and barn and cleared and fenced 20 acres (8 ha). He then applied for permission to buy more land at Beaver Point.

Ashdown Green, the government surveyor of Salt Spring in 1874, recorded that Ruckle was unmarried and had seventeen cattle and twenty pigs but no horses or sheep. Green was evidently impressed with Ruckle: "This man has the making of a good farm and he seems an industrious fellow if his work for the last two years may be taken as a criterion. He has about 30 acres cleared and fenced and has more land available for clearing."[3] By 1877, Ruckle had bought a total of about 340 acres (136 ha). He was able to pay for all his land at a dollar per acre by 1879.

Henry Ruckle was fairly isolated and soon realized that he needed a wife and compatible neighbours. He solved his first problem when he married Norwegian-born Ella Anna Christiansen in 1877. The couple originally met in Tacoma, Washington, in the early 1870s when Ella Anna was married to her first husband and Henry was on his way from Ontario to British Columbia. When they met again a few years later, Henry was working in a hardware store to earn money so he could pre-empt on Salt Spring. They eventually married in December 1877 in Victoria, after Ella Anna's husband had been killed in a mining accident. Marriage was a good arrangement for both parties, according to Henry's granddaughter Gwen Ruckle. Henry needed a wife to help him look after his Salt Spring farm, and Ella Anna needed a father for her infant son, Alfred. Altogether they had four children: Alfred, Ella, Agnes, and Daniel Henry.

SALT SPRING SURVEYED

On June 8, 1874, Ashdown Green was given the task of surveying Salt Spring. His instructions were to register all pre-emption claims on "the rectangular or square system where practicable." His challenge was to reconcile this with a haphazard settlement pattern and the range and section plan that had been used to record settlers' claims.

Green landed at Burgoyne Bay two days later. He started his survey in the south end with Joseph Akerman's land and continued with Frederick Foord's. Green's diary contains a wealth of information on Salt Spring's early settlers. In his itemized list, "X" indicates an aboriginal woman. The spellings are Green's.

List of Settlers	Men	Women	Children	Horses	Cattle	Sheep	Pigs
Mitchell	1	1	3	2			
McDonald	1	1					
Carnes	1	1	2		9		
Purser	1	X	3	—	7	—	20
Ford	1	1	0				
Williams	1	1	0				
Sparrow	1	X	3	1	30		
Gyves	1	X					
Welsh	1						
Meinersdorf	1			1	12		
Trage	1	X	1		13		28
Maxwell	1	X	4		100		30
Sparrow	1	X	2		33		30
Ruckles	1	0	0		17		20
Howmere (Kanaka)	1	X			2		12
Nuan	1	X					
Shepherd	1	X	4				
Pimburys	3	0	0	0	2	350	0
Ackerman	1	1	4				
Spikerman in partnership with Trage							
Weston	1	0	0				

As they worked, surveyors buried small pieces of china a metre or so below their stakes. If there was any dispute about the location of a stake, the presence of the china could confirm the accurate location.

Like many settlers, Henry Ruckle became active in local affairs. In 1877, he was appointed to form a Court of Revision and Appeal for the polling division of Salt Spring. Later, he built a wharf at Beaver Point, which became an important connection between the area and its Vancouver Island markets and suppliers. He also served as postmaster at Beaver Point and as one of

Henry and Ella Anna Ruckle on their Beaver Point farm, c. 1890. SSIA

three trustees on the Beaver Point School District. For a while, he earned extra income as a road foreman for the Beaver Point area.

Ella Anna was also very active. As well as running the home and raising their four children, she occasionally acted as a midwife and was very involved in the day-to-day running of the farm. In fact, the community considered Henry the businessman of the family and Ella Anna as the farmer.

When Henry died in 1913 at seventy-seven, his farm of almost 1200 acres (480 ha) was the largest on Salt Spring. Ella Anna lived on the farm until her own death seventeen years later. In 1998, the Ruckle farm was the oldest family farm in British Columbia. Salt Spring residents will always remember the Ruckles for the beautiful provincial park created from their property.

Over the years, Henry Ruckle managed to lure several families to Salt Spring. His first conscript was Scottish-born Alexander McLennan. McLennan had taught school in Ontario, worked as a surveyor, gone to the Cariboo to seek gold but taught the assayers' children instead, and worked in a men's clothing store on Johnson Street in Victoria. There he met Ruckle, who persuaded him to settle on Salt Spring, where he bought 350 acres (140 ha) in 1882.

The McLennans' Glenshiel Farm was on Beaver Point Road near present-day McLennan Drive. Japanese workers helped clear the land. A mixed-farming and poultry operation in 1895, the farm grew to 600 acres (240 ha), and the farmhouse eventually had ten rooms. A 350-tree orchard was one of the farm's most outstanding features. McLennan worked as the postmaster at Beaver Point from 1886 to 1908 and briefly as a justice of the peace, a job he disliked. He also served as school board secretary for a time. Elizabeth McLennan was a source of strength to everyone around her, both in her own home and in the community. Friends and neighbours knew that they could always count on her help. Granddaughter Mary Davidson fondly remembered the McLennan home as a friendly, popular place where even strangers were welcomed and often invited to stay the night. With eight children—four sons and four daughters—and often the Beaver Point schoolteacher as a boarder, the McLennan house must also have been a busy centre.

Another south-end community got its start in 1874, when four brothers—Edwin, John, Phillip, and Augustus Pimbury—established a large sheep farm on the western flanks of Mt. Bruce and Mt. Tuam. The Pimbury brothers came from England via Cobble Hill on Vancouver Island. They were the first settlers in the Musgrave area of Salt Spring and probably built the first wharf at Musgrave Landing. Of the four, only John died on Salt Spring, and only Augustus married—at an advanced age. Edwin represented the constituency of Cowichan in the legislative assembly for two terms from 1875 to 1882, when he moved to Nanaimo. The Pimbury holdings on Salt Spring were bought by Edward Musgrave in 1885.

Salt Spring's south end acquired its first school in 1873, when the Burgoyne Bay School District was formed. The new one-room schoolhouse was built across from what is today the Burgoyne United Church on land donated by John Sparrow, a Norwegian-born logger who had come to Salt Spring in 1860. (The school later burned down.) In 1880, Burgoyne Bay also acquired a post office with Frederick Foord as its first postmaster.

A MAN OF RELIGION

Born in Bristol in 1826, Charles Horel lived in the United States for more than twenty years before coming to Salt Spring in 1878. The devout Methodist had a reputation as a fire-and-brimstone lay preacher. His grandson, another Charles Horel, wrote of his grandfather with humour, in a family history:

> Besides building his farmhouse and barns and clearing the land, he also logged with oxen down into Fulford

Harbour and constructed a number of buildings on the Island, including the little Methodist church in Burgoyne Valley. . . .

Grandfather was a hard-working, earnest and pious Methodist. He ran a strict, bible-guided household and could not bear to look upon a sinner in that group. A story in the family was that the little girl who left the family in San Francisco to sing on the stage later married a quite wealthy man of that town. She and her husband sailed up to Salt Spring in their own sailing ship and anchored in Burgoyne Bay. However, sanctimonious old Grandfather refused to go aboard or have them visit at the farm-house. . . .

When Grandfather felt the breath of the angel of death, he transferred his Burgoyne hilltop farm over into the name of his eldest son, our Uncle Jim. In November of 1892, he was struck by a generous impulse and he made out a will leaving his faithful wife, Sarah, the rest of his estate, which was itemised for probate two years later as:

One span of horses	$200.00
One Waggon	40.00
Two cows	20.00
Three heifers	70.00
Three hogs	30.00
7 small pigs	5.00
12 Hens	10.00
One plough	10.00
One Harrow	5.00

. . . Father said she sometimes mentioned how overwhelmed by gratitude she was at the benison of seven small pigs and twelve hens.

Vesuvius Bay, in the north end of the island, was largely dominated by Estalon José Bittancourt, a Portuguese born in the Azores in 1845. In some ways, Bittancourt was a romantic figure. According to one story, he went to sea at about fifteen by swimming out to a sailing ship. When he reached Vancouver Island, he was refused shore leave but swam ashore at Royal Roads. In the early 1860s, on the advice of another Portuguese, John Norton, he moved to Salt Spring and became a successful entrepreneur.

In 1873, Bittancourt opened a store—on the site of today's Vesuvius Inn parking lot—which he enlarged thirteen years later, adding a post office. He brought goods for his store from Victoria on his own sloop. During his life on the island, Bittancourt operated sandstone quarries, farmed, mined coal, and built several fine houses. In 1878, Father Gustave Donckele from Saanich Mission said the first mass on Salt Spring in a private chapel on the second floor of Bittancourt's house. About ten years later, Bittancourt built a chapel in a separate building, which he called "The Ark." This building was still standing in 1998.

Vesuvius Bay, c. 1890, showing the houses that Estalon Bittancourt built. Note that the area has been extensively logged. SSIA

GETTING ON AND OFF THE ROCK

Marine service to Salt Spring improved steadily through the mid-1860s. In 1865, the propeller-driven *Sir James Douglas* was launched for government service on the coast. The ship carried freight, mail, and settlers, and its crew also tended lighthouses and helped shipwrecked vessels. From 1881, another steamship, the Victoria-built *Emma*, offered passenger service in competition with the *Sir James Douglas*.

In 1883, the Canadian Pacific Navigation (CPN) Company was formed when the Pioneer Shipping Line, Hudson's Bay Company shipping interests, and the East Coast Mail Line amalgamated. The CPN was acquired in 1901 by the Canadian Pacific Railway, the company that launched the famous *Princess* ships.

The Hawaiian Community

HAWAIIANS COME TO SALT SPRING

I n the late eighteenth century, ships from Europe began stopping at the Hawaiian Islands, which Captain Cook named the Sandwich Islands in 1778. Some ships took Hawaiians—or Sandwich Islanders as they were then called—with them when they left, occasionally as passengers but more often conscripted as crew. Then, in the early nineteenth century, American and British employers began to hire Hawaiian men to work in the whaling industry and in fur trade posts on the northwest coast of North America. (Hawaii was the closest source of labour for this area.) These people were known as *Ow(h)yhees* (a variation of Hawaiians) or *Kanakas*, a Hawaiian word meaning "person" or "human." Several thousand British Columbians probably descend from these Hawaiian immigrants.

KEY DATES

1778 Captain Cook is the first European to land on Kauai Island.

1868 Kiave, the first Hawaiian to pre-empt land on Salt Spring, settles at Fulford Harbour.

1875 William Naukana and John Palua pre-empt land on Portland Island.

1885 St. Paul's Catholic Church, built largely by Hawaiians, is consecrated.

1902 Maria Mahoi inherits and moves to Russell Island.

The Hawaiian men who left their country may have been fleeing poverty, debts, or unhappy marriages (such manoeuvres were aptly termed "north-west-coast divorces"[1]). Or, if they were Catholic, they may have been escaping persecution in Hawaii, since Hawaiians considered Roman Catholics to be idol worshippers. Or they might simply have been looking for adventure. In any event, these men were respected for their hard work and loyalty, as well as their boat-handling, boat-building, swimming, diving, and fighting skills. Those who ended up in the fur trade often found themselves working alongside French Canadians and Orkney islanders as labourers, boatmen, millhands, farmworkers, and blacksmiths.

Many Hawaiians returned to Hawaii after their contracts ended, but others

An Unceremonious Arrival

Karey Litton of Victoria, a descendant of part-Hawaiian settler Maria Mahoi, said the Hawaiians were unwilling arrivals. Jean Barman recorded her version of the story:

> Natives, local natives tell the story that when the early sailing ships arrived with the cattle, etc., they often picked up supplies in Hawaii and they took on Hawaiian crews and then when they got up off of San Juan, rather than pay the Hawaiian crew, they simply threw them overboard. That's how the natives say some, not all, of the early Hawaiians arrived here. They were just thrown off the ships out on the San Juan Islands.

According to another story, recorded by Eric Roberts in *Salt Spring Saga*, Hawaiian seamen regularly "moved" to Salt Spring Island by jumping overboard and swimming to the island as their ships passed Isabella Point. Ships' captains are said to have been so concerned that they would chain all Hawaiians before passing Salt Spring. This story, though highly unlikely, is a romantic explanation of how Hawaiians reached the island.

remained in North America, where the Hudson's Bay Company (HBC) encouraged them to marry aboriginal women as an incentive to settle down and continue their employment. At first, these were mostly common-law arrangements, but many couples later had church marriages.

As island dwellers, many Hawaiians found the San Juan and Gulf islands congenial. Some settled on Piers, Coal, Portland, and Russell islands, while about eighteen chose the Beaver Point and Isabella Point areas at the southern end of Salt Spring, which became known as "a Kanaka settlement."

A man named Kiave was the first Hawaiian to pre-empt land on Salt Spring. He brought with him his aboriginal wife, Mary, and his baby daughter, Lucy. Kiave pre-empted about 150 acres (60 ha) along the shore between Isabella Point and the head of Fulford Harbour in 1868. He and Mary cleared a little over 6 acres (2.4 ha) and built a house and seven-foot fences—all within one year. He then applied for a government survey so that he would be eligible to own the land. When Kiave died in the early 1880s, his wife married a Songhees man. Although Mary moved away from Salt Spring, in 1885 she sought title to the Kiave land in the name of her son, Frank. By that time, another Hawaiian, William Naukana, may have been living on it.

William Haumea brought his aboriginal wife, Mary, and teenaged daughter (also named Mary) to Salt Spring in about 1873. The Haumeas first settled near Eleanor Point (directly south of Beaver Point), where Haumea officially pre-empted land in 1877. A reference in surveyor Ashdown Green's 1874 diary probably refers to Haumea:

> Sept. 26 Passed a Kanakas claim (Bill Howmore). This is another hard place for a ranch. He has about 4 acres under cultivation, principally with Indian corn or potatoes, and estimates that he can get about 7 acres more on his claim. The rest is rock. [Green also notes that Haumea had two cows and twelve pigs.]

In 1886, Haumea acquired Russell Island, where he grew vegetables and fruit.

A PATRIARCH: WILLIAM NAUKANA

Some Hawaiians who were living on San Juan Island in 1872 when it became US territory moved to British Columbia. One was William Naukana, probably Salt Spring's best-known Hawaiian settler. Naukana, perhaps

BY ANY OTHER NAME

Many immigrants to Canada had their non-English names changed. Sometimes only the spelling changed, but often the names themselves changed, usually because other people found the names too difficult to pronounce or remember. This was especially true of Hawaiian immigrants. Traditionally, Hawaiians were given only one name. One Beaver Point man was always known simply as "Kanaka Bill."

The following people of Hawaiian descent settled on or near Salt Spring between 1868 and 1885. Their names are italicized, and some alternative spellings of their names are given in parentheses: *Kiave* (Kaiwe, Chowy); William *Nawana* (Nuana, Onawon); John ("Peavine" or "Pevines") *Kahon* (Kahou, Kahow); William *Haumea* (Haamea); Maria *Mahoi* (Mahoy); William *Naukana* (Naukanna, Nanton, Manton, Nowkin, Likameen, Lagamin, Lackaman, La-Gamine); John *Palua* (Pallow, Pellow, Polua). No wonder it's often difficult to find out what happened to these people!

related to the Hawaiian royal family, is thought to have been born in Hawaii in 1813. He worked for the HBC in various BC locations from 1845 to 1856. He claimed to have been hired by HBC chief factor James Douglas. Naukana was tall, strong, and bearded. He was probably illiterate, as he signed his name with an X.

After his HBC contract ended, Naukana apparently returned to Hawaii where he found his family's land had been sold. Disillusioned, he returned to settle on San Juan Island. In 1872, he moved back to BC, where he was allowed to become a citizen, own land, and vote, which had been impossible in the United States. Naukana and his close friend John Palua would become naturalized British subjects in 1889.

In 1875, when Naukana was sixty-two and Palua fifty-eight, they pre-empted most of Portland Island and developed an extensive farm, with sheep and cattle, fruit trees, and vegetable gardens. They may also have earned money transporting people and freight from island to island by canoe.

With at least two aboriginal women, Naukana fathered six daughters and a son who died as a child. Two daughters married other Hawaiian descendants. The oldest, Sophie, married and had five children with Naukana's partner, John Palua, almost forty years her senior. Palua died in 1907, the same year Naukana sold Portland Island. Naukana died two years later.

Children of Hawaiian immigrants such as Sophie Naukana tended to marry within their own community, as Jean Barman's extensive research indicated:

William Naukana, c. 1880. Many of Naukana's descendants continue to live on Salt Spring. Courtesy Dick Toynbee

> More often neighbors' children married each other, as with the...
Naukanas, Mahois, and Nawanas on Saltspring. As had their parents, many descendants had two or more relationships in their lifetime. As one has observed: "A lot of families married and separated and remarried." Perhaps not surprisingly, only at the end of a long afternoon of conversation with me did two long-time friends realize that they shared common great-grandparents of mixed Hawaiian and Native descent.

A MATRIARCH: MARIA MAHOI

One Hawaiian descendant we know much about is Maria (pronounced Ma-RYE-ah) Mahoi, who eventually settled on Russell Island. She is of particular interest because many islanders are descended from her and because she lived the kind of hard life typical of most early Salt Spring settlers.

A CLOSE CALL

Salt Spring author Bea Hamilton, whose family's property adjoined William Naukana's after he arrived from Portland Island, recorded (in *Salt Spring Island*) a story of Naukana's from his Hudson's Bay Company years.

A sudden snowstorm trapped Naukana and a small fur-hunting party in an unmapped area. After several days, out of food and horse feed, they decided to kill a horse for meat but found that all the horses had wandered off into the blizzard. So the men decided to draw lots, with the loser to be that night's dinner:

> That really alarmed Naukana as he wasn't in on the bizarre draw and he figured they would naturally choose him to be sacrificed as he was the servant—the only native amongst them. To him this was a normal procedure, as in his native land in far off days he knew that for any sacrifice, a slave or servant was always the choice.

In fear, Naukana ran off into the snowstorm and hacked a hole in a snowbank to hide himself.

> As he dug down with his hunting knife, he came upon a mound that was pretty solid and he dug quickly hoping that this might be a log where some sleeping grubs would ease the gnawing hunger in his stomach. Suddenly he shouted aloud in his joy—he had stumbled onto the dead and frozen body of one of their poor horses! This was his miracle indeed! Naukana managed to hack off a chunk of meat and he hastened to retrace his steps before they became obliterated by the still falling snow.

In camp, Naukana and his prize were a welcome sight. The next day, the men were rescued by aboriginal people with dogsleds.

Maria was born on the Saanich Peninsula in 1855, the child of an unknown aboriginal or part-aboriginal mother and a Hawaiian father employed by the HBC (she gave her father's name as William Mahoya on her 1900 marriage certificate).

Maria's first relationship was with a man twice her age—an American sea captain, Abel Douglas. In 1870, at fifteen, she became pregnant with Douglas's child. Douglas pre-empted land near Beaver Point in 1877, and four years later, the family could afford a twelve-year-old aboriginal house servant.

In 1887, like many Catholic working-class parents, Maria sent two daughters to St. Ann's Convent School in the Cowichan Valley. Salt Spring girls had boarded at St. Ann's since four-year-old Emma Palua attended in 1874. Maria, herself illiterate, probably wanted her children to acquire an education and basic Catholic religious instruction. Poor families who sent a child to St. Ann's also had one less mouth to feed at home.

A SALT SPRING GHOST STORY

An old log house hidden away on the southwestern corner of Ruckle Provincial Park has a tragic history. The Peavine House was built in about 1883 by John "Peavine" Kahon, a Hawaiian who pre-empted 160 acres (64 ha) near the home of William Haumea and his family. Kahon married Haumea's daughter, Mary, and the couple had a son. Kahon, known for his violent temper, reputedly beat Mary when she was next pregnant. Perhaps as a result, in 1892, Mary and her twins died in childbirth.

According to local legend, thunder and lightning marked the funeral in Haumea's orchard, and the guests shuddered with fear. The orchard was considered haunted from that time on. The year after Mary's death, John Kahon sold the Peavine House to Henry Ruckle and left Salt Spring. People still live in the Peavine House today.

When Douglas disappeared from Salt Spring and Maria's life around 1890, the couple had seven children. Still an attractive woman in her mid-thirties, Maria and her children were soon living with George Fisher, ten years younger than her and the godfather of her last child with Douglas. Fisher was the son of an English father and an aboriginal mother. A devout Catholic, he had been educated by the Christian Brothers in Victoria after his father's death. Fisher had joined his mother and her new partner, George Purser, on Salt Spring. Maria and Fisher had another six children, not all of whom survived to adulthood. The last was born in 1899, when Maria was about forty-four. A Catholic priest married the couple a year later.

A TRAGIC DISPUTE

Alfred Douglas, Maria Mahoi's thirty-six-year-old second son, was fatally shot by Beaver Point neighbour George Williams in 1907. The testimony at the inquest described a small gathering at the Williams property opposite Beaver Point Hall on the afternoon of the murder. Those present included neighbours James and Emiek Sparrow (Douglas was married to one of John Sparrow's daughters), William Norton, Alfred Douglas, Susannah Trage (Emma's mother), and George and Emma Williams and their young daughter. The men had been smoking, drinking, and possibly playing cards. At one point Williams had appeared angry with Douglas.

Between three and four in the afternoon, Williams left to go to bed, and Douglas followed him. A shot rang out and Douglas was found dead. The murder had no clear motive, although newspaper reports suggested that Williams was angry about Douglas's advances to his wife. Williams was arrested and taken to Victoria, where he was tried, convicted, and sentenced to fourteen years in prison. Douglas's widow later married Dick Maxwell, Williams's brother-in-law. That's how interconnected many islanders' lives were!

When he died in 1902, William Haumea left Russell Island to Maria. No one is sure why. It is not even absolutely certain that "Mary Ann Haumea"—named in Haumea's will as his beneficiary—was really Maria. But as his only daughter, Mary, had died in childbirth, there seemed no other obvious heirs. Within six weeks of Haumea's death, Maria's lawyer registered her claim to be legally declared Haumea's daughter, a claim supported by affidavits sworn by her son Alfred, Haumea's widow, and two neighbours, John Pappenburger and Alexander McLennan. It may be that Haumea had adopted Maria, or she may have cared for him in his old age.

Maria Mahoi Douglas (later Fisher) at thirty, 1885. Courtesy Karey Litton

Maria and George Fisher built a small frame house, which still stands on Russell Island (today a provincial marine park). There they lived a self-sufficient lifestyle, providing for almost all of their family's needs. They raised sheep and chickens, kept a cow for milk, and caught fish, clams, crabs, and other seafood. They also grew apples, peaches, grapes, and strawberries, which provided a valuable source of revenue. They gathered and dried seaweed for Chinese and Japanese traders who sold it in Victoria and Vancouver. George earned additional money by pruning trees on Salt Spring and by fishing, and Maria bartered her skills as a midwife for whatever families could afford. Anything they couldn't produce themselves Maria and George bought from the Sidney Trading Company. They felt Sidney's lower prices repaid the effort of rowing 16 km.

Like other Salt Spring pioneers, the Fishers lived a hard life on Russell Island by today's standards. Maria was constantly busy caring for her many children, and cooking, drying, and preserving plentiful produce for the winter. She made wine, smoked herring and salmon, and created her own canning jars from glass bottles. Having no refrigeration, she hung perishables down the well.

Despite almost ceaseless work, Maria and George seem to have had a rich life. Maria loved to swim and boat. Maria's grandchildren remembered their swimming lessons:

> "She would take you swimming with her nightgown on. That was her bathing suit."
> "She put me on a board and I was on her back and she would swim along the water with me on her back."
> "I thought she was trying to make me drown, but she was trying to make me swim. I got on her back and she taught me."[2]

In 1936, at eighty-one, Maria Mahoi died. Her husband, George Fisher, lived on Russell Island until his own death in 1948.

Maria's psychic powers

Maria Mahoi's grandchildren testify to her psychic powers. Granddaughter Violet Bell told how Maria, on seeing a snake in the garden, unenthusiastically, but successfully, predicted the arrival of a less-than-welcome guest. Another grandchild, Harry Roberts, remembered that Maria was always assured of wind to propel her sailboat. If the wind died, she just whistled, and it magically reappeared. It seems she'd inherited this power from her Hawaiian ancestors.

THE HAWAIIAN LEGACY

People of Hawaiian ancestry living on Salt Spring or nearby islands significantly contributed to and used Salt Spring's institutions. The Naukana children from Portland Island and the Fisher children from Russell rowed to Salt Spring each day to attend Beaver Point School, and St. Paul's Church in Fulford Harbour was a centre of Hawaiian life for many years. Among the church's first events were the baptisms of Hawaiian children. By the 1930s,

Isabella Point School opened in 1904. This photo was taken the next year when Willie Palua (left) received the Roll of Honour from teacher Adelaide Bailey. SSIA

thirty to thirty-five members of Hawaiian families were buried in the church's graveyard.

Among the Hawaiians' traditions was the desire to party and have a good time. Their parties, or luaus, featured food roasted in beach fire pits, music, dancing, and much drinking. These parties would often continue for days, moving from island to island, home to home. The community must have boasted talented musicians, since several Hawaiian descendants from Salt Spring were working as musical entertainers in the late nineties. In *Salt Spring Island*, Bea Hamilton wrote a colourful account of the Hawaiians' parties:

> At the first inkling of a luau all the Hawaiians would load up their canoes with food, family and friends, not forgetting the home brew, a special Salt Spring mountain dew made by experts in that line and cached away in some dark hole for just such an occasion as an all-out party.... The party would gather speed day by day and many a group could out-wiggle any Hawaiian affair ever staged in their native land.

Some aspects of Hawaiian culture never reached the island, especially elements such as the hula that passed through the female line, since no Hawaiian women came to Salt Spring. Maria Mahoi was an exception: her descendants report that she spoke some Hawaiian and taught her children and grandchildren to dance the hula. The Hawaiian language also failed to survive:

> Most families spoke English, possibly in combination with Chinook, the trading jargon long used across the Pacific Northwest. According to a granddaughter, "the wife of Grandpa Naukana spoke Indian and Chinook, but he wanted children to speak only English and Chinook, not Native Indian and not Hawaiian.[3]

Today, the only obvious evidence of the Hawaiian influence on Salt Spring is a couple of names—Kanaka Road and the Kanaka Restaurant in Ganges—and the Polynesian features of some Hawaiian descendants. Visitors to St. Paul's Roman Catholic Church can learn a little about the Hawaiians on the island from the Salt Spring Island Historical Society plaque and the gravestones of Hawaiians and their descendants.

St. Paul's Church was consecrated on May 10, 1885. Note the large number of dark-skinned Hawaiian descendants celebrating the occasion. SSIA

ROBBING PETER TO PAY PAUL

Since most Catholics lived in Salt Spring's south end, Fulford Harbour was the obvious choice for a church site. Father Gustave Donckele, the first Catholic missionary to the Gulf Islands, had been enthusiastically and frequently rowing to Salt Spring from his mission at Cowichan since 1878. St. Paul's was founded that year and built under his direction between 1880 and 1885.

Horace John Shepherd, though not a Catholic himself, donated about 5 acres (2 ha) for the church. Community members, especially the largely Catholic Hawaiian population, did most of the construction. Estalon José Bittancourt (the first store owner at Vesuvius), John Pappenburger, Joseph and Ted Akerman, John Maxwell, John King, Dick Purser, and Michael Gyves also worked on the church, as did some Cowichan people.

Lumber for the church was brought from Cowichan by dugout canoe to Burgoyne Bay and then by ox-drawn stoneboat through the Fulford-Burgoyne Valley. The windows (including one stained-glass window), door, and bell came from a dismantled stone church at Cowichan Bay, often called "the Butter Church" because the proceeds of butter sales from Father Pierre Rondeault's farm had partly paid for it. For this reason, people often said that the Catholic church at Fulford had been built by "robbing Peter [Rondeault] to pay Paul [St. Paul's]."

Dedicated on May 10, 1885, St. Paul's is Salt Spring's oldest church building. Its little graveyard contains—unfortunately in unmarked graves—the remains of many Hawaiians, including several Paluas and Tahouneys, Mary Haumea, William Naukana, and Maria Mahoi.

8

Connections and Communities

1884–1899

A TIME OF GROWTH

Communities, a social framework, and services had evolved on Salt Spring Island by the mid-1880s. The arrival of the first settlers had marked the first phase of development. Next followed basic connections and services: a few rough roads, wharves, schools, some policing, and the establishment of sketchy political organizations.

This phase of Salt Spring's growth seems dynamic and exciting today, but it must have been disturbing for many early settlers. Between 1881 and 1891, the island's population grew by more than 50 percent. Many new residents, arriving from Britain and Ireland, were generally more affluent, better educated, and more class conscious than the first settlers. Services on the island also grew enormously. Between 1884 and the end of the century, Salt Spring acquired two new schools (Beaver Point School and Ganges School in the Divide), two new post offices, two boarding houses, more steamer calls at several island wharves, the island's first full-time doctor, four churches, a community hall, and at least six stores and businesses. By 1900, the island was a well-established community.

NEWCOMERS TO THE SOUTH END

Several new families, mostly of mixed race, joined the Ruckles and McLennans near Beaver Point. They included brothers Thomas and John Pappenburger, whose father, George Pappenburger, had immigrated from Bavaria to Vancouver Island in 1857 and married a Cowichan woman. In 1886, twenty-two-year-old Thomas came to Salt Spring and had a son with Emma Purser, also of mixed race. However, Thomas almost immediately left to work on sealing ships, and the couple may never have lived together. Thomas drowned when his ship, the *Triumph*, sank in 1904.

John Pappenburger pre-empted land southwest of the Ruckles and in 1889 married Mary Ann Pielle (or Pierre), a Penelakut from nearby Kuper Island. They had eight children. John was the first mail carrier for Beaver Point and later picked up south-end farmers' milk for the Ganges Creamery.

Joseph King, who came to Canada from Greece, married a Songhees woman named Mary Tegurviei who already had a daughter, Emma. Joseph and Mary settled near the Pappenburgers, where Joseph farmed and worked on boats. In 1883, Emma married another Greek immigrant, John Stevens.

The Kings gave the young couple 4 acres (1.6 ha) of their land as a marriage gift. Stevens, who had worked on freighters, now fished commercially. The couple had seven children. When Emma decided to return to the Esquimalt Reserve, Stevens cared for the children on his own.

The Musgrave area remained relatively unsettled. The Pimburys' 7000-acre (2800 ha) farm with its 350 sheep was sold to Edward Musgrave in

KEY DATES

1884 Joseph Akerman opens The Traveller's Rest, which houses the first store in the island's south end.

1885 Beaver Point School opens.

1887 The Union Church (now Burgoyne United Church) is built and consecrated.

The Stevens Boarding House opens in the north end.

1891 The population of Salt Spring reaches 435.

1896 The first fall fair is held on the grounds of the newly completed Central Hall.

1897 The first telephone wires are erected on Salt Spring.

WORKING IN JAPAN?

Many young men, including islanders, went sealing near Japan, almost 5000 km away. Each January, sealers would leave Victoria to return in September or October. Each man would bring back one or two thousand dollars. But they didn't always return. The *Triumph's* 1904 disappearance, for example, claimed the lives of several young Salt Spring men, including members of the King, Palua, and Pappenburger families.

1885. Musgrave, the fourth son of an Irish aristocrat, lived in a house near Musgrave Landing. Nearby were hired hands' cottages; cow and hay barns; an orchard; fenced fields for hay, oats, and root crops; and three or four fenced paddocks. Musgrave sold the farm to Clive and Edward Trench just seven years later, but left his name on the landing built by the Pimburys.

The Musgrave ranch was isolated—essentially cut off from the rest of the island. The nearest community was the Vancouver Island village of Cowichan Bay. Aside from the steamer *Isabel's* twice-weekly visits, contact with the outside world could be made only by private launch. The Musgrave community in 1891 included the Musgrave family members, shepherd Alexander Aitken, the Musgraves' Chinese cook and field foreman, and a few nearby residents. Aboriginal people passing Musgrave Landing in their canoes were also regular visitors.

Several settlers joined the Akerman, Gyves, and Sparrow families in the Fulford-Burgoyne Valley during this period. Edward Lee, arriving in 1886 from England by way of Ontario, and his brother Thomas, arriving six years later, left more than the Lee name behind. Edward settled at the bottom of what is now Lee Road and Tom at the top. They cleared their heavily timbered land, burned the timber, planted fruit trees, and developed a beautiful herd of Jersey cattle. Like most early Salt Spring farmers, they operated mixed farms. An 1895 promotional brochure on Salt Spring said: "Mr.

Edward Lee owns 400 acres, and with the aid of his brother, Mr. T. Lee, cultivates 150. Last year he raised 700 bushels of wheat, 50 tons of hay, and 75 tons of potatoes." The Lees reportedly had 250 fruit trees.[1]

John Carter Mollet and his wife Elizabeth brought their family to British Columbia from Ontario. In 1896, they bought a large farm on Ford Lake which they called Mereside. The family raised cattle, pigs, and geese, which they shipped to Victoria by steamer from Fulford Harbour and Burgoyne Bay. After about ten years, the Mollets sold their Ford Lake property and bought ten acres in the Fulford-Burgoyne Valley, where they lived for many years. John's elaborate garden made him a local celebrity. Lukin Johnston, travelling through BC in the late 1920s, visited Mollet's masterpiece:

> Through an ivy-covered gateway, I caught a glimpse of a most lovely garden ablaze with flowers. I heard a voice calling the chickens to supper and so, entering the gate, I met John Carter Mollet, eighty-one years old in March last, and still in love with every flower in his garden.
>
> He took me round the well-kept beds. "You seem to love your garden?" said I. "My garden? It is my life," he said earnestly. "I work from five in the morning till dark, and I am never done with the flowers!" Then, his snow-white hair and beard and his battered hat making him a quaint old figure, he took me to see his water-ram—a simple device by which he controls all the water he needs from his never-dry spring. . . .
>
> We stood and chatted awhile at the gate, and he gave me a buttonhole of pansies. Then he said: "Well, young man, I must go to my chickens. I've been living all alone for fourteen years, you know, and I'm busy. Good-bye—and come and see the old man's garden if you pass this way again."[2]

Other newcomers in the Fulford-Burgoyne Valley during this period included Joe Nightingale and Frederick and John Reid.

The Isabella Point area was mainly settled by Hawaiians until 1897, when Irishman William Hamilton and his English wife Caroline Louisa bought 66 waterfront acres (26 ha) halfway down the west side of Fulford Harbour. The upper-class Hamiltons had grown up with servants and must have found life on Salt Spring challenging, especially since most of their ten children[3] had

John Mollet's beautiful garden, c. 1900, which he loved to show to passersby. Today only a line of poplars marks its location. SSIA

physical disabilities.

Educated at the Royal School of Mines, William Hamilton is supposed to have invented one of the first incandescent light bulbs, but may never have worked for a living. On Salt Spring, the family had a two-storey house built, naming it Dromore after the Hamilton family's estate in Ireland. William Hamilton puttered about his hobby farm, indulging in gardening and animal husbandry. The Fulford-area Hamiltons identified most closely with the north end's English and Irish immigrants. William Hamilton was the Salt Spring correspondent for two Vancouver Island newspapers, a role that his daughter Bea was to take on in later years.

AND IN THE NORTH END

Among new north-end residents were brothers Henry and William Caldwell. As boys they had accompanied their widowed mother from Ireland to Scotland, moving to Victoria in 1884 after two years in Montreal. William

A VERY SPECIAL ISLANDER

Joe Nightingale, a cousin of Florence Nightingale, the famous English nurse, came to BC from Ontario in the 1880s. On Salt Spring, he met and married Fanny, the oldest child of Joseph and Martha Akerman. The couple settled near the school in the Fulford-Burgoyne Valley and had three children—George, Isabel, and William. Like many other island farmers, Joe supplemented his living by logging and working on Salt Spring's roads.

Schoolteacher Leonard Tolson remembered Joe Nightingale, whose daughter Martha married Gilbert Mouat, as a popular islander and a very strong man:

> My brother told me that the muscles of his back stood out like pieces of rope. He was a fine horseman and I was told of a very difficult thing he did....The Old Divide Road was very steep and a man was driving a loaded wagon down the hill without brakes and the load was too heavy for the horses to hold back and they got out of hand. Joe galloped up from behind (on horseback) and bending down held a spoke of one of the wheels, thus putting on the necessary brake—a good piece of work....(Joe was afterwards killed when his horse ran away on Cranberry Rd.)

found a stonemason's job at Estalon Bittancourt's sandstone quarry at Vesuvius, while Henry sought work in Oregon. William fell in love with a piece of land in the Walker Hook–Mansell Road area and summoned Henry home. The brothers bought 640 acres (256 ha) along Trincomali Channel, including the beautiful tombolo-peninsula known as Walker Hook. They

H. Lavigne and the original class of Beaver Point School. Sam Beddis and his sons built the school in 1885 with building materials hauled by stoneboat through the thick Beaver Point forest. The 1886-87 Public Schools Report lists ten boys and fourteen girls enrolled in the first year, with an average monthly attendance of twenty-two. Provincial school authorities were pleased with the school's total cost that year of $505 ($21.04 per student). Courtesy Gwen Ruckle/SSIA

built their first home in 1888. The Caldwells rowed their garden produce and fruit from their large orchard to Vancouver Island, selling to smelter-workers' families at Crofton. Henry supplemented his farm income for decades by working as road foreman.

British-born Samuel and Emily Beddis, their five children, and Emily's brother, Raffles Purdy, arrived in Victoria via San Francisco in 1884. Thirty-four-year-old Sam purchased a sloop in Victoria and the family sailed for Salmon River on northern Vancouver Island. A storm threw them off course and the Beddises ended up on San Juan Island, where US Customs agents asked them to leave. They eventually reached North Saanich. There they met Henry Ruckle, who was selling eggs and butter from his Beaver Point farm. He praised Salt Spring's good farmland and invited the Beddises to see for themselves. They liked what they saw and bought land south of Ganges

Harbour on the west shore near the outlet of Cusheon Creek.

The Beddises lived in a large tent while they built their first home, cooking over open fires and clearing the land laboriously without the help of horses or oxen. They planted trees from seeds gathered en route and later grafted cuttings from more than forty varieties of apples mailed from Ireland. (Each cutting survived the voyage embedded in a potato.) The Beddis orchard was well established by 1890.

Sam Beddis and his son Charles earned their living as builders, and their success won them building contracts on other Gulf Islands. Despite the few years they were in business, they built many of Salt Spring's heritage buildings—including Beaver Point School, the Stevens Boarding House on North End Road near Central, and the interior of St. Mark's (Anglican) Church.

Tragedy struck during the hard winter of 1893. After a heavy January snowfall, Sam Beddis caught a cold, which soon turned into pneumonia and pleurisy. His family bundled him up in blankets and rowed him out to catch the steamer to Victoria, where he died the following June. Salt Spring's most

The Beddis homestead after extensive clearing, c. 1885. Courtesy Rob Beddis/SSIA

popular beach and one of the island's prettiest country roads preserve the family's name.

Henry and Anne Stevens also arrived on Salt Spring in 1884 and settled first at Ganges Harbour. Three years later, they moved to a log farmhouse at Central Settlement, donating half an acre of their land to the Anglican church. After St. Mark's was consecrated in 1892, the Stevens farm next door became known as Church Hill Farm. Leonard Tolson's reminiscence, written for his daughter, painted a picture of Henry and Anne Stevens:

> From their way of speech they were Devonshire (said "Yer be I", etc.)....Old man Stevens used to sing songs (after a few) but could never remember the words, but had them written out in his pocket, and said he must go out to relieve nature and came back remembering two or three lines about a girl with "a Roman-shaped (h)eye and a cast in her nose." He was a fine old man— came out to B.C. on the construction of the C.P.R.—and was the first man to have a team of horses on S.S.I.
>
> Mrs. Stevens, affectionately known to us all as "Aunty," ran a boarding house (she had come out too on [the] C.P.R., running a camp at rail head). All the young men went there for dinner on Sunday (25¢). The best meal I have ever known at the price. (I once swallowed a wasp with the mint sauce, but it came up again later and I was none the worse.) Aunty was a dear old lady. She had one big front tooth which was very loose and the boys used to say that if she didn't do what they said, they would take it from her. The Stevens had no children [of their own], but had an adopted son, Walter. (I was told by C. Abbot that he was a side-line of old Stevens.) Mrs. Stevens adopted Eva Jenkins (who later married Walter and now has a large grown-up family).

The Stevenses ran Salt Spring's second rooming house from their home. Joe and Martha Akerman had opened the first in their home below Lee's Hill on the Fulford-Ganges Road to paying guests in 1884. The Akermans' Traveller's Rest and Stevens Boarding House were the only places visitors to Salt Spring could stay. Both charged a dollar a day or $5 a week.

A flurry of commercial activity on the island began in the mid-1880s. The Akermans began running a general store from The Traveller's Rest, and

The Traveller's Rest, somewhat run-down, was still standing in 1998. SSIA

Stevens Boarding House. SSIA

SALT SPRING'S
FIRST SUBDIVISION

As early as 1891, some early Salt Spring entrepreneurs had dreams of property development. They went so far as to have plans drawn up for what they hoped would be Salt Spring's main residential and commercial centre. (Of course, Ganges did not exist at this time.) The location was near Beggsville, on land on the west side of Walker's Hook Road, where Edward Mallandaine, Edward Walker, and some businessmen and land speculators owned property.

Grantville, as the development was to be called, was named after Victoria Mayor John Grant, a friend of Edward Mallandaine. A plan dated December 1891 and registered in Victoria shows that the land was surveyed and laid out in quarter-acre lots. Like many dreams, this one never went anywhere. The one legacy of Grantville is a sub-division with lots that are among the smallest on the island. And, of course, one of the streets in this little development is still called Grantville.

Estalon Bittancourt enlarged his Vesuvius store, offering a postal service as well as goods.

Joel and Mary Amanda Broadwell created the largest store on Salt Spring in 1892 in their Central Settlement home. They had come to the island with their two children ten years earlier with enough money to buy a large farm that extended from the west side of St. Mary Lake to the area now called Channel Ridge (for years it was known as Broadwell's Mountain). Joel was English and Mary Amanda was American. Joel became Salt Spring's second postmaster in 1883 and served until 1901.[4] Mary Amanda ran the store until her health failed. The Broadwells gave up the store in the late 1890s, although Joel continued to run the post office and opened a second store in

1900. After 1898, the post office also housed Salt Spring's first lending library, with a start-up collection of about sixty books.

By 1894, the Broadwells were Salt Spring's largest landowners, with 1260 acres (504 ha), including a market garden around their house and a sheep ranch on Broadwell's Mountain. The family joined the lively social life and growing fraternal and commercial associations of the island's north end, like other mainly British newcomers in the 1880s. After Mary Amanda died in 1901, Joel moved to Vancouver. Joel Broadwell, Jr., ran the farm briefly but then moved off-island. Their daughter, Anna Laura, who had married Henry Caldwell in 1888, remained. Both Joel Broadwell and his son died in 1909 and, with Mary Amanda, lie in the public cemetery at Central.

Raffles Purdy, who had taught school in London, accepted a job at Vesuvius School (locally known as Central School) soon after arriving on Salt Spring, "as they had such trouble keeping lady teachers, as they were in great demand by the single men."[5] From 1885 to 1897, Purdy taught all eight grades for $50. To be closer to the school, Purdy roomed with

The Broadwell house and store at Central (c. 1889), across from today's Portlock Park. Seated (on the fence) are Llewelyn Wilson and Joel Broadwell, Jr. In the foreground (from left) are Minnie Mouat, William Mouat, Jane Manson Mouat, and Jane Laurenson Mouat. Note St. Mark's Church in the distance. SSIA

8

Methodist, Presbyterian, and Anglican volunteers, working under the direction of Charles Horel, built the Burgoyne United Church in 1887 on land donated by Arthur J. Robinson. Known as the Union Church, it was meant to serve the needs of all Protestant settlers. Salt Spring's Anglicans later preferred to worship separately and used the Fulford-Burgoyne Valley schoolhouse across the road. Both are visible in this photo. Courtesy Mary Davidson/SSIA

the Stevens family. In his final year of teaching, Purdy bought land near his brother-in-law, Sam Beddis, where he established a fruit farm. One of Purdy's two daughters, Mary Inglin, recalled the development of Purdy's farm in a letter to historian Jean Barman:

> During the time he was teaching he found land on Beddis Rd., fronting on Ganges Harbour, where he pre-empted 125 acres for 50¢ an acre. He rowed across the bay on week-ends [at this time Purdy was probably living at the head of Ganges Harbour] & started to clear the land with the help of 2 Japanese men. He planted an orchard of apples, pears, plums, cherries & peaches,

- 124 -

& sold fruit in Victoria, & some even went to the Yukon. There was a good sale for apples before the Okanagan came in. He also made apple cider & vinegar, selling the cider for 30¢ a gallon until about 1924 when it became illegal to sell an alcoholic beverage over 8%, the cider being 11%.

In 1910, Purdy and his sister, Emily, visited their family in England. There he met his future wife, Alice Mary Waymouth, whom he married the following year in Victoria when he was fifty.

One of Salt Spring's best-known families arrived in 1885. Thomas William Mouat and his wife Jane had emigrated from the Shetland Islands in 1884 to Nanaimo, but left because of the lung-irritating coal dust. On Joel Broadwell's recommendation, they bought Abraham Copeland's farm on what is now Tripp Road on St. Mary Lake.

Farm life demanded long hours of hard work, particularly for Thomas Mouat, whose health was poor. When he died in 1898 at forty-five, he left

St. Mary's Church was completed in 1894 on land donated by John Sparrow as a memorial to his son, Babington, killed in a hunting accident. When Rev. E.F. Wilson arrived on Salt Spring, the lumber was already waiting on the beach at what is now Drummond Park. Wilson's "church bee" moved the wood to the site in one day and completed the church in four months. Total cost, including furnishings: $705. SSIA

Jane with eleven children: Thomas William—a son from his first marriage to Mary Manson—and ten children from his marriage to Jane—Margaret Janet, William Manson, Gilbert James, Mary Jane, Laurence, Lydia, Gavin Colvin, Jeremiah, Jessie, and Grace. The older children were a great help on the farm.

Also in the early 1890s, Socrates Tobias Conery and his wife Sibble (as it is spelled in the 1901 census) settled in the Divide on a large property on what is now Blackburn Road. S.T. Conery was born in Vermont and raised in a mining camp in Butte, Montana. Leonard Tolson was impressed with Conery:

> I think he was the hardest working man I have ever known, and he turned Mountain Meadow into what I thought a perfect farm, and the land around the lake [Blackburn Lake] and up the valley was cleared and brought into cultivation. He had his own dairy and appeared to be comfortably off, but it was a queer household.

Consecrated by Bishop George Hills in 1892, St. Mark's (Anglican) Church was built on land donated by Henry Stevens. Lumber and other construction materials were brought by scow to Vesuvius Beach and then dragged by ox team to Central. Twenty-three-year-old Rev. James Belton Haslam, sent to the Gulf Islands as "missionary priest" in 1891, oversaw the church's construction. Rev. E.F. Wilson replaced him three years later. SSIA

THE BRIEF, CONTENTIOUS LIFE OF "HOPE OF SALT SPRING, LODGE NUMBER 7"

On the evening of February 1, 1886, thirteen men and five women, mostly north-end Methodists (about half Blacks), met in a lamp-lit room in Central School to form "Hope of Salt Spring, Lodge Number 7." Emblazoned across its crest was the word *Prohibition*.

A representative from the Grand Lodge at Nanaimo chaired the meeting and provided the new "templars" with "proper instructions as to grips & signals and all rules necessary to the proper conduction of a Lodge." The first regular meeting struck a committee to draft laws, but "considerable argument here ensued which, however, took no definite effect."

Subsequent biweekly meetings argued about organizational matters such as who would be accepted or rejected for membership. Resignations, disciplinary action, and reinstatements often followed. Meetings closed with various members singing songs, reciting poems, telling stories, or giving speeches. The minutes never mention temperance and prohibition, but perhaps the acrimonious discussions of by-laws covered such matters.

Formal debates at meetings were popular. Members debated "Which is happier, an old bachelor or an old maid?" (the old maid, judges decided) and "Which are the most useful to mankind, the services of the agriculturist or those of the artisan?" (The artisan side won.)

Finally, "in view of the want of harmony," the lodge was closed in September 1888. During its thirty months of activity the lodge had a total of forty-nine members. Of these, six had resigned, thirteen had been suspended, and one had been expelled.

One time, when his wife was ill, Winifred Wilson went to look after her and had to double-bunk with Florence Conery [a daughter]. A pig got into the garden in the night, and Florence got up to chase it back into its pen, paddled all around the barnyard and into the pigpen, in her bare feet, and then hopped back into bed.

George and Walter Dukes also settled in the Divide area during this period. Other north-end newcomers included Alfred Few and Arthur Cartwright, Thomas and Adeline Mansell, Benjamin and Ann Lundy, Nels and Matilda Nelson, and a few years later, Nels's brother Erik.

In 1896, Ganges School opened in the Divide area. Socrates Tobias Conery donated the land on what is now Blackburn Road about 1 km from the Fulford-Ganges Road. The school closed for brief periods, when student enrollment fell below the required minimum. To keep the school open one year, the community ingeniously enrolled five-year-old Rosie Conery, who was underage. Rosie ran away one day when the school inspector was expected, and everyone searched to find her so the school could stay open. In 1921, the school's name changed to Divide School, because another Ganges School had opened four years earlier, this time in Ganges.

A NEW KIND OF IMMIGRANT

Much late-nineteenth-century population growth on Salt Spring resulted from word-of-mouth advertising, particularly among affluent "better classes of society" in England and Northern Ireland. The island increasingly attracted, especially from the 1890s, "gentlemen settlers" of means.

Many of these immigrants came with brothers. In the late 1880s, Henry Louis Mahon and Ross Mahon, grandsons of an Irish aristocrat, arrived. In 1891, they bought land on Long Harbour, at the head of Ganges Harbour, and on Walter Bay (1.5 km south). Ross Mahon owned a small steam vessel named *The Mist* and brought out another Irishman, Hugo Robertshaw, to run it.

Thomas and Jack Scovell were another pair of Irish brothers. Of Thomas we know only that he died of typhoid fever in a Banff sanitarium in 1898. Jack Scovell pre-empted 160 acres (64 ha) on Ganges Harbour from today's Fulford-Ganges Road east to what is now Churchill Road. He and Robertshaw became good friends. Engineer E.R. Cartwright described them when he lived on Salt Spring in the early 1900s:

> Jack Scovell . . . was well past middle age when I first met him, but
> even then he had one of the soundest practical brains and an
> extremely forceful personality. He gave and demanded of his
> friends absolute trust and loyalty.
>
> Jack was a bachelor, and with him lived a strange character,
> Hugo Robertshaw. . . . Hugo was a man of great strength and a
> small squeaky voice, a eunuch we always supposed, a good gar-
> dener, splendid cook and a very willing hairdresser who knew
> how to sharpen his own scissors. His devotion to and dependence
> on Jack was almost pathetic. Fortunately perhaps he died of
> pneumonia just at the time when Jack himself was going into hos-
> pital for his last illness.[6]

John and Charles Tolson arrived next, around 1888, and brother Leonard
joined them the following year. The Tolsons came from a family of ten children whose father owned cotton mills in England. Each had an independent
income. Charles had an annual 300 pounds, for example, then a respectable
$1500. John soon moved to Nelson, but Charles bought a 160-acre (64 ha)
ranch on Salt Spring and in 1895 married Evelyn Wilson, a daughter of Salt
Spring's Anglican minister, E.F. Wilson. The Tolsons' lives on Salt Spring
seemed carefree compared with those of the less affluent south-end farmers.
When nineteen-year-old Leonard Tolson arrived from Victoria, he met an
unusual welcome:

> Captain Butler ran a little boat called the *Amelia*, and it took us
> nearly all day to get to Vesuvius Bay. Charlie met me there with an
> ox wagon. He also met two gallons of Scotch. Scovell was there. He
> met two gallons of rum. And Mansell—he met two gallons rye, all
> for Christmas. They took a shot of each in turn all the way to
> Ganges (I was a strict teetotaller), and when we got to Ganges we
> found HMS *Acorn* anchored in the harbour and there was an invi-
> tation for Charlie and me and the Scovells to dine with the captain.
> It was dark when we got to Ganges and I did not see anything. A
> boat came for us to Craig's Beach and we went—a most curious
> experience—into the ward room and were given sherry and bitters,

and for dinner a bottle of Bass. So you can imagine the results. Scovell had to be lowered into the boat with a rope.

The Tolsons travelled extensively, often going back to England to see family and friends. Charles and Evelyn Tolson eventually moved to Victoria, and Charles sold the ranch to Leonard in 1897. Charles, suffering from tuberculosis, returned to England, where he died two years later. Leonard spent many happy years on Salt Spring.

The Scott brothers—Frank, Geoff, W.E. (Will), and Harold—came to Salt Spring from England in 1892. Will bought Louis Stark's Ganges Harbour pre-emption and developed the north end's largest, most successful orchard. Actively involved in the Salt Spring Island Club, which was dedicated to "the progress and improvement of Salt Spring Island," he also served as deputy minister of agriculture for British Columbia from 1910 to 1916. In 1896, Frank Scott bought Thomas Mansell's Ganges area farm. Mahon Hall was built on land bought from Frank.

A fourth family of brothers—Alfred (Fred), Ernest, and Frank Crofton—arrived from Ireland in 1898. Fred, the first to arrive, initially worked on

Having fun: from left (back row) Fred Smedley, Leonard Tolson, Frank Scott, Gerald Young, Hugo Robertshaw, Tom Scovell, Harold Scott; (front row) Frederick Foord, Jack Scovell, Dennis Baker, Howard Horel. Fred Smedley and Harold Scott drowned in 1898 when their boat overturned as they were crossing Ganges Harbour to the Scotts' farm. SSIA

Jack Scovell's Ganges area farm, later buying and renaming it Harbour House after the Croftons' family home in Ireland. Ernest bought the house and land on Booth Canal that became Acland's Resort and later the Booth Bay Resort.

These immigrants created a new social class on Salt Spring. Many sought a "civilized" society like the one they'd left. Their clubs, private schools, and leisure activities were often exclusive. Leonard Tolson described his rather easy lifestyle at Ganges Harbour at the turn of the century:

> That summer on the Ranch was very lovely. There was not much stock and I found that with morning and evening chores and working in the mornings, we had the afternoons free. We had a 17 ft. boat with centre board and lug sail, but most afternoons we used to row across to the shady side of the harbour with the English papers. We got a London daily paper and 3 or 4 weeklys...and with plenty of cushions and sometimes a book, we had lovely, happy, contented times....

The relatively affluent English and Irish immigrants dominated the island's institutional life in the 1890s. Farm society became more complex. Social distinctions, conspicuously lacking in the early pioneering days, appeared. The mainly Church of England newcomers lived on "ranches" or "homesteads," dressed well, and often had servants. More humble were the Scots, often Methodist or Presbyterian, who lived on plain "farms."

The best-known moneyed English immigrant was Harry Wright Bullock, the single younger son of a wealthy English family. Bullock arrived in 1892 at twenty-four and soon made a stir on Salt Spring. Like many newcomers, he first stayed at Stevens Boarding House, boarding for five years while his twelve-room house was built on a 300-acre (120 ha) estate on the edge of Bullock Lake. He developed a thriving farm and a busy social life (with himself at its centre) that made him a legend. Bullock lived in this home on Salt Spring until his death in 1946 and considerably influenced island life for six decades (see chapter 11).

John Collins, a dairyman from Bristol, evidently knew Bullock well. When he arrived on Salt Spring with his family in 1895, he rented a cottage on Bullock's estate. Two years later Bullock backed him in opening a creamery in a converted barn on Bullock's property, but the business failed. Collins eventually bought Levi Davis's pre-emption on what is now North End Road.

SNOBBERY ON
SALT SPRING?

Historian Jean Barman feels that the arrival of new, more affluent immigrants from England and Ireland in the late 1800s created social problems on the island. In "The Worth of an Everyday Woman," she wrote:

> The Fishers were of mixed Aboriginal descent and so increasingly dismissed by the dominant society with a sweep of a hand or wag of the tongue as "half breeds." Even though Saltspring had a considerable proportion of persons of colour, including American Blacks as well as Hawaiians, Aboriginal women, and their mixed-race offspring, it was rapidly becoming White.... Newcomers established their own social set, one in which families of mixed race settled around Fulford Harbour had no place. As recalled about a wealthy Englishman arrived on Saltspring in 1892, "he didn't think much of the Fulford people," telling a contemporary that "it was very wrong of her to buy property down on Fulford because that was just like living across the tracks."

But it's unclear how much the two different Salt Spring communities influenced or even noticed each other. Outlook, interests, distance, and difficult on-island travel separated them. Those in the south end no doubt knew of the snobbery of some in the north, but it probably had little effect on their daily lives.

AN ENERGETIC CLERGYMAN

In 1894 another newcomer arrived who would greatly influence the island. Edward Francis Wilson, born in London in 1844, took over the Anglican parish of Salt Spring. Wilson had studied farming and then theology in Ontario, eventually running an Indian residential school. An intense, energetic individual, Wilson had a nervous breakdown in 1880 and, following his doctors' advice, avoided another breakdown by coming to British Columbia in 1893.

Wilson first came to Salt Spring on his own, leaving his family at their Victoria suburban home of Barnsbury Grange, named after the family home in London. He bought early Black settler Armstead Buckner's 100-acre (40 ha) property complete with a dilapidated log house at Central for $900. (Today, the property is home to the Salt Spring Golf and Country Club.) Salt Spring real estate prices were rising; it was no longer possible to buy land for a dollar an acre. Improvements—clearing the land for pasture and developing orchards and gardens—accounted for much of the increased value.

The grounds of Wilson's new Barnsbury Grange required a lot of work.

> Scarcely anything had been done hitherto towards improving the land & it had been lying waste & unfenced ever since old Buckner died. Most of it was still virgin bush, so there would be a great deal to do before it could be brought even partly under cultivation & made profitable.
>
> Day after day, whenever time could be spared, father [Wilson always referred to himself in the third person in this way] & Norman [Wilson's son] & young Moule [Frank Moule, whom Wilson had hired for $10 per month] were chopping down the young fir trees or dragging them out by the roots. A Jap was engaged to dig necessary drains, & Mr. Cundell came with his ox team to plough. The ploughing of course could only be done in very small portions, just where there were no big trees or huge stumps. In the course of the spring about an acre & a half was put in with wheat for chicken food, & potatoes; & a small vegetable garden was planted surrounded by a log fence & adjoining the shack an old chicken house was also fixed up, a yard made with poles stuck in the ground & some chickens purchased.

Wilson also had to renovate the house before he could move his family into it:

> The house . . . was a tumbledown old concern, & most of the people advised to pull it down or burn it. But in those days it was necessary to be economical & to save all we could, so we patched it up & made a new place of it:—and to this day (1911) it is still in existence & would scarcely be believed to be Buckner's old shack.
>
> To begin with . . . there was no floor to the two lower rooms, & cattle & sheep had had free ingress & egress; the upper part was reached by a wide sloping ladder; & the windows were miserable little 6 pane concerns. In the larger of the two rooms was a hearth made of rough flat stones, a stone fireplace, made of rough stones set in mud, & a mud chimney; the roof was of shakes, through which daylight gleamed; & the log sides of the house were but partially "chinked" with moss & mud. However, a transformation scene soon began. New doors, new windows, new floors, new staircase, rooms partitioned off; walls chinked, lined inside with dressed lumber; outside plastered & whitewashed & covered with lattice work for creepers to grow on; a porch made at the front door, & a woodshed erected at the back.[7]

Wilson was soon able to send for his wife, Elizabeth Frances, and the rest of their ten children.

In some respects, Wilson was a Renaissance man: he wrote prolifically; he painted workmanlike watercolours that he sold for any number of causes; before Salt Spring's first official full-time doctor arrived, he often gave medical help; he was an avid and able promoter and organizer, especially for the church or the island itself; he was an inventor (he patented an "Apple Harvester" in 1904); and, most important to historians, he kept meticulous journals and issued monthly newsletters that recorded much of what happened on the island.

Like many middle-class fathers of his time, Wilson supported both evangelism and temperance. He required that his children attend church every Sunday, sometimes more than once when services were at St. Mark's. They were not to play cards or dance on the Sabbath, and drinking alcohol was

SALT SPRING'S FIRST "RESIDENT PHYSICIAN"

Trained at St. Bartholomew's Hospital in London, England, Dr. Gerald Ramsay "Paddy" Baker first worked as a doctor and armed guard—an odd combination!—for Wells Fargo in Nevada. He later practised in Alaska and Victoria before bringing his family to Salt Spring in 1897. On Salt Spring, the government appointed him "resident physician" and gave him a yearly grant for his medical services. Islanders soon became accustomed to seeing him make his rounds on foot, on his pony, or by boat. His love of hunting, fishing, and the outdoor life was also well known on the island.

In 1904, Paddy Baker—accompanied by Joe Nightingale, Frank Scott, Arthur Llewelyn Wilson, and Daniel Keith Wilson—left for the Yukon gold fields for six months. While he was away, Dr. Lionel Beech moved to the island to take care of Salt Spring residents. Perhaps upset by the competition—and by the departure of his wife and daughter to England in 1908—Dr. Baker himself left Salt Spring, eventually spending his last forty-one years in the BC Interior. In 1955, Quesnel residents honoured Baker by naming their new hospital after him.

forbidden at all times, though not all family members complied. Granddaughter Denise Crofton remembered that Wilson refused to baptize her sister Diana because he disapproved of the baby's non-Christian name. Bea Hamilton wrote of Wilson's near-conflict with Harry Bullock, whose personality was probably equally strong:

> Mr. Bullock had laid a cross, with the wounded Christ attached, on the altar. He hadn't asked permission and in those days when

Anglicans and Roman Catholics hardly recognized each other, one can imagine what it did to Mr. Wilson to go into St. Mark's one morning and find a crucifix on the altar! Mr. Bullock was an Anglican but to him a cross was a cross—and unfortunately he had chosen the wrong kind according to Mr. Wilson's strict standards. Mr. Wilson was about to heave the cross out—he was always heaving things out of the church, it seemed—but he thought of the possible consequences of offending Mr. Bullock, so he compromised. He took the body of the Christ off and left the Cross. Indeed he probably saved a split in the Church.[8]

The arrival of the Wilsons intensified Salt Spring's social upheaval, according to Leonard Tolson:

One of the big social cataclysms came about this time. The Wilson family having arrived, there were social distinctions, hitherto unknown. My brother, Charlie, was giving a dance, Mrs. Stevens not invited but asked to make some cakes—She said, "It's no use to tell, Mr. Tolson, 'hi' wunt! [I won't!]"

But Wilson's daughters were a welcome addition to Salt Spring society, as Tolson made clear:

The Wilson family settled on Salt Spring, five girls and five boys, and they certainly made things hum. Charlie was the first to succumb [married Evelyn Grace Wilson], then Frank Scott [married Kathleen Manorie Wilson], then Fritz Walter [married Winnifred Lois Wilson], then Fred Crofton [married Frances Nona Wilson], then George Borradaile [married Florence Muriel Wilson]. It was quite a flirtatious time for all of us.

Immediately after his arrival, Wilson started several projects. He persuaded the provincial government to give him $100 to write a pamphlet promoting Salt Spring to prospective settlers. Wilson's passion and flair for compiling statistics makes *Salt Spring Island, British Columbia, 1895* a fine source of information. Wilson's demographics for this time of transition were especially interesting:

IT WASN'T ALL WORK

Dances and musical events were popular on nineteenth-century Salt Spring. Many talented residents played for their neighbours, including violinist Alfred Ruckle and his wife Helen, who played the piano; pianist Percy Lowther; Jack Judd, who could play any instrument; and in Fulford, Frank Downie, Arthur John "Pop" Eaton, and Bill Hague. People would row or walk long distances to hear these musicians. Concerts—often school, church or fund-raising events—were popular.

Many people fished, cycled, or played competitive sports. Some, like the Musgraves, could afford to join the Cowichan Valley Tennis Club. Everyone enjoyed countless community picnics and fall fairs, the social events of the year.

The present population of the island is estimated to be 450. A large number of different nationalities are represented. There are approximately, old and young, 160 English (or Canadians), 50 Scotch, 20 Irish, 22 Portuguese, 13 Swedes, 4 Germans, 2 Norwegians, 34 Americans, 90 Halfbreeds, 40 Colored, or partly colored people, 6 Sandwich Islanders, 10 Japanese, also 1 Egyptian, 2 Greeks, 1 Patagonian.

Religious connection is about represented as follows:—Church of England, 220; Presbyterian, 30; Methodist, 50; Roman Catholic, 80; Baptist, 2; Lutheran, 13; Greek Church, 2; Congregational, 3; Salvation Army, 2; leaving about 40 whose religion is unknown.

There are about 62 married couples on the island, 35 single men or widowers, 7 single women or widows, 50 young men, 20 young women, 85 boys, 80 girls, 16 babies.

The Scotts picnicking at Cusheon Lake, c. 1896. The fishing cabin behind them was built in 1896 for the Tolson brothers by F.M. Phillips. On April 16, 1890, the crew of the HMS Acorn and their mascot, a Skye terrier named Jo, were using the then abandoned cabin. As the sailors gathered wood for the fire, a piece of wood struck and instantly killed Jo. The distraught crew buried the terrier and erected a teak cross to mark the dog's grave. The cross was still in place in 1998, although the cabin was about to be demolished. SSIA

Trades and occupations are represented as follows:— Carpenters and builders, 4; engineers, 2; blacksmiths, 3; bricklayers, 1; tavern-keeper, 1; boarding house keepers, 2; stonecutters, 2; hunters, 2; fishermen, 1; seal hunters, 10.

In addition to Wilson's listed occupations on Salt Spring, the 1891 census registered the following: millwright, dressmaker, miner, logger, gardener, sailor, baker, painter, painter in oils (perhaps the beginning of the island's attraction for artists and craftspeople), teacher, cook (mainly Chinese men working in logging camps), hunter, and domestic. In 1892, the BC Minister of Agriculture estimated "nearly 100 farmers live on the island."

Wilson also recorded the following services and businesses on the island:

There is an Odd Fellows' lodge with a membership of 38.... There are five Post Offices on the Island, viz.: Vesuvius (Joel Broadwell); North End (Levi Lakin); Burgoyne Bay (S. Maxwell); Fulford Harbor (H.N. Rogers); Beaver Point (A. McLennan). Five steamboat wharves, viz:—Fernwood, Vesuvius Bay, Ganges Harbor, Burgoyne Bay, Fulford Harbor. Two boarding houses, (1) by Mrs. Stevens, at Vesuvius [Central], roomy and home-like, with accommodation for 12 guests; charges by the day, $1, by the week, $5. (2) by J. Akerman, in the Valley, charges the same. One tavern, with barroom at Fulford harbor, by H.N. Rogers. One general store, Vesuvius Bay, by E.J. Bittancourt.

New business and social organizations formed quickly in the next few years, including several agricultural organizations (see chapter 10) and the Salt Spring Island Club, an 1896 forerunner of today's chamber of commerce. By the turn of the century, Salt Spring society was still young, but the number and variety of services had increased greatly in just fifteen years.

GETTING ON AND OFF THE ROCK

Two rival companies—the Canadian Pacific Navigation Company (CPN) and the People's Steam Navigation Company—provided steamer service between Victoria and Nanaimo with stops in the Gulf Islands. Their somewhat unreliable service to Salt Spring improved when the Esquimalt & Nanaimo Railway started a marine division in 1886 with the *Isabel* and later the *Joan* (pronounced Jo-Ann by some islanders), as Wilson described in his pamphlet:

> The usual way of getting to Victoria or Nanaimo, and also of sending produce to or receiving stores from the city, is by steamship "Joan,"—a very comfortably fitted up passenger vessel of 544 tons register. The charge for

The Joan *at Fulford dock, c. 1895. SSIA*

single passage to or from Victoria is $2.00, return ticket $3.00; to or from Nanaimo, $1.50, return $2.25. Freight to Victoria $2.50 a ton; to Nanaimo $2.00. Meals on board, very good and well served, 50 cents. Stateroom for the night, extra 75 cents. . . .

The arrival of the steamer was always an important event on the island, as Wilson attests:

There is always a great gathering at the wharf on "steamboat day;". . . there are crates of poultry, boxes of eggs, cases of butter, lambs or sheep lying uncomfortably on their sides with their legs pinioned, little pigs carefully boxed up, and great old hogs with their feet tied firmly to a pole by which they will be carried, yelling and struggling but incapable of resistance, on board. All around the

wharf under the trees are picturesquely grouped the settlers' saddle ponies and conveyances, ox-teams, one-
horse carts, heavy waggons with horses, spring buggies,
etc. The boat comes, ropes are thrown—all is bustle for

*The first piledriver on Salt Spring (c. 1895) at the Vesuvius wharf. This rig was
used to construct those all-important landings. Seated centre, Ted Akerman;
standing right, Al Raynes. Courtesy Bob Akerman*

awhile—then a deep whistle, plank drawn in, and off she goes again. Settlers crowd around the little Post Office window to get their mail and their freight bills, then all disperse, and the wharf is left empty and deserted.

Despite Wilson's glowing description, islanders were not satisfied with the service. They complained of high freight rates and inconvenient schedules.

By 1895, the Victoria & Sidney Railway ran two trains daily between Sidney and Victoria. The trip cost 50 cents and took fifty minutes. But islanders lacked a connection between Salt Spring and Sidney. They had to hire a boat for $1.50 from Burgoyne Bay or Vesuvius Bay and walk several kilometres to the railway, or hire a boat from Fulford Harbour or Beaver Point to the railway terminus in Sidney. In summer, Leonard Tolson often used his own boat for the complicated trip:

> The idea was to go out in the evening when there was often a land breeze and sail down to Beaver Point and camp, and leave there about 4 a.m. and get to Sidney in time for the train to town at 9 a.m. (known as the Cordwood Ltd.)....There was a rather steep grade near Elk Lake, and one time when I was on board, the train could not quite make it and had to back down and make another run at it. When we got near the top, the conductor asked all the men to jump out and push! And we just managed to make it. The return trip was much the same—out by the evening train, camp at Beaver Point, leave about dawn and be home in time for breakfast.

9

Into the Twentieth Century

1900–1918

SLOW BUT STEADY DEVELOPMENT

During the early twentieth century the island continued, quietly but steadily, to change. In 1900, both the Fulford Harbour and Burgoyne Bay post offices were transferred to R.P. Edwards's store in the Fulford-Burgoyne Valley, about 1.5 km from the head of Fulford Harbour, under a new name—the South Salt Spring Post Office. Edwards was already considered eccentric, and his new role as postmaster only enhanced his reputation. Bea Hamilton wrote in *Salt Spring Island*:

> He would wait until he heard the whistle of the steamer just before it rounded the point. Then he would close the mail bags, dump them into his cart and start on his slow trip down the Valley road to the wharf. His old sorrel horse being a bit lame never went very fast and invariably the mailboat reached the docks first. That delighted the people who gathered in groups on the wharf to watch mailboat day fun.
>
> The Captain [A.A. Sears, part owner of the *Iroquois*] would storm up and down the deck, shouting for someone to "go and hurry the old so and so up." ... What made it so annoying for the Captain was that he could watch the mail cart ambling down the road for a

KEY DATES

1901 The population of Salt Spring reaches 508.

1902 Ganges and Victoria are connected by telephone.

1905 The Vesuvius Bay Methodist Church is consecrated.

1911 Alan Blackburn acquires Salt Spring's first car.

1912 The Salt Spring Island Trading Company is born.

The island's population swells to about 900.

1913 Salt Spring has its first bank—but only for a year and a half.

The first speeding ticket is issued.

1914 Lady Minto Gulf Islands Hospital opens.

Ganges Water and Power Company is founded.

1915 Rev. E.F. Wilson dies and is buried in St. Mark's churchyard.

mile or two. When he did finally arrive, the old Londoner would give back to the captain as good as he got only in more picturesque terms. These little set-tos were the delight of the day.

Also in 1900, two new stores opened in the north end. Joel Broadwell opened his second store at Central, having closed the first when his wife's health failed. Only a year later, however, after Mary Amanda's death, Broadwell sold his store to partners Joe Malcolm, a blacksmith, and Percy Purvis, who had both arrived in 1889.

In 1904, Malcolm and Purvis—cousins from Ontario who each had married a sister of the other—decided the business centre of the island was shifting to Ganges. (Abraham Reid Bittancourt had been running a store on Ganges Hill since 1900.) Malcolm and Purvis's second store was the largest the island had yet seen. It included sheds and a blacksmith shop at the end of the Ganges wharf, from which the partners operated an export business using two boats, the 30-foot *Nomad* and the 60-foot *Ganges*.

Edward R. Cartwright, who worked for Malcolm and Purvis in 1906, described Purvis, then around forty, as "a quick-moving, active-brained man with a real flair for business" who "had go-ahead ideas" that included selling Salt Spring Island produce on Vancouver Island. Malcolm was less ambitious, "a delightful, easy-going countryman."

All that remains of the Edwards store today is a somewhat larger weeping elm (centre). The store opened in 1896 and closed with the death of its proprietor in 1918. The post office was then moved to the White House hotel run by A.J. ("Pop") Eaton.

Purvis started immediately to develop a thriving export business; buying everything that the ranchers of the Island could produce, except milk and cream, which went to the local Government Creamery [the Salt Spring Island Creamery]. This was good for the ranchers who up till then had been in the habit of sending their fruit, pigs, sheep, etc., to Victoria via SS *Iroquois* and the rail from Sidney, and having to take any prices they were given. Now they were able to bargain, or imagine they were bargaining. They did get better prices and Purvis got his bills at the store paid.[1]

In 1907, after Joe Malcolm's sudden death, Jane Mouat and her son Gilbert James, who had been working for Malcolm and Purvis, bought the business and renamed it G.J. Mouat and Company. The Purvis family moved to the United States.

Reid Bittancourt's store, c. 1907. After the store was sold in 1910, the building housed at different times meetings of the Ganges Methodists, the Canada Customs office, the police station, a jail, a courthouse, and, from 1945 to 1965, the nursing home of Dr. Arnold Francis. Bittancourt Collection/SSIA

The company did so well that in 1910 it was able to purchase Reid Bittancourt's business. Years later, in "Our Tribal History," Chuck Horel remembered Mouat's as "a general store that was really more of a community emporium than a store":

> You could buy groceries and shoe polish, horse harness and blacksmith tools, blankets and furniture or a cemetery lot or a farm complete with stock, everything was available at Mouat Brothers. In addition, G.J. bought and sold logs and poles and piling, and he financed the loggers while they were getting their timber ready. Mouat Brothers also sold hunting and fishing licences, registered births and deaths and bought and graded eggs from the local farmers, as well as beef, lamb and fowl. You see, you could hardly draw breath on Salt Spring Island without getting involved with Mouat Brothers Ltd.

A SUMMING UP

Rev. E.F. Wilson summed up the state of the island in the *Salt Spring Island Church Monthly* in 1905—the eleventh anniversary of his arrival:

> The moral condition of the Island, taking it all over, has, I believe, improved. There is no tavern now on the Island [Rogers Saloon burned in 1901] and not nearly as much drinking as there used to be. Many bachelors have married and new settlers with families have come in. Bicycles are now numerous. Lawn tennis and rifle shooting, with an occasional concert or dance, seem to be the principal amusements. There is, I think, very little gambling, and even card-playing does not seem to be much indulged in. I would like to be able to feel that there was some increased interest taken in spiritual matters, but of this I fear there is not very much outward evidence.

Despite his usual business acumen, Gilbert sometimes made mistakes. In 1912, John Charles Lang, a retired but still energetic railway construction engineer, found an article he wanted in Mouat's and asked its price. Unsure, clerk Walter Norton called up to Gilbert's office where the president was sitting in his wheelchair (he'd been disabled by polio some years earlier), "What does this cost?" "Who's it for?" was the response. Lang decided it was about time Mouat's had some competition. He and others who felt the same way—Will, Frank, and Geoff Scott, Harry Bullock, and T.F. Speed—launched the Salt Spring Island Trading Company. (For another version of the company's founding, see chapter 11.)

These men had something else in common: they were all Conservatives.

G.J. Mouat and Company became Mouat Bros. Co. Ltd. in 1909, and in 1912 the store moved into new premises next door. The old Malcolm and Purvis store eventually housed the Ganges Inn, also known as Granny's Boarding House because it was run by "Granny" Jane Mouat. SSIA

The original Mouat's store (c. 1908) is visible at the extreme right, its boat—the Ganges—on the left, and Reid Bittancourt's the Victor in the foreground. Boats were essential to merchants, who had to be mariners as well as storekeepers. SSIA

The Mouat family, c. 1908: (left to right) Jerry, Laurie, Will (W.M.), Gilbert, Gavin, Mary, Mrs. Jane Mouat, Lydia, and Jessie. SSIA

The inside of Mouat's store, c. 1912, with the paint and oil department upstairs. SSIA

The Trading Company quickly became identified as the place for Conservatives to shop, while Liberals traded with Mouat's. Winnifred Best, shortly after moving to Ganges from Galiano, entered Mouat's to buy the Anglican Sunday School's Christmas gifts. Thinking she'd mistakenly entered the wrong store, the clerk told her that the Trading Company, not Mouat's, was Conservative and Church of England. Mrs. Best thanked the clerk but still made her purchases at Mouat's.

CATERING TO TRAVELLERS

The Ganges Inn opened in the original Mouat's store when a new store was built next door in 1911–12. Store employees, members of the Mouat family, and travelling salesmen lived there, as did manager Jane Mouat until she died in 1935.

The White House hotel, a predecessor of the Fulford Inn, opened in 1913 on the site of Rogers Saloon. The same year, the *Sidney and Islands Review* reported, Charles Taylor of Vancouver opened "a thoroughly up-to-date and splendidly appointed" waterfront hotel at the other end of the island beside the Trading Company in Ganges. The Ganges Hotel cost $15,000 to build and had thirty guest rooms, each with hot and cold water, four with private baths. Room rates started at $2.50 per night including meals. Shortly after opening, the spacious dining room served lunch to three hundred Conservatives from Vancouver. But less than three months later, fire destroyed the new hotel.

In 1914, four hundred Canadian Pacific Railway (CPR) employees came to Salt Spring for a picnic and six to seven hundred Conservatives returned for their annual picnic. It seemed that Ganges might become a convention centre, and boosters called for more accommodation facilities.

In 1916, Nona Crofton and her brother Norman Wilson partly solved this problem by converting her home, Harbour House, into a guest house. A dining room was added to the house with five or

The Ganges Hotel (1913). SSIA

six bedrooms above it, and guests could also sleep in five or six tents on the grounds. Harbour House could then accommodate up to twenty-five visitors. The first of three tennis courts and additional guest space were added just after World War I.

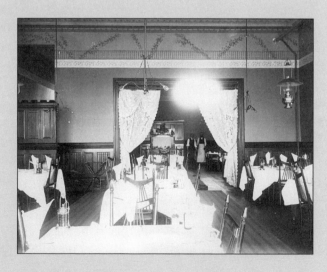

The dining room of the Ganges Hotel (1913). SSIA

The Vesuvius Lodge c. 1920, opened in E.J. Bittancourt's former house in about 1918. It burned down in 1975. BCARS A-09781

As Salt Spring land values increased after 1900, some people saw more opportunity in land development than in farming. Leonard Tolson noted that in 1903 his ranch was making no profit. "I began to realize that with $6,000 invested something was wrong with the works. The only advantage was cheap living—milk, eggs, butter, vegetables, fruit cost nothing, and as I was quite a good shot, we seldom had to buy meat."[2] Tolson sold his property to Arthur Ward for exactly what he had paid for it a few years earlier. Perhaps he should have waited, as Salt Spring real estate was about to rise sharply.

In 1909, Rev. E.F. Wilson estimated the Barnsbury property he had purchased fifteen years earlier for $900 had increased in value, with improvements, to $16,000. Jonathan Begg's former Fernwood farm, bought by the Legh family when then-owner John Booth died in 1902, was sold again in 1910 for the princely sum of $15,000.

In 1912, Arthur Ward subdivided the property he'd bought from Leonard Tolson, selling all of the lots within a year. (This included modern-day McPhillips, Jackson, and Hereford avenues). Another 1912 subdivision of 704 acres (282 ha) in the Long Harbour–Ganges area offered 5-acre (2 ha) parcels for $1600 to $2550. And in 1913, Fred Crofton's land around the Harbour House Hotel was being surveyed and subdivided. Land was becoming a commodity not to farm but to buy and sell.

Perhaps hoping to benefit from the active Salt Spring market, the Merchants Bank of Canada opened a branch in Ganges in 1913 to great fanfare. It was unsuccessful, however, and closed down about a year and a half later.

Rivalry continued between Salt Spring's north and south ends. So did the influence of English and Irish immigrants settling mainly in the north end, many of whom expected all "the English amenities." For example, Brownlow Villiers Layard sent his sons, Arthur Raymond ("Togie") and Henry Camville ("Cam"), from southern England to Salt Spring in 1905. Togie and Cam Layard were totally unsuited to farming, according to Togie's daughter Louise Wolfe-Milner, but their father envisioned them living an idyllic life on an estate in the colonies.

The many British newcomers—described in the *Sidney and Islands Review* in 1913 as "retired Old Country people of an excellent class"—vexed some islanders with different backgrounds. Margaret Garner, whose parents came to Salt Spring from South Carolina, recounted problems with pronunciation and accent:

> It was at grade school that we realized we spoke differently. Our parents had particularly broad Southern accents. The majority of the population on Saltspring was English, and their accents were rather exaggerated. It was natural that we were teased about our speech. . . . The arrogance and pomposity of the English population irritated me for many years.[3]

Portuguese descendant Len Bittancourt had his own view of the class distinctions these people brought to the island:

> We still have this class thing here. In those days a lot of people were sent out from England because they were no good back there. They sent them out here and kept them alive out here with a remittance. We've had a lot of it on the coast here. A lot of those old English families; some of them outstanding some maybe not so good.[4]

Despite differences, a spirit of co-operation also existed, as Bea Hamilton suggested:

> In Ganges there were homesteads owned by gentlemen's sons—scions of what one is pleased to call the "good families" who came out from the Old Country, some bringing their servants and help with them. They ran ranches and owned a dress suit. In other parts were what one might call the "working class" of various nationalities, including English and Irish. They owned farms and wore good sturdy denim overalls, and bought ready-mades. That was the only difference between the farmers and the ranchers. They were good neighbours and pooled their agricultural knowledge, worked out problems together, assisted each other in times of stress, attended meetings and between them helped to straighten out marketing problems. They respected each other and poked fun at each other.[5]

NEW ARRIVALS

James and Charlie Monk and their families came to the island in the early 1900s. James, who taught at Beaver Point School, bought a farm in Beaver Point near the Pappenburgers in 1904 and settled there with his wife, May. Charlie lived first in the Peavine House (see chapter 7) and later in his own house on 40 acres (16 ha) across from today's Beaver Point Hall.

John and Janet Hepburn bought their farm toward the end of Beaver Point Road in 1911. John Reid wrote in his autobiography that Hepburn was innovative, if impractical:

> This farmer was quite a genius. He had a Cadillac car, a Chevrolet, and an Avory tractor, and he figured that, if he made a scow with three pontoons on the bottom with a propeller on each pontoon, which were arranged so that he could back the Cadillac's back wheels to turn between two pulleys and the same for the Chevrolet and tractor on the other pontoons, that there would be lots of power to run the scow. The cars and tractor and propellers worked fine but there was too much backwater and the scow hardly moved. I was with them one Sunday afternoon,

and it took us all afternoon to go up Fulford Harbour a short distance and we were lucky to get back. He built the scow on the beach by the Catholic Church at Fulford Harbour. I wonder what happened to it.

A small community developed on rough, rocky Musgrave Mountain, where people may have pre-empted to avoid escalating land prices elsewhere on Salt Spring. Edgar Brantford successfully ran his "upper ranch" where the road to Mt. Tuam Buddhist Retreat now branches off Musgrave Road. Another homesteader, George Laundry, in 1910 established a sheep ranch farther down the road toward Musgrave Landing.

The Smith brothers from Lancashire—Frank, Arnold, and Walter—were among the last early settlers to choose this area. They homesteaded below the Laundry ranch near Musgrave Landing. Arnold Smith's Mill Farm (now a park) was named after the ponderous, whimsical mill his brother Frank designed. Miles Smeeton described it almost thirty years later, in his book *A Change of Jungles*:

> Frank had taken more pleasure in designing his water-wheel than in constructing it, and more pleasure in constructing it than in making it work. Indeed, it could only work in winter when the stream was running, and it was really a tremendous and impracticable construction for the amount of work that was required of it, for it was only used for sawing up an occasional plank or a few shingles for the roof. He should really have been a scholar and a mathematician, and would have been if the right opportunities had been available.

Arnold and Walter Smith were equally eccentric. Here's Smeeton's charming description of them:

> Arnold was the older and really the farmer of the family. He had kept more of the homely accent of his birthplace than the others. He had a great long nose, deep furrowed lines on his cheeks, and clear blue eyes that always kept something of childhood's wonder in them. He was tall and spare, with huge horny hands, hands that had achieved wonders of work in hewing out of the woods the

small primitive farm. Now that his hands were resting the forest was coming back again, rather slower than at Frank's place, because it had been attacked more savagely in the first place, but the split cedar fence-rails were down and the young firs back in the field.

Arnold had always been fond of painting and now it occupied all his time, but other than self-portraits he believed in no original inspiration and preferred always to copy other pictures....

Walter, the youngest of the Smith brothers, grey-haired, lean, haggard and intense of feature, but always with a friendly smile and salty North Country humour, was...the reader and the philosopher of the family, extremely well-read and up to date in all that was going on. One day Beryl handed him back some huge volume of Toynbee's that he had lent her. "What are you reading now?" she asked. "Oh, I'm on to something serious now," he said, "Relativity!"

The Musgrave homesteaders were nearly all sheep farmers, as the mountain pastures wouldn't support dairy herds. In 1915, fifty-nine residents in seventeen families were homesteading on the mountain. Work started on a road from Fulford to Musgrave Landing about the same time, but Musgrave Landing remained accessible only by water for years. At least once, pre-emptors served their required residency and then left en masse, disappointed with the lack of progress on the road.

A few people settled in the Cranberry Marsh area—named for the berries growing there before it was drained—before 1900, but most came in the early 1900s. In 1903 a road was built through the Cranberry to Maxwell Lake. British-born John Rogers and his Canadian wife, Martha, arrived around 1902 and successfully established an 800-acre (320 ha) mixed farm. As a sideline, John discreetly sold homebrew. Neighbours reported that most traffic on Cranberry Road headed for the Rogers farm.

Other pre-1918 Cranberry settlers included Charles Gardner, John and Annie Brown, the Toynbee brothers (Charles, Albert, and Richard), Edward

(Opposite) The original of this map showing where Salt Spring families were located in 1912 was drawn by a teacher and was donated to the Bittancourt Heritage House Museum by the Crawford family. Some of the map's errors and omissions have been corrected from information supplied by John Bennett.

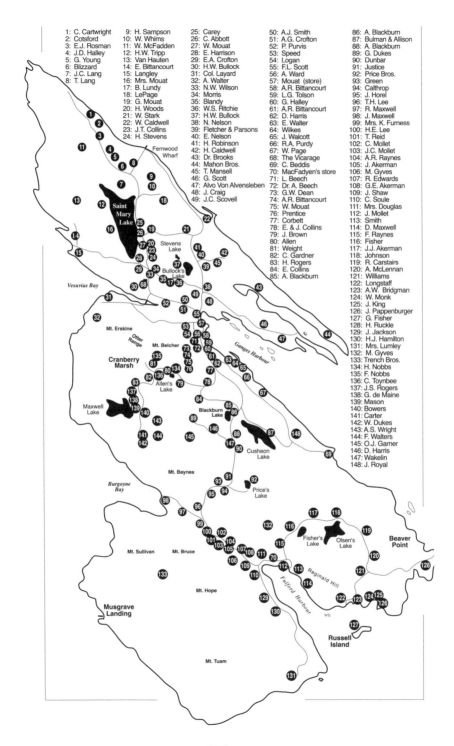

1: C. Cartwright
2: Cotsford
3: E.J. Rosman
4: J.D. Halley
5: G. Young
6: Blizzard
7: J.C. Lang
8: T. Lang
9: H. Sampson
10: W. Whims
11: W. McFadden
12: H.W. Tripp
13: Van Hauten
14: E. Bittancourt
15: Langley
16: Mrs. Mouat
17: B. Lundy
18: LePage
19: G. Mouat
20: H. Woods
21: W. Stark
22: W. Caldwell
23: J.T. Collins
24: H. Stevens
25: Carey
26: C. Abbott
27: W. Mouat
28: E. Harrison
29: E.A. Crofton
30: H.W. Bullock
31: Col. Layard
32: A. Walter
33: N.W. Wilson
34: Morris
35: Blandy
36: W.S. Ritchie
37: H.W. Bullock
38: N. Nelson
39: Fletcher & Parsons
40: E. Nelson
41: H. Robinson
42: H. Caldwell
43: Dr. Brooks
44: Mahon Bros.
45: T. Mansell
46: G. Scott
47: Alvo Von Alvensleben
48: J. Craig
49: J.C. Scovell
50: A.J. Smith
51: A.G. Crofton
52: P. Purvis
53: Speed
54: Logan
55: F.L. Scott
56: A. Ward
57: Mouat (store)
58: A.R. Bittancourt
59: L.G. Tolson
60: G. Halley
61: A.R. Bittancourt
62: D. Harris
63: E. Walter
64: Wilkes
65: J. Walcott
66: R.A. Purdy
67: W. Page
68: The Vicarage
69: C. Beddis
70: MacFadyen's store
71: L. Beech
72: Dr. A. Beech
73: G.W. Dean
74: A.R. Bittancourt
75: W. Mouat
76: Prentice
77: Corbett
78: E. & J. Collins
79: J. Brown
80: Allen
81: Weight
82: C. Gardner
83: H. Rogers
84: E. Collins
85: A. Blackburn
86: A. Blackburn
87: Bulman & Allison
88: A. Blackburn
89: G. Dukes
90: Dunbar
91: Justice
92: Price Bros.
93: Green
94: Calthrop
95: J. Horel
96: T.H. Lee
97: R. Maxwell
98: J. Maxwell
99: Mrs. K. Furness
100: H.E. Lee
101: T. Reid
102: C. Mollet
103: J.C. Mollet
104: A.R. Raynes
105: J. Akerman
106: M. Gyves
107: R. Edwards
108: G.E. Akerman
109: J. Shaw
110: C. Soule
111: Mrs. Douglas
112: J. Mollet
113: Smith
114: D. Maxwell
115: F. Raynes
116: Fisher
117: J.J. Akerman
118: Johnson
119: R. Carstairs
120: A. McLennan
121: Williams
122: Longstaff
123: A.W. Bridgman
124: W. Monk
125: J. King
126: J. Pappenburger
127: G. Fisher
128: H. Ruckle
129: J. Jackson
130: H.J. Hamilton
131: Mrs. Lumley
132: M. Gyves
133: Trench Bros.
134: H. Nobbs
135: F. Nobbs
136: C. Toynbee
137: J.S. Rogers
138: G. de Maine
139: Mason
140: Bowers
141: Carter
142: W. Dukes
143: A.S. Wright
144: F. Walters
145: O.J. Garner
146: D. Harris
147: Wakelin
148: J. Royal

Carter, and the Nobbs brothers (Harry, Fred, and Charlie). The isolated Cranberry seemed to attract eccentric, solitary bachelors such as Charlie and Bert Toynbee and Abraham Secord Wright. Harry Nobbs's daughter Jessie Wagg later remembered one Cranberry bachelor who hung his telephone by his bed so he could listen in on party-line conversations.

Oland and Lona Garner settled on Dukes Road in the nearby Divide area in 1905. Two years later, Alan and Esther Blackburn bought Socrates Tobias Conery's beautiful farm and renamed it Ostaig after the Blackburn family's home in Ireland. Blackburn hired Charlie Beddis to build a large house with a Catholic family chapel, semicircular apse, and attached tower. In 1913, Blackburn ran out of money and abandoned his unfinished house, leaving many suppliers unpaid. The house was eventually completed and, most recently, housed the Salt Spring Centre.

NEW AND IMPROVED SERVICES

Salt Spring grew less isolated after the turn of the century. Telephone cable was laid between Salt Spring and Vancouver Island in 1901, and Ganges and Victoria were somewhat undependably connected by telephone the next year. The transportation of goods and services improved dramatically when the CPR bought the Canadian Pacific Navigation Company (CPN) in 1901 and four years later acquired the Esquimalt & Nanaimo Railway and its steamship division. Different steamships now visited each of the island's six ports two or three times a week bound for Victoria, Nanaimo, or Vancouver. Residents could also flag down ships en route.

In 1913, another passenger service to Victoria began. It ran three days a week from Deep Cove on the Saanich Peninsula to Ganges and if necessary Fulford. The trip took about two and a half hours, and islanders could now reach Victoria in four hours, conduct business for three hours, and return to Salt Spring the same day.

Roads still presented many problems—such as fallen trees, which often made them impassable. In 1910, Kyrle Symons, the founder of Victoria's St. Michael's School but then the teacher at Beaver Point School, couldn't get his wife to the doctor by road when she was in labour. He had to row her to the Beddis home where Emily Beddis helped deliver the baby. Symons's account of his return home, in *That Amazing Institution*, reveals the problems travellers faced:

The SS Iroquois *in Pender Island Canal, c. 1911. The* Iroquois *began serving the Gulf Islands in 1901 and continued until it sank off Sidney in stormy weather in 1911. Twenty passengers and crew drowned in the accident. The vessel was overloaded, and part-owner Capt. A.A. Sears was indicted for manslaughter and lost his licence. BCARS 12868, F-335*

Mrs. Beddis saw us into a small row-boat I had borrowed; hot bricks were put on the floor and a shapeless bundle of rugs, etc., that was my family, was installed in the back. We rowed to the Bulman saw-mill [in Cusheon Cove], now no more, where the foreman boosted them up a steep ladder to a little cottage. Here a short rest and some hot cocoa did wonders. The next step was to board the old steamer *Iroquois*.... On it we reached Beaver Point wharf in a gale and deluge. Here another good friend,... Mr. Ruckle, lent us a horse and buggy and we drove home, avoiding falling branches with more luck than skill.

The roads were apparently so bad that Beaver Point and Fulford residents communicated more easily by mail than by visiting. Polly (Mary Galloway) Ruckle exchanged postcards with her stepsisters, the Lees, between 1908 and 1912.

Improvements were on the way, however. In 1902, only $2000 was budgeted for widening the island's roads under the supervision of Joe Nightingale, the road foreman. Nightingale had only $150 to build a road between Burgoyne Bay and Beaver Point, following 19 km of cattle trail. When Alan Blackburn acquired the first automobile on Salt Spring in 1911, the roads were inadequate. (Rev. E.F. Wilson's daughter Kathy Scott wrote that Blackburn's car made "noise enough to frighten 100 horses."[6]) The *Cowichan Leader* reported in May 1911 that "the roads were not built sufficiently wide nor are they straight enough to give room for such traffic [cars] ... so that it is no wonder that those compelled to travel on them [in horse-drawn vehicles] are alarmed at the introduction of the speeding motor."

In Salt Spring's first car accident in 1913, a dog was run over and badly injured. By then Salt Spring had five cars. The first speeding ticket—with a fine of $15, a significant amount in those days—was given to A.R. Bittancourt the same year. Mouat Brothers, now Ford agents, built a garage and installed a 10,000-gallon (45,460 L) gasoline tank a year later. By 1914, the Salt Spring fleet had reached nearly twenty autos, Mouat's garage had started a taxi service, and the Ruckles had acquired Beaver Point's first car.

Until 1914, Ganges drew water by pipeline from a mountain spring above the area now called Ganges Hill. This pipeline also supplied the Salt Spring Island Creamery, Reid Bittancourt's home and store, and Arthur Ward's property, which included most of today's Lower Ganges. John Charles Lang wanted to extend this primitive water system and give Ganges electrical power. He established the Ganges Water and Power Company in 1914 with many of the same directors as the Salt Spring Island Trading Company. The company raised capital of $50,000 by selling 25-dollar shares. It then bought land on Ganges Hill and installed a 10,000-gallon (45,460 L) water storage tank. Since the supply from the hill was limited, the company had a 5180-metre trench dug and wood-stave pipe laid by hand to bring water from Maxwell Lake. A wooden pipeline required different maintenance from an iron or clay pipeline. It was a formidable task:

> The wood pipe is made of staves of wood which are held together with spiral wrappings of wire. Most leaks occur where, for one reason or another, two neighbouring staves separate and thereby sprays of water are produced of various shapes and sizes. The work crew carried a sack full of fine wooden wedges and repairs were made by driving them into the split, side by side, until the leak was stopped. It took a delicate touch to drive the wedges tight enough to stop the leak without spreading the staves further apart and making matters worse. During the process, the repair-man was usually in line of fire of the leak so rubber clothes were most essential.[7]

Several new schools improved Salt Spring education in the early 1900s. In 1904, Isabella Point School opened on land donated by John Palua about 1.5 km past the junction of Roland Road and Isabella Point Road. Initially the school often had to enroll children below school age to meet the minimum enrollment for government grants. The school had one classroom and a cloakroom, but no plumbing or electricity. A wood stove provided heat. Each school day, students were responsible for chopping wood, keeping the stove going, bringing in water from a well nearby, and raising the flag. The school closed in 1951, and the building no longer exists. The school board donated the property to be used as a park, and the community was still holding picnics there in the late 1990s.

A school for the Cranberry opened in 1910 in an old cabin belonging to Charles Gardner, which was also used for church services. A one-room schoolhouse at the corner of Wright and Nobbs roads replaced the cabin in 1912. At first, it was called Ganges School because the Ganges School in the Divide was closed at this time, but by 1911, it was known as Cranberry Marsh School. Longtime Salt Spring teacher A.J.W. Dodds, who came from England in 1905, taught here that year.

Students in farming families had a long school day. Before school they had chores to do, such as feeding farm animals. Then there was often a long walk of an hour or two to school. After school, children often did more chores before doing their homework.

A number of private schools opened at this time. At the urging of Rev. E.F. Wilson, who estimated that there were seventeen children needing a school, Leonard Tolson returned to Salt Spring in 1906 and opened Ganges Private School the next year. Business was slow at first, since another teacher, Edward Cartwright, had opened a school in the old creamery shed and enrolled most of the seventeen students. But by spring, students were trickling over to Tolson's school, and Cartwright closed his school and left to teach at University School in Victoria. In 1917, Tolson followed Cartwright's example, closing his school and taking a job at University School.

In 1914, Nora Halley opened a small but successful school on what is now Margolin Road to educate her own and her neighbours' children. Her school closed in 1936, when her youngest child matriculated.

Kathleen Ashton opened Formby House School for boys in 1915 on Ganges Hill at the corner of Bittancourt. She soon advertised in England for a second teacher and hired A.K.N. Oxenham, whom she later married. In 1920, the school moved to larger quarters in Tolson's old schoolhouse. After Oxenham died in 1927, Kathleen operated the school for another eight years until she and her daughter moved to England. After a few months, Leonard Cropper reopened the school in late 1935. The school closed for good in 1940.

Improving health care led to some of Salt Spring's most important events of the early twentieth century. A retired British army doctor, Surgeon Colonel Lionel Beech, replaced Dr. Gerald Baker in 1904 soon after he left for the Yukon. The well-regarded Dr. Baker returned to the island after only six months but left for good in 1908. Dr. Beech rented one of Harry Bullock's cottages, then bought a house and 8 acres (3.2 ha) on Ganges Hill from A.R. Bittancourt. He felt he had too much work—after all, he had already retired once—so the community invited his son, Dr. Alan Beech, then practising in Quesnel, to join him.

Dr. Lionel Beech started building support for a hospital in the Gulf Islands, aided by the Guild of Sunshine, a local women's group founded to help those in need. Dr. Beech donated land, and by the end of 1913 he and the Guild of Sunshine had raised more than $3000. The Gulf Islands (Cottage) Hospital opened in 1914 with two three-bed wards and added a third ward the same year. The hospital was renamed the Lady Minto Gulf Islands Hospital after it received $1000 from the Lady Minto Fund, named

A NEW CHURCH FOR CENTRAL

Ever since Rev. Ebenezer Robson visited Salt Spring in 1861, north-end Methodist services had taken place in schoolhouses, community halls, and private homes. The south end acquired a Methodist church in 1887, and in 1900, the Methodists decided it was time to build a church at Vesuvius Bay. The next year, the provincial government provided an acre of land for the church, part of a 100-acre (40 ha) parcel set aside at Central in 1864 for community use. Now the congregation needed only the money to build.

The Methodist church built at Central in 1904 was moved to Hereford Avenue in Ganges in 1926 and modified. It was being used as a stationery store in the late nineties. SSIA

Jane Mouat, who worked untiringly until she raised the necessary $650, reportedly drove her horse-drawn buggy from one end of Salt Spring to the other, often with her daughter Jessie at her side. Construction began in 1904, and the Vesuvius Bay Methodist Church was dedicated the following year.

after the Canadian governor general's wife, who sponsored local or "cottage" hospitals throughout Canada. The original hospital building is now the Salt Spring Community Centre.

The new hospital was opened by the provincial secretary, Dr. Henry Essen Young, who noted it was the first hospital he'd opened that was already debt-free. Although money was short during the war years, a voluntary hospital insurance scheme supported the hospital. Subscribers were ensured a hospital bed and nursing care for annual premiums of $6.00 per adult and $1.20 per child. The hospital was staffed by a nurse or "matron"—Annie R. Colhoun—and a male attendant—Corporal Newens, formerly of the Royal Army Medical Corps.

JUST FOR FUN

Almost everyone on the island enjoyed picnics, school and church concerts, and dances. They provided welcome relief after the long, hard workdays. However, the leisure pursuits of some early twentieth-century islanders—particularly the English and Irish settlers—reflected a more carefree and affluent lifestyle, since they could afford to hire workers for field clearing and heavy farm work. For example, one newcomer, twenty-one-year-old Basil Cartwright, arrived from England in 1904, bringing in his luggage a cricket bat and ball and an inflated soccer ball.

Both women and men played grass hockey, introduced to Salt Spring by Ethel Wilson. The first hockey sticks were made from curved cedar roots and old buggy shafts. Islanders also enthusiastically played soccer, baseball, water sports, badminton, and tennis. There were about thirty private tennis courts, mainly clay, on Salt Spring before 1914. Dances often followed big games or tennis matches, and these occasionally lasted into the wee hours.

The north and south ends of the island competed keenly in sports. Fulford formed a football (soccer) team in 1910 with the intent of beating the Ganges team's English boys. The Fulford and Ganges teams were the chief competitors for the McPhillips Cup, named after Victoria lawyer Albert Edward McPhillips, who had represented Salt Spring in the provincial legislature from 1907 to 1913. The cup went back and forth between Ganges and Fulford until 1928, when Fulford won three times running and claimed it permanently. Ganges and Fulford also competed in baseball after starting teams in 1913.

The Salt Spring Dramatic Club, formed in 1913, was so successful that the company took its production to Sidney, where the plays were well received. SSIA

This beauty contest took place in Drummond Park at Fulford around 1917. Courtesy Bob Akerman

WORLD WAR I

World War I took its toll on Salt Spring. Of nearly 150 men enlisted, 25 were killed. Some volunteers joined the 16th Battalion (later called the Canadian Scottish) of the Canadian Expeditionary Force. The departure of so many men left too few workers to maintain the farms and businesses, disrupting the relatively prosperous rural economy.

Islanders took pride in their support of the war effort. Men died at the front, but many women also took part. The hospital's first matron, Annie Colhoun, volunteered in 1915. Dr. Marjorie Blandy, the daughter of R.R. Blandy who ran the White House (on the site of today's Fulford Inn), was one of seven female surgeons in the Women's Hospital Corps. Meanwhile, on the home front, Salt Spring chapters of the Imperial Order Daughters of the

The memorial set up in 1917 contained the names of Salt Spring men who died in World War I: C.C. Hedges, J.R. Lumley, H.T. Lumley, C.P. Storer, S.A. Storer, G.F. Haydon, N.C. Heaton, P. Falkner, A.N.H. Churchill, E. Cartwright, G.R.C. Calcott, R.P.P. Norton, G.H.C. Milnes, F.H. Corbett, J.D.B. Craig, C.M. Blandy, A.T.B. Charlesworth, H. Emerson, H. Longdon, L. Carter, C.G. Dean, A.G. Kemp, J. Mason, M.T. Myles, J.D. Whims. SSIA

Empire (IODE), founded in 1906, organized many bake sales, concerts, plays, and other events to aid the Red Cross Society and Belgian relief.

Quiet growth marked the prewar years on Salt Spring. No longer a frontier society, the community had sufficient wealth to support various complex undertakings—from the Ganges water pipeline to buying a piano for Mahon Hall, the community hall completed in 1902. By 1912, the island's population had reached about nine hundred and services were expanding quickly. So too were land development and tourism. Although the "Great War" rolled back growth (the population fell by about 10 percent during the war), once it ended a prosperous peacetime sparkled on the horizon.

LADY MINTO'S FIRST MATRON

Annie R. Colhoun was born in Londonderry, Northern Ireland, in 1876. She graduated at the top of her nursing-school class and was asked to stay on and teach, but later told her son Frank "she didn't want to become a prune-faced old biddy like her teachers." She worked as a private nurse for a few years, coming to Canada around 1911 on a holiday. When she arrived in Montreal, she was conscripted by the Victorian Order of Nurses and soon moved first to Burnaby and then to Salt Spring to become Lady Minto's first matron.

When war was declared, as the only nurse, Annie Colhoun stayed on at Lady Minto until September 1915, when she enlisted. She was wounded in the bombing of the Salonika hospital where she was stationed in Greece but continued to tend to her patients anyway. John Crofton, her grand-nephew, remembered hearing that she had picked up and disposed of a live shell when it landed in her tent. For her bravery, she was awarded more medals than any other islander, male or female. While in England, Annie married Frank Crofton whom she'd met on Salt Spring before the war. Although she did not return to her former job at the hospital, for years Annie did relief work at Lady Minto.

10

Farming the Hard Way

FROM LOG CABINS TO FRAME HOUSES

Though most settlers came to Salt Spring Island to farm, few found farming profitable. Eighty percent of Salt Spring is rugged, rocky mountainside. The 20 percent suitable for agriculture is mainly scattered in low-lying pockets where soil has accumulated since the glaciers retreated. Large-scale farming was—and is—impossible.

A pioneer farmer's life, given these environmental limitations, was not easy. In the first generation of settlement, people had little time to do anything but work. Life for field-crop farmers was a routine of planting, harvesting, and storing crops. Dairy farmers milked seven days a week, year round, in sickness and in health. Poultry farmers fed their fowl and gathered eggs. Farm work could also be dangerous, and farmers were regularly injured in accidents involving their equipment or their animals.

By the 1880s, the more tenacious and best-located farmers were well established. Markets opened up for their produce, neighbours moved in, and a sense of community developed. Frame houses replaced log cabins, big barns went up, and imported farm machinery appeared. Though still far from Easy Street, farmers could expect more from life than their predecessors.

By 1905, farms were no longer isolated clearings in the forest. Open fields lined many roads, and farms clustered around Fernwood, St. Mary Lake, the head of Ganges Harbour, the Cranberry, and the Fulford-Burgoyne Valley.

Small-scale farming, still geared to basic survival, was typical on the limited arable land. Families like the Ruckles and Musgraves, with farms of a thousand acres or more, were exceptional, and they left most of their land in forest or sheep grazing. Rev. E.F. Wilson wrote in 1900, "Of 45,440 acres, the entire area of the Island, only about 3,700 acres is as yet 'slashed'; and of that, not more than 1,700 acres are actually under cultivation."[1] Each of the island's hundred farms had an average of only about 17 acres (7 ha) under cultivation.

Salt Spring family farms were small but versatile. Every farm had an orchard, a garden, pigs, chickens, and at least one milk cow. Many had turkeys, ducks, and geese, as well as sheep grazing the hills. Field crops included hay, grain, and root crops for livestock feed.

Livestock husbandry dictated most farm activities. Farmers spent nine or ten months of the year raising feed—peas, timothy, clover, and other forage crops. Small acreages grew prodigious quantities of root crops—for both feed and market—including sweet mangel (a large, yellow beet), kale, and carrots. Every farm needed its own root cellar.

KEY DATES

1885 The CPR rail line to Vancouver is completed, making it easier to ship farm produce to eastern markets.

1896 Central Hall is built for use as an agricultural exhibition hall.

1898 The Salt Spring branch of the Farmers' Institute is founded.

1902 Mahon Hall, the island's new agricultural hall, is ready for use.

1904 The Salt Spring Island Creamery opens in Ganges.

1918 The Islands Farmers' Institute (named in 1937) results from the amalgamation of the Islands' Agricultural and Fruit Growers' Association and the Farmers' Institute.

1957 The Salt Spring Island Creamery closes.

1982 The fall fair is held for the first time on the Farmers' Institute's new grounds on Rainbow Road.

1991 About 5 percent of Salt Spring's labour force is involved in agriculture.

1992 Island Natural Growers is formed to support Salt Spring's organic farmers.

As raising feed grain—wheat, oats, and some barley—was so time consuming, the island never had enough. When the *Iroquois*—Salt Spring's primary link with Vancouver Island—sank in 1911 and was not immediately replaced, dwindling feed supplies caused near panic.

Every farmer needed to raise some surplus for cash to buy household and, increasingly, farm necessities: nursery stock, livestock, seed grain, hay, and basic equipment. Potatoes, lambs, wool, and homemade butter were the main cash crops. With so many expenses, even the most prosperous farmers were hard pressed just to break even.

Nature presented farmers with many other problems. The weather might be too hot, too cold, too wet, or too dry. The damp, warm coastal climate fostered diseases (scab, blight, scale) and insect pests (green fly, borer, bark louse, green and black aphids) that attacked the apples, plums, and cherries. Then, as Rev. E.F. Wilson recorded in his monthly newsletter, there was the caterpillar blight of 1900:

> They are entirely destroying the second growth of clover, and are swarming in the pea fields, eating both vine and pod. Nursery men are suffering very severely as they are destroying young fruit trees and plants of every description. Whole fields of carrots have been destroyed, the worm gnawing round the crown of the root until the top falls over. Many potato fields are left bare of all green—nothing but yellow naked stalks, and the tubers below perforated by the horrible worms. Nothing was ever seen like it before, we believe, in British Columbia.

Diseases and pests increasingly responded to spraying and control programs developed by the agriculture department. Breeders were also developing disease-resistant fruit varieties.

The deer were almost as destructive as the diseases and insects, but farmers could legally kill them if they were caught eating crops. By 1900, wolves and bears no longer caused problems, but cougars occasionally killed sheep and raccoons stole chickens.

TECHNOLOGY LIGHTENS THE LOAD

At first, only a few ox- or horse-powered machines—mainly horse-drawn mowers, hay rakes, and binders—lightened farm labour. Around 1890, Salt Spring's first horse-powered threshing machine—probably Joe Nightingale's—revolutionized grain growing on the island, though oldtimers like Willis Stark still threshed their grain with flails. In 1901, Edwin Rosman started custom threshing with his ten-horse-drawn thresher. Threshers were so useful that farmers gradually got their own, sometimes buying them co-operatively. Horse-powered stump pullers, such as the "Canada Stump Puller" introduced in 1912, helped farmers clear land. By 1914, horses had nearly replaced oxen as draught animals. Then, after 1920, tractors slowly—because of the expense—replaced horses.

Horse-powered haying on Ted Akerman's farm, on the site of today's Fulford firehall, c. 1910. Farmhands are James Akerman, Mike Gyves, Sr., Mike Gyves, Jr., Tom Jackson, and Ted Akerman. Courtesy Bob Akerman

The old spirit of co-operation survived despite mechanization. Moving threshing machines and other equipment from farm to farm, neighbours still helped each other with heavy or specialized work such as threshing, filling silos, digging potatoes, or butchering pigs.

This steam-powered monster felled trees and cleared parts of the Maxwell property around 1883. Most farmers considered land-clearing the greatest hurdle to establishing a farm. BCARS 11251, F-2519

GROWING SPECIALIZATION

To get past the subsistence level, some Salt Spring farmers specialized, first in fruit growing, later in dairying, poultry, specialty crops, and organically grown produce.

Commercial orchards were the first agricultural specialty on the island. In the 1880s or early 1890s, farmers planted large orchards, which were in full production by 1900. By the end of the century, fruit growing was big business.

Anna and Henry Caldwell in their orchard, with Clark Whims in the background, c. 1900. SSIA

In 1894, BC's agriculture department reported 13,739 apple trees, 1689 plum trees, 1161 pear trees, 474 cherry trees, and 279 other fruit trees on Salt Spring.[2]

In a good year, Harry Bullock, Theodore Trage, and Ed Lee each reportedly shipped about two thousand 40-pound (18 kg) boxes of fruit. The Scott brothers—Frank, Geoff, Will, and Harold—at Fruitvale were harvesting big prune crops (up to 10 tons in 1902) and the next year they hired ten Chinese workers to pick an expected 40-ton crop. The annual shipment of apples alone from Salt Spring was twenty thousand boxes. The 1913 harvest must have been worth about $16,000, then a substantial sum.

Farmers struggled to find enough affordable labour, particularly at harvest. In the early 1890s, itinerant whites and people of mixed race worked for one or two dollars a day, but farmers liked to hire Asians, who would work hard for lower wages than others. Japanese men, for example, would work for only 50 cents a day and often provided their own board.

After 1900, labour was more expensive and difficult to recruit, yet commercial fruit growing made island farmers more and more dependent on hired help. As early as 1903, lack of seasonal labour reportedly made harvesting difficult. By 1911, labour was two to three times more expensive than twenty years earlier. Competing with US produce, which was less expensive and often more attractive, grew increasingly difficult.

Transportation was also a hurdle. The island was isolated from markets, and its population and production were too small to support local transportation services. Salt Spring farmers still depended heavily on somewhat infrequent, unreliable steamer service. In response, the government replaced older wharves with new ones at Ganges in 1902 and at Beaver Point in 1910; and in 1914, a new 1000-foot (304 m) wharf at Ganges provided deepwater docking on any tide. But there were still insufficient steamers for the island's needs.

Joe Malcolm and Percy Purvis alleviated a growing transportation crisis in 1904 by using their 30-foot *Nomad* and 60-foot *Ganges* to transport produce to off-island markets. G.J. Mouat and Company, and later the Gulf Islands Trading Company, continued this service. Some farmers shipped their fruit directly to market. For example, Will Scott's apples, pears, and plums travelled by scow from his private wharf at Fruitvale. After about 1890, the Ruckles—and later the Monks—shipped fruit from their private wharves near Beaver Point, and Fulford-Burgoyne Valley fruit went from the public wharf at Burgoyne Bay.

Early in the twentieth century, BC's fruit-growing areas—the Okanagan, Saanich Peninsula, and Gulf Islands—were not in serious competition. Together they made BC a major exporter to the east, and by 1903, the volume warranted a daily fruit train from Victoria to Winnipeg. But by the 1920s, Gulf Islands orchards could no longer compete with well-serviced, large-scale Okanagan and US operations.

DAIRY FARMING

Dairying was Salt Spring's next agricultural specialty. From the time Louis Stark's cattle swam ashore in 1860, almost every Salt Spring farmer kept at least one cow to provide the family's milk and butter. Other than the Maxwells on Burgoyne Bay who concentrated on raising beef cattle commercially, farmers kept beef cattle only for home consumption or as beasts of burden in place of oxen.

Cattle thrived in the island's mild conditions, and by the 1880s and

1890s, farm families with a milk surplus were earning spare cash by selling butter. S.T. Conery on Blackburn Lake managed to produce a thousand pounds of butter from his dozen cows in 1895. He was the exception, however. To make dairy farming commercially significant, most farmers needed a creamery to buy their cream and convert it into butter.

By 1896, enough Jersey cows were producing rich milk to prompt John Collins, who had recently brought his family from England to live on his friend Harry Bullock's farm, to open a creamery. An old barn on Bullock's property became a small butter factory, the Salt Spring Island English Creamery Company. However, Collins couldn't make a go of it (perhaps because islanders complained of the foul-smelling pig farm nearby) and the creamery was closed. Today the building, on Upper Ganges Road, is a residence.

But the need was still there, so Harry Bullock helped to establish another creamery. The Salt Spring Island Creamery Association, which opened in 1904, was a co-operative modelled on creameries in Victoria and Duncan and financed by the sale of five hundred 10-dollar shares.

Assembly-line milking on the Bullock farm, c. 1912: (left to right) "Bowsie" Bowes-Elliot (?), Betty Dunnell, Steve Dunnell, Bill Palmer. Photo by Jesse Bond, courtesy Malcolm Bond

SALT SPRING GOLD

Only Ganges area farmers sent cream to the Salt Spring Island Creamery when it opened in 1904. Weekly butter production averaged 750 pounds (340 kg) during the first year. The creamery reached its peak output of about 140,000 pounds (63,504 kg) in 1928, when 136 farmers on Salt Spring and the Outer Islands—Galiano, Mayne, the Penders, and Saturna—supplied cream. Salt Spring butter at this time was so well regarded that the creamery often had trouble producing as much as it could sell. Eventually most Salt Spring farmers sold to the creamery.

The creamery sterilized the cream and stirred it in two large churns, one producing 1000 pounds (454 kg) of butter and the other producing 500 pounds (227 kg). Buttermilk ran off into a tank behind the creamery, where farmers could collect it free to feed their pigs and chickens. The butter itself was shipped via the Canadian Pacific Railway (CPR) ferry to Northwestern Creameries in Victoria, which sold it to the stores.

For more than fifty years, the famous creamery was a mainstay of the island economy. Not only did it win prizes at the Canadian National Exhibition in Toronto, but it also churned a special batch for the king and queen when they visited Victoria in 1939.

POULTRY FARMING

From early days, almost every island farm kept some poultry, and housewives earned grocery money by selling surplus eggs at 25 to 30 cents a dozen. In 1895, Thomas Mouat claimed, "my poultry alone pay their own cost and find us in flour and groceries, which is pretty well for a family of ten."[3]

John Armstrong, buttermaker, standing in the doorway of the Salt Spring Island Creamery, c. 1909. The creamery was built of local stone at the foot of Ganges Hill. In the late 1990s the building was being used as a bakery. SSIA

By 1910, some dairymen—unable to find dairy workers or pay their high wages—turned to poultry farming. Three years later, the Salt Spring Island Poultry Association was organized. After World War I, three large poultry operations began.

Paul and Marie Bion, originally from Paris, started the first large poultry farm north of St. Mary Lake and eventually kept about a thousand Leghorn hens. In the late 1990s, ninety-year-old Simone Chantelu, one of the Bions' twin nieces, still kept ninety birds and was selling three to four dozen eggs a day.

Another large chicken farm belonged to Ted Parsons, who bought his 160-acre (65 ha) Mansell Road farm in 1911. He raised four thousand Leghorns, and his eight incubators hatched almost twelve thousand chicks a year. The Parsonses sold their eggs through Mouat's, where they bought up to twenty tons of feed each month. Son Gordon remembered taking the family boat to collect the Parsonses' secret ingredient—clamshell—which they ground up and mixed with the chicken feed, the shell providing the lime necessary for strong eggshells. By the late thirties, the Parsonses were selling about twelve hundred dozen eggs (worth $600) a week to a commercial hatchery in Langley. Ted Parsons' sons, Gordon and Doug, bought their father's business in 1946 but ceased operations about eight years later.

In the 1920s, Leo and Peggy Chaplin, raising thousands of birds as breeding stock for sale on- and off-island, had the biggest industry at Vesuvius Bay. One of the Chaplins' Barred Rocks was Canada's champion producer in 1924, and three years later, the company won awards at the World Poultry Congress in Ottawa and exhibited prize birds as far afield as London and Tokyo.

SPECIALTY FARMING

Specialty farms have operated on Salt Spring over the years, but the greatest economic impact came from the James Brothers Seed Company. P.T. James, a trained horticulturist from England, and three of his sons started this family business in 1915 on Parker Island (just west of Galiano Island). Their mail-order flower and vegetable seed business grew so rapidly that only two years later they sold Parker Island and moved to Salt Spring. For four years they leased Norman Wilson's Barnsbury farm and then, from 1922 to 1930, John Charles Lang's larger Fernwood farm, which had better soil and a good water supply.

After the war, the James family sold their fruit and vegetable seeds worldwide and also shipped much produce to markets in Vancouver. The Jameses developed, among other specialized machinery, a transplanting machine that could plant eight hundred cabbages an hour. Eventually, the James seed operation became too big to function effectively on the Lang property, given Salt Spring's irregular mail service and thrice-weekly steamships. In 1930, the company moved to a 300-acre (120 ha) farm on Cowichan Bay, where it operated as the James Canadian Seed Company until the late 1940s.

Other small specialty farms also operated on the island in the 1920s, including a violet farm at Vesuvius, Betty Shaw's silver-fox farm at Fulford Harbour, a mink farm between Fulford and Ganges, a chinchilla rabbit farm near St. Mary Lake, and the Bryants' and Smiths' goat-cheese factories (see chapter 13). However, none of these highly defined businesses lasted long.

Seeding on the James family farm, c. 1918. Courtesy Val Watt/SSIA

SHEEP FARMING

Almost all island farmers raised a few sheep—usually relegated to hillier, less productive areas—for their meat and wool. Farmers with large flocks in the north end included John Patton Booth at Mt. Erskine, Joel Broadwell west of St. Mary Lake, John Maxwell around Burgoyne Bay, and Theodore Trage toward Beaver Point. The Ruckles focussed on sheep-raising only after World War I, although Henry Ruckle shipped some lambs to market before then.

The relatively isolated western slopes of Mt. Tuam and Mt. Bruce (then called Musgrave Mountain) were the island's major sheep ranching area. Here three wealthy landowners in succession ran sheep in large numbers: the Pimbury brothers in the mid-1870s, Edward Musgrave from 1885 to 1892, and later Edward Trench.

The 1891 diary of young Scottish shepherd Alexander Aitken, who worked on the Musgrave ranch for just over a year, gives us precious details about the Musgrave operation. More than eleven hundred sheep, raised primarily for their wool, ran wild over the whole mountain and were rounded up two or three times a year with help from Cowichan people and Hawaiians from Fulford Harbour. After shearing in June, nearly 4000 pounds (1814 kg) of wool were sacked and shipped to Victoria from Musgrave Landing. About a hundred "fat sheep" were sent to market that summer, Aitken recorded, and each week the family slaughtered a sheep for food.

NURSERY FARMING

Salt Spring nursery farming began in 1860 when Jonathan Begg started raising fruit trees, ornamentals, and shrubs at his Fernwood nursery. Richard Brinn and Thomas Griffiths took over his business, but we don't know if it survived the 1870s. In the 1880s and early 1890s, when farmers were planting orchards all over the island, they probably bought their nursery stock in Victoria. In 1896, professional nurseryman Ambrose A. Berrow opened a nursery southwest of Central, but sold it five years later to Harry Bullock.

No dedicated nursery operation served the island for much of this century, although Mouat's, Patterson's, and the Trading Company sold farmers some supplies. In 1976, recently arrived Tom and Mimi Gossett opened a small store in Upper Ganges. The Gossetts' Foxglove Farm and Garden Supplies, named after their farm on Mt. Maxwell Road, first catered to farmers' needs but expanded to bedding plants the next year. It moved to the corner of Atkins and Lower Ganges Road in 1979. As Salt Spring's population grew, the Gossetts' nursery business expanded, and other nurseries opened. By the late

Kumanosuke Okano built the island's first greenhouse, 55 m by 91 m, on his Booth Canal farm around 1930. A few years later, his daughter, Kimiko Murakami, started selling fruit and vegetables from a stall on her 17-acre (7 ha) farm on Sharp Road. The quality of Mrs. Murakami's produce was widely known; much went to the Empress Hotel in Victoria. Courtesy Mary Kitagawa

nineties, the island supported about a dozen nurseries, including one specializing in native plants and another in water plants.

SUPPORT FOR THE FARMING COMMUNITY

Three important farmers' organizations formed in the late 1890s: the Central Hall Association, the Islands' Agricultural and Fruit Growers' Association, and the Farmers' Institute. The last two especially, with government support, helped improve island agricultural methods.

In 1895, local farmer and Member of the Legislative Assembly John Patton Booth led a move to create a limited liability company with shares at $5 each to build a public hall mainly for agricultural shows. Central Hall housed Salt Spring's first agricultural exposition on October 14, 1896. The hall soon proved more suitable as a community centre, and the fair moved to Rainbow Road. Central Hall at North End and Vesuvius Bay roads still functions as an island meeting place.

The Horticultural and Fruit Growers' Association, formed in 1896, soon changed its name to the Islands' Agricultural and Fruit Growers' Association, broadening its membership to all the Gulf Islands. Its objectives also grew to include both agriculture and horticulture.

Salt Spring founded its branch of the Farmers' Institute in 1898 to educate farmers and improve agriculture through lectures and demonstrations. John Collins, Rev. E.F. Wilson, Edward Walter, James Horel, and Ed Lee were among the most active members and officers. The institute's educational efforts focussed largely on co-ordinating government-sponsored lectures by experts on topics such as clearing land with stumping powder, tuberculosis and dairying, animal husbandry, creamery management, and orchard care.

The Islands' Agricultural and Fruit Growers' Association, sponsors of the fall fair, soon realized it needed proper exhibition grounds with an adequate hall, livestock facilities, and space for athletic and social events at the annual celebration. Land on Rainbow Road was purchased from Frank Scott, and by fall 1901 a new hall was under construction. Even before it opened in 1902, the society borrowed $1000 from landowner Ross Mahon to enlarge the hall and buy additional exhibition grounds. Mahon died in 1903, and in 1904 the Mahon family forgave the mortgage and the hall was named the "Mahon Memorial Hall." (It's been known simply as Mahon Hall ever since.)

Fairs from 1896 to 1914 were a great success, each proclaimed "the best

Mahon Hall during an early fall fair. Photo by Jesse Bond. SSIA

ever" in local newspapers. Widely supported by farmers and business people alike, the fairs became prime social events drawing up to a thousand people each year. The CPR ran a special ferry to bring visitors from Victoria and the other islands.

The Islands' Agricultural and Fruit Growers' Association and the Farmers' Institute amalgamated in 1918, and after several name changes, became the Islands' Farmers' Institute in 1937 and eventually the Salt Spring Farmers' Institute.

No fall fairs took place during World War II. After the war, as farming declined, much smaller fairs were held in Fulford Hall and the nearby Shaw farm. From the late fifties no fairs were held until Mike and Bev Byron took the initiative and resurrected the annual agricultural show in 1976 on the school grounds on Rainbow Road. Three years later, the Farmers' Institute bought its own exhibition grounds farther up Rainbow Road and held its first fall fair on the new site in 1982. From then on, fall fairs once again became Salt Spring's most popular annual event.

No WAY TO EARN A LIVING

British Columbia suffered a general economic downturn from 1912 to 1914. Farmers' profits fell to record lows. Things got even worse when

World War I began. Nearly 150 Salt Spring men, many of them farmers, enlisted. On many farms, women or older men were left to do the farm work. Low prices and reduced soil fertility resulted from the strain of all-out war production.

Despite prolonged worldwide economic recession after the war, some farmers succeeded in the 1920s. But many took nonagricultural work, such as working on the island's roads, to make ends meet. Farm life lost its appeal for young people.

The Depression of the 1930s hastened the decline of a farming livelihood for many islanders. Farming virtually ended in peripheral areas such as Musgrave Mountain, the Cranberry, and even Vesuvius. Nearly every agricultural specialty on the island was dealt a crippling blow.

Economic conditions picked up somewhat from 1939 to 1945. Lotus Ruckle remembered that farmers could sell anything they grew during World War II and that there was finally some spare cash to buy new farm equipment and a new car. But farming's decline continued after the war. Most farmers still had to find other work. For example, Bill Crawford, who ran a dairy farm on Beddis Road, opened a shoemaking shop in a shed behind Mouat's store in the late 1940s. A few new agricultural enterprises started, such as the large turkey farms of Ted and Daisy Gear in the Fulford-Burgoyne Valley and Arthur and Joane Millner at Central. But one old farm after another stopped production.

Miles Smeeton, who settled at Musgrave in the 1940s, witnessed the end of one old farm:

> At its best he had run perhaps twenty ewes, kept a couple of breeding sows, a cow or two, and some hens for the house. This he had achieved with immense labour, courage and initiative. Now he was too old to battle any longer with bramble and thistle and the invading bush, and the old age pension had made it unnecessary. The weeds and thorns grew almost unnoticed about the yard and the farm buildings that he had made. Beryl and I— knowing a little what it takes even to re-make a place—were continually humbled by the thought of all the hope and effort that must have gone into making these small farms, and what little visible reward it had reaped in rest and comfort.[4]

Even the once-flourishing dairy industry dwindled. For years a major island business, the Salt Spring Island Creamery began to falter after the war. In 1948, a new law required that all milk in BC be pasteurized—but many Salt Spring dairy farmers still lacked the electricity to do so. This forced many of them out of business. Arthur Drake, who had run the creamery for thirty-seven years, retired in 1949. Don Mackenzie, who owned and ran the creamery in the early 1950s, complained that he was losing money by importing cream since fewer people had dairy cows. But the general opinion was that under the new management the creamery's butter quality had slipped. In 1957, the creamery closed forever.

Farming on Salt Spring, as we look back, seems to have been farming the hard way. For most island families, farming was too small-scale to really be profitable. It demanded almost endless hard work for meagre, precarious financial rewards. No fortunes were ever made farming on Salt Spring.

Today few on Salt Spring can make a living solely from farming, but a number of residents still keep sheep, pasture beef cattle, raise poultry, and maintain excellent produce gardens. In 1991, just under 5 percent of the island's work force, almost two hundred people, worked in agriculture. Very few of these, however, earned their income from farming alone.[5] While the island's large orchards and farms of the past no longer exist, small-scale, full-time farming has enjoyed a resurgence, much of it connected with the back-to-the-land movement in the seventies and eighties and interest in organic farming in the nineties.

In the past, many Salt Spring farmers farmed organically simply because they couldn't afford fertilizers and pesticides. In the 1990s, concern over how these chemicals affect human health made organic farming appealing to many growers, but still not financially viable. In 1992, Island Natural Growers, a local trade association, formed. In 1997, nine Salt Spring farmers were part of the Islands Organic Producers Association. These certified organic growers joined other longtime island farmers, many raising Salt Spring's famous lamb or growing produce for the local market.

Salt Spring's first farmers faced the huge obstacle of clearing the land and planting the first crops and orchards. Successive generations of farmers have contended with the island's generally rugged, rocky terrain. Like their predecessors, most farmers today still rely on mixed farming—and often on outside work to supplement meagre incomes.

11

The Squire of Salt Spring

A MYSTERIOUS NEWCOMER

One Salt Spring islander greatly influenced almost everyone and everything around him. Not everyone liked Harry Wright Bullock, and few understood him, but he was truly larger than life.

The single, rich, twenty-six-year-old Englishman who came to Salt Spring Island in 1892 must have intrigued islanders. Bullock was short (about 5'8"), broad, bespectacled, and balding, with a large beard and a round kindly face. Donald "Goodie" Goodman, who worked for Bullock from 1922 to 1926, said his employer "was a man of very much regular habits, including a fair amount of eating, usually about five meals a day, and he showed it all right."[1]

Bullock's somewhat mysterious quality led many people to exaggerate when discussing him. His dress and demeanour were consciously that of an upper-class English gentleman. Almost every photo or description portrays him formally dressed in a starched white shirt, tie, vest, black waistcoat or long black frock coat, and satin top hat. He even kept his beard black and shiny with a product called Beardblack. In the frontier community of late-nineteenth-century Salt Spring, where most people survived by hard physical labour, Bullock's fanciful appearance sometimes inspired far-fetched stories of outlandish behaviour. Bullock's wealth, lifestyle, and eccentricities—he liked islanders to call him "The Squire"—invited discussion and anecdote.

Bullock, the second son of a wealthy Bristol family,[2] was born in 1866 near his mother's home of Chalfont, Buckinghamshire. His family provided ample financial support when he left for the colonies. Denise Crofton, a frequent guest in Bullock's home, remembered hearing that Bullock was in love with his brother's wife and left England to avoid painful encounters.

For five years, Bullock rented two rooms at Stevens Boarding House and lived there while his house was being built. Anne Stevens was a good cook, and the boarding house at Central was next door to St. Mark's Church, very important to the devoutly Anglican Bullock.

Bullock purchased land on the lake that now bears his name and hired Reid Bittancourt to build a twelve-room mansion, which reputedly cost

Bullock in his finery on the way to church, c. 1910. Photo by Jesse Bond. SSIA

$2000. Fruit and nut trees were planted almost immediately.

One of Bullock's first housekeepers was Miss Hind, a former matron of Victoria's Protestant Orphans' Home, who came to Salt Spring in 1903. Mary Palmer replaced her three years later.

Over the years, Bullock's house grew. Bill Palmer, his employee for years, said the house had ten bedrooms, a dining room, a drawing room, a huge hall, Bullock's den, a sitting room, a small dining room where the household staff ate, and a large kitchen. Donald Goodman remembered that Bullock had a furnace in the entry hall, "which only a bachelor would do, because no wife would ever arrive and let him get away with it." He said the house contained "a helluva lot of antiques," and the walls were covered with valuable paint-

Bullock's house was probably the largest house on the island when it was built. Two of his Japanese employees stand at right, c. 1910. SSIA

ings. The indoor plumbing, perhaps the first on the island, required an unsightly network of exposed pipes on inside walls.

Bullock was a knowledgeable farmer, but left most farm work to Japanese labourers. Each year, his 300-acre (121 ha) farm produced about two thousand boxes of apples, plums, pears, and cherries—80,000 pounds (36,288 kg) of large, high-quality fruit. Bullock also produced cream from his Jersey cows, pork, poultry, lamb, garden crops, and honey from his hundred or so beehives. Ham and fish were cured in a smokehouse.

Bullock's state-of-the-art equipment included one of the island's first tractors in about 1922, a gasoline generator, and a steam engine to thresh grain. Day-to-day operations were overseen by a succession of competent managers. The first, in 1905, was Keith Wilson, Rev. E.F. Wilson's youngest child. Three years later, Bill Evans came to work on the farm and eventually replaced Wilson as estate manager. Bullock built a house for Evans and his wife, Nellie Dowson, who arrived from England in 1912. When Evans left to manage a farm at Duncan in 1917, Bill Palmer took over.

Bill Evans, Bill Palmer, and "Bowsie" Bowes-Elliot cutting hay on the Bullock farm, c. 1912. Photo by Jesse Bond. SSIA

Cocking hay on Bullock's farm, c. 1911. Photo by Jesse Bond. SSIA

THE PALMERS

Mary Palmer was forty-seven and living in Victoria when she became Harry Wright Bullock's housekeeper. She and her nine-year-old son, Bill, lived in the Bullock house. Mary cooked for Bullock for twelve years. After retiring, she gained a reputation as a fine piano teacher of island children.

Bill Palmer began managing Bullock's estate in 1917. Palmer's wife-to-be, Irene, came from New Westminster in 1927 at twenty-two to teach at Beaver Point School. She and Bill met at a Fulford Hall dance and married in 1929. Bill, Irene, and Mary then lived together in Bullock's small cottage.

After Mary Palmer's death in 1940, Bill and Irene moved to a house they built on 44 acres (18 ha) on St. Mary Lake. For some time, Bill rented Bullock's farm, paying the rent in firewood, milk, and labour. He managed the 12-acre (4.9 ha) orchard and sold the apples himself. Irene fondly remembered Bullock as "a very kind man" who gave them a goose every Christmas, helped "his boys" develop their interests, and shared magazines with the Palmers.

BULLOCK'S BOYS

After 1900, Bullock always hired a couple of twelve- to sixteen-year-old boys to care for his house and property. Most came from the Protestant Orphans' Home in Victoria. After Mary Palmer retired, the senior boy would serve as cook—taught by Bullock, himself a good cook—and the junior as houseboy. The cook was also responsible for preparing the shopping lists. The houseboy cleaned the house, served at table, and did the dishes. In winter, the boys cleared snow and brought in well water, as Bullock Lake was too boggy to provide drinking water; in spring, they helped plant the gardens.

THE PHOTOGRAPHER-FARMER

Jesse Bond in his houseboy uniform, c. 1908. SSIA

Jesse Bond came to work as Bullock's houseboy in 1906. Jesse's mother, unable to support three children, had placed him in the Protestant Orphans' Home after his father died in 1903.

Bullock was good to Jesse, teaching him many skills, notably photography. An avid amateur photographer himself, he transferred his enthusiasm to Jesse and gave him photographic equipment. Many wonderful photographs from this period of Salt Spring history were taken by Jesse Bond.

After serving in World War I, Jesse bought a farm under the government's Soldier Settlement program. He farmed for eight or nine years, using the skills he'd acquired at Bullock's. During the Depression, he sold the farm and left to log on Vancouver Island. But in 1932, he returned to Salt Spring and bought a 200-acre (81 ha) farm on LePage Road. Four years later, he married Mary Dahl from Saskatchewan. Jesse and Mary and their children, Malcolm and Moira, lived on their farm Bon Acres, which became well known for its high-quality produce.

Although Jesse gave up photography after the war, his professional-quality pictures survive as a record of early twentieth-century Salt Spring.

Each boy received room and board plus $10 a month in his first year, with an increase of $2 a month for each successive year. A boy needed to buy only clothing from his wages, as Bullock supplied everything else. Donald Goodman remembered Bullock investing $125 in a radio just for the boys' use.

Bullock was very strict with his boys, insisting on proper behaviour and dress (he dropped the requirement for elaborate uniforms after World War II). Although Palmer said his employer occasionally caned him and made the boys "toe the line," Goodman said that Bullock never really mistreated them. Still, Bullock's class biases were apparent in his "upstairs-downstairs" household. He ate only in the dining room, for example. Occasionally he would break his own rules, Palmer recalled, by having a cup of tea in the kitchen. He also did not believe that working-class children required schooling, so his boys never attended school. The only exception was Bill Palmer, who attended a Salt Spring private school and completed Grade 13 in Victoria, perhaps at his mother's insistence.

Bullock with two of "his boys." Apparently he had his playful moments. SSIA

GOODIE

Donald "Goodie" Goodman was born the youngest of four children in Saskatchewan in 1910, but his family soon moved to Victoria. Goodie's childhood was marred by his father's alcoholism, his parents' estrangement when he was only six, and his mother's death from tuberculosis. Goodie's brothers were placed in an orphanage in England, and in 1919, after his mother's death, Goodie's father placed him and his sister in the Protestant Orphans' Home.

Goodie worked for Bullock from 1922 to 1926 but left to try other jobs. He worked as a porter on the *Island Princess* and harvested wheat in Vermilion (now Princeton), BC. Back on the island, Goodie survived the Depression in various jobs. His favourite was working from 1928 to 1930 with the Gulf Islands Trading Company. Goodie married Isabel Howard in 1934, and the couple had three children.

After working for the Trading Company for another three years in the mid-forties, Goodie ran the Ganges Shell station until 1954. In the early fifties he trained for the business he's best known for—undertaking. He drove the ambulance, the fire truck, and the truck used as a hearse. Eventually, Goodie became an agent for Hayward's Funeral Parlour in Victoria.

Goodie acquired many skills in his profession. When a friend asked him for a badly needed haircut one day, Goodie agreed but asked his friend to lie down. His usual clients were never in an upright position!

Donald Goodman recollected one Bullock failing: "One of his bad faults was that he couldn't tolerate seeing you without something to do." The boys started work at 8:00 or 8:15 a.m. but dragged it out until 9:00 p.m., "because if he caught you without a job, he'd find a new one for you.... When he went out, we'd finish up within ten minutes and be gone." It was the only way they could get time off.

Some felt that, when Bullock was older, the boys took advantage of him, as Donald Goodman reported:

> [Bullock] was foolish to an extent, especially years after I left. He was loanin' the kids money with no thought of ever getting it back. . . . They could touch him for 20 dollars any old time they wanted. And he'd give it to them and smile. He knew he wasn't gonna get it back, but he'd still loan it.

Over the years, Bullock hired as many as sixteen boys from the orphanage.[3] Bullock's boys must have learned valuable skills from him, because most did well after they left the estate. Today people might suspect the motives of a man who had such close involvement with young boys. However, no hint of scandal attached to the man in his own day, and Bullock's boys continue to speak highly of their mentor.

A GENEROUS AND ENTERPRISING MAN

Bullock was a strong supporter of the Anglican Church. St. Mark's was built and consecrated the year he arrived, and St. Mary's soon after. Bullock donated land for St. Mark's vicarage and money for some church furnishings. He also served as church warden for several years and provided a carriage and team of horses for funerals. When he died, Bullock left the Anglican Church $5000.

Bullock also gave generously to individuals, community groups, and causes. He was active in many organizations, although his focus was the island's Anglican community. In 1896, he was a founding member of the Salt Spring Island Club, a social club, which used his billiard table for years. He was first president of the Salt Spring Island Creamery Association, a member of the Central Hall Association building committee and the Salt Spring Island Development Association, and a director of both the Ganges Water and Power Company and the Gulf Islands Trading Company.

Apparently Bullock liked to have the upper hand in his dealings with others, as Ivan Mouat pointed out in a revealing anecdote. One day his uncle Gilbert Mouat was helping Hiram Whims carry his many purchases to his

An IODE picnic on Bullock's estate, c. 1917. SSIA

wagon. Bullock pulled up in his gig and called, "Gilbert!" Mouat answered, "Just a minute, Mr. Bullock," and made another trip to the wagon. Again Bullock called, somewhat irately, "Gilbert!" But Mouat concentrated on loading Whims's wagon. "Gilbert, in England when the squire of the village drives up, the shopkeeper comes out and takes his order." "Well, Mr. Bullock, this isn't England and I didn't think you were the squire, so you will just have to come in like everybody else and get your order." According to Ivan Mouat, Bullock's reaction was to start the Salt Spring Island Trading Company. (Another version of the company's founding is given in chapter 9.)

Bullock started several other enterprises, including his ill-fated creamery (see chapter 10), and rented out many homes and buildings. Rents varied with his mood and feelings about the renter. In 1937, Bullock had a building constructed at the corner of Hereford Avenue and Lower Ganges Road to help his former "boy" Alf Hougen, a good cook, start a restaurant called The Ship's Anchor. The restaurant was later known as The Log Cabin, The Ship's Inn, the Ship's Anchor Inn, the Tides Inn, Rita's Inn, and, again, the Tide's Inn.

A number of undocumented stories suggest that Bullock lent money to many Salt Spring people, sometimes at high interest rates. He was generally kind and generous to those he liked, stern and forbidding to those who did not court his favour. One relationship that seemed to go bad was that between Bullock and John Collins, who followed Bullock to Salt Spring in 1895. After Bullock's English Creamery Company run by Collins closed (see chapters 8 and 10), Bullock sued Collins over the money invested in the creamery. In 1900, in "Our Life on Salt Spring," Rev. E.F. Wilson wrote tersely in his diary, "Report that Mr. Collins had got 9 months in gaol, being result of Bullock's action to recover $4329. People nearly all with Mr. Collins and against Mr. Bullock."

One story has it that Bullock wanted to marry Collins's daughter, Alice, but Collins refused. A letter Bullock wrote to Alice Collins while vacationing in Bristol suggests that he was strongly interested, if not in love, with her. Bullock planned to buy Alice a riding habit:

> Please remember I cannot in the least promise, so you must not be disappointed if I do not bring one. If I do, would you like it to be made with a 18 in. or 21 in. waist. I suppose you would like some new stays to fit it, in fact you had better send me your complete measure & be careful not to get it too wide across the back. To use a slang expression I want you to cut the shine out of the rest of them.[4]

SETTING THE FASHION

Bullock's contribution to the social life of some islanders—especially the wealthy, north-end English families—made a lasting impression. Bullock placed so much importance on dressing well that he provided clothes and incentives so people would dress as he thought proper. Mabel Davis, who attended several lunches and dinners at Bullock's, remembered his specific dress code for women:

> They had to have 18-inch waists. Well, I couldn't get below 22. And he wanted high-heeled shoes 5 inches high, which was very high in those days. He liked them to have earrings and a veil. Oh, yes, gloves! He used to give us gloves every now and again. Oh he was awfully good![5]

Bullock's drawing room. Much has been written about Bullock's lavish balls, but it's unlikely that much dancing took place in rooms like this one crowded with furniture.

The earrings were for pierced ears, and Bullock would arrange piercing to be done by a doctor, although sometimes he'd do the job himself. However, not all women wanted pierced ears and the tightly laced corsets required for the small waists Bullock favoured.

Bullock delighted in having guests in his house, and guests delighted in coming. (In later years, Bullock often entertained at the Harbour House Hotel run by the Croftons.) Margaret Cunningham, a frequent guest, remembered her host as a wonderful character who "really entertained" with splendid seven-course dinners including soup—he insisted that diners put a spoonful of sherry in their oxtail soup—grapefruit, large servings of fish and red meat, and three or four beautiful desserts. Later there would be choices of drinks for the men and chocolates and coffee for the women.

Bullock's boys and their friends would share leftovers from these lavish dinners in the kitchen. In later years, a turkey or side of beef would often leave the table almost intact, so those in the kitchen frequently ate even more than the guests.

Bullock's cellar was well known on the island. Donald Goodman remembered that it contained mainly hard liquor, sherry, and beer rather than wine. He recalled Bullock having a drink only twice in the four years he worked for him, once simply to check a sherry's quality. However, after Bullock's death, his nephew and heir, Gerard (sometimes referred to as "Gerald") Bullock, discovered twenty inexplicably empty whiskey bottles.

"The squire" also liked visiting and was not averse to inviting himself over, as Margaret Cunningham's sister Mary Inglin recounted:

> He'd write me a note and say, "Dear Mary. I shall come to tea with you on Thursday if it's convenient. Yours faithfully, H.W. Bullock." So then he would come and I'd make cream puffs, which I knew he liked. Then he just opened his mouth and threw in a cream puff. Because he had a long beard and moustache, it was difficult to get this cream puff in.[6]

Bullock also regularly had tea with his sister Mary, who had come to Salt Spring in 1900 and married Ernest Crofton. Mary and Ernest Crofton were often dinner guests at Bullock's house.

THE TROUBLE WITH CARS

Harry Bullock's 1912 Model T Ford was Salt Spring's second or third car. Like other cars it caused problems on the narrow roads—especially with horses, the only transportation most people could afford. Bullock once received a letter from J. Compton Kingsbury, the secretary of the Islands' Agricultural and Fruit Growers' Association, requesting that he not drive his car during the fall fair to avoid terrorizing the animals. In conversation with Ruth Sandwell, Daisy Gear remembered hearing that Bullock drove his car only on designated days of the week so that other islanders could drive their horses in peace.

Bullock driving his new Model T, with Bill Palmer getting into the back seat, c. 1912. SSIA

Mastering the gearshift seemed to elude Bullock. Manson Toynbee remembered Bullock's driving as "a continuous lurch." Bullock had a real problem with Salt Spring's first stop sign at the corner of Lower and Upper Ganges roads. To avoid coasting back down the incline as he approached Lower Ganges Road from the north, Bullock would enter the intersection and carefully stop right in the middle, halting any traffic coming along the road. Perhaps his inadequacies as a driver encouraged him to leave the driving to his boys.

Bullock's dress standards were not confined to females. He also encouraged local boys and employees to dress for church, sometimes with bribes of 5 or 10 cents. However, this occasionally led to problems, as Mabel Davis recalled:

One day Mr. Bullock came and asked Mrs. Wilson [the minister's wife] if she would allow him to supply Eton suits and silk hats for her two younger boys so that they could wear them to church. So she finally got persuaded that it would be all right.... Then one day the boys opposite, who were considered quite a bit lower down on the scale, came dressed the same. She was so horrified that I think she sent the Eton suits and hats back to Mr. Bullock.[7]

Mrs. Wilson was less critical than her husband, who felt Bullock's lifestyle was excessive for a good Anglican. He especially disliked the dancing in the early days. John Crofton neatly summed up the Rev. E.F. Wilson's relationship with Bullock:

He had his puritanical ideas of how people should behave, but at the same time he needed money for his parish. And Mr. Bullock provided that conflict of interests because of his lifestyle, but at the same time he had the money which he gave to the church.[8]

MAKING SENSE OF IT ALL

Islanders had difficulty understanding Bullock, who distanced himself from others because he considered respect and status his due. Bullock was interested in ideas and history, but we have no idea if he read widely or whether his extensive art collection represented a personal interest or merely an inheritance. We do know he was religious and had fears some would consider foolish. For example, Dr. Raymond Rush remembered Bullock giving him these unusual instructions:

"Now in my will, there's an envelope there with five dollars in it." And he was desperately afraid of being buried alive. So he says, "Now I want you to cut my throat to make sure I'm dead." But I never got the five dollars because I moved off the island before he died.[9]

Most people felt Bullock was eccentric, as he no doubt was. Daisy Gear thought he was just a "lonely old gentleman." Anne Mouat felt he was just "trying to build a community like an English town. He wasn't very popular so he had to try to make himself popular."[10] Mary Inglin believed he was a true altruist:

> Mr. Bullock was quite a wonderful man, really, very kind-hearted, and he was always doing good turns for people. If anybody was very hard up, he would send a good lot of groceries from the store just at dusk when nobody could see what he was doing.[11]

But perhaps Bullock wasn't entirely altruistic. Donald Goodman felt that Bullock evidently enjoyed having people grateful for his kindnesses and in his debt.

In one way or another, most of Bullock's boys benefited hugely from their exposure to the squire. Most were encouraged to return if they had problems, as several did when jobs were scarce during the Depression. In his will, Bullock left small sums of money to Bill Palmer and Jesse Bond and forgave Bill Currie's $2500 mortgage. Bill Palmer summarized many islanders' view of Bullock: "He was a very kind-hearted man, and you had to put up with his eccentricities. He was very, very good to me. He gave me a start."[12] Malcolm Bond also remembered that when his father, "a very slight lad at the time, left to serve in World War I, Bullock told him that he was too frail to go, but that if anything happened to him in the war, there would always be a place for him to come back to."

When Bullock died at eighty in 1946, his nephew Gerard Bullock inherited his property, which he sold to Ernie and Brenda Lowe fifteen years later. The Lowes named the property Lakeridge and started a summer camp for youth there. In 1964, Bullock's "manor house" burned to the ground, and by the late nineties, little remained to remind islanders of Bullock, other than the lake named after him and the stories told by Salt Spring elders who knew him.

12

Logging, Mining, and Red Ink

HARD PHYSICAL WORK

Timber was an obstacle to eliminate rather than a resource to exploit for most early farmers. When Salt Spring Island's first settlers cleared land, they slashed and burned much of the timber they felled.

Some recognized the resource's potential, however. In 1860, for example, four German-born settlers in Fulford Harbour were shipping cedar shakes and staves for salmon casks to Victoria. A few years later, Michael Gyves chose his pre-emption in the Fulford-Burgoyne Valley specifically for its fine stand of cedar, which he used to make cedar shakes for the Victoria market.

Many farmers soon supplemented their meagre income with logging. Charles Horel logged around Dean and Drake roads in the 1880s, using oxen to drag logs from the bush to a bank where he rolled them into the sea. He likely sold his logs in Mill Bay.

A few people logged full-time. The 1891 census identified nine loggers, mostly on Salt Spring's south end. Many farmers logged to augment their income, and some also worked as teamsters. Their horses and oxen dragged logs from as far as Weston Lake to Fulford Harbour along skid roads still partly visible today.

There was a log dump at the head of Fulford Harbour by about 1900. Much of the timber was exported for mine props and piles in Mexico and wharves and bridges in China. Islanders also burned logs to make charcoal for salmon canneries and to fuel steam boilers on steamships. Rev. E.F. Wilson noted a charcoal-burning crew on Edward Walter's property (around

KEY DATES

1859 Saltspring Island Stone Company operates near Southey Point on the west side of the island.

1860 Four settlers produce shakes and barrel staves for the Victoria market.

1891 The census lists nine Salt Spring residents whose primary occupation is logging.

1924 F.M. Singer Lumber Company brings several portable tie mills to the island.

1926 The wharf of the Bulman sawmill at Cusheon Cove collapses; the company soon closes.

1960 Prince Thurn und Taxis of Bavaria begins buying 6000 acres (2428 ha) of Salt Spring forest.

1962 The Holdfast Pozzolan plant on Welbury Bay begins production.

Walter Bay) in 1901. About twenty thousand bags sold for 16 cents a bag.

A building boom early in this century, especially in Vancouver, boosted the logging industry. By 1908, logging made up 40 percent of BC's economy, a growth of 31 percent in six years.[1]

Salt Spring's largest operation was the Bulman sawmill (originally the Bulman and Allison sawmill) at Cusheon Cove, established between 1906 and 1908. Its bunkhouse eventually accommodated about 150 men, many of them Norwegians and Swedes. Because Salt Spring timber was considered inferior, most of the mill's timber came from off-island, although small-scale independent handloggers working around Cusheon Cove also supplied the mill. After milling, the lumber went to market in large ships that came to the company's wharf.

The Bulman mill at Cusheon Cove had more than its share of problems, including lack of road access to Beddis Road. When a Japanese employee lost three fingers in a planing machine in 1911, the mill had to phone Captain Good to bring his launch from his Beaver Point store to take the accident victim to Dr. Beech in Ganges. Also in 1911, the company closed temporarily after its manager, a Mr. Profit, drowned when the *Iroquois* sank. Later the same year the mill burned but was quickly rebuilt, since the demand for

The Bulman sawmill under construction at Cusheon Cove. Courtesy Gordon Cudmore/SSIA

lumber was increasing rapidly. The final blow was the 1926 collapse of the mill's dilapidated wharf when it was overloaded with lumber waiting to be shipped. Estimates of the load vary from 1 to 3 million board feet. Most of the wood was lost, and the company soon ceased operations.

Two main "logging shows" operated in the island's south end around 1912. The Maxwell family on Burgoyne Bay used a large steam donkey engine to yard logs and horses to drag them down to the sea. (The land had been logged since the 1870s, with oxen pulling logs over skid roads to tidewater.) Meanwhile, the Fraser Logging Company worked the west shore of Fulford Harbour. Salt Spring-born logger Joe Garner described the operation in "Logging on Salt Spring Was Vital to the Island":

> To start with they had to drive piling for a combination log-dump and wharf. This allowed them to put a huge steam donkey far enough out from shore so the logs could be dumped into deep water and boomed. Up in the woods they had a second steampot to yard the logs to their roads.

Mr. and Mrs. Stephen Carter watch a scow being loaded at the Cusheon Cove wharf, c. 1912. Courtesy Bob Akerman/SSIA

A wedding party in front of the Cusheon Cove cookhouse, c. 1912. Courtesy Bob Akerman/SSIA

Mike Lumovitch's steam donkey drags logs out of the forest. SSIA

Bill McAfee's mill on Vesuvius Bay Road was one of the first Singer mills on the island. Left to right, (standing) Florence McAfee (Bill's mother), Jim Gava, Art Longbottom, Tony Gava, Ted Parsons, Andrew "Shorty" McAfee, Ed Hoyles, Bill Evans, Archie Hoyles; (seated) Bill McAfee, Jock Goodrich. Courtesy Ivan Mouat

This operation was a hazard to the pioneers living on Isabella Point as the one and a half inch steel main line lay across their path looking much like a huge snake, but it was actually much more dangerous. One snap of this line could cut a person in half or toss him 60 feet in the air. Two large signs were put up to warn people to signal the donkey engineer before stepping over this cable. Logging continued there for several years with no one being injured.

When World War I started in 1914, lumber production in BC fell 40 percent from its 1910 level. It picked up again after the war.[2] In 1924, the F.M. Singer Company and others brought portable tie mills to the island to process mainly small timber. Much local timber could now be milled on-island. The portable mills also processed lumber that was too far from the sea for booming, so only the finished product needed transportation. The Cranberry produced much lumber in this way. At one time, there was even talk of building a railway to carry wood from the area.

Piles, props, railway ties, and telephone poles were the main end-products of Salt Spring timber in the 1920s and 1930s. Many camps—engaging seven or eight men, a donkey engine, and one or two teams of horses—moved around the island seeking suitable timber. Around 1916, Joe Garner and his older brother Tom—at ages seven and nine—cut and peeled about sixty cedar telephone poles in one month for Jim Horel, who was responsible for setting poles and stringing telephone wire from Fulford Harbour and Burgoyne Bay to Ganges:

> He gave us a contract to supply as many poles as we could and place them along the road where he had put marker stakes. These poles had to be 25 to 30 feet long with a top size of 6 inches. The price per pole was $1.50 unloaded at the markers.[3]

As teenagers, Joe and Tom Garner worked for the Singer Company. In 1929, dropping lumber prices bankrupted the company. Many Singer employees were left holding worthless paycheques.

Jim Horel's brother, Howard, ran a small logging show and sawmill in North Vancouver and Surrey, before moving back to Salt Spring in 1924 with his wife Winnie, his family, his equipment, and his skilled Japanese employees.

At one time, Howard had a Japanese partner on Salt Spring, a Mr. Nakamura. Later, with partner Peter Perfect, Howard cut and milled logs on his own and others' timber lots.

Howard and Winnie took a typical small-operator's approach to logging. They would lease timber rights or buy a quarter-section or more, cut as much timber as possible, and move on. They sold the logged land they couldn't afford to keep. Howard's son, Chuck, remembered attending more than half the island's schools as his family moved around.

The owners of these small logging shows made a living, but their income and disjointed lifestyle were miserable. Many, including Howard Horel, were often nearly broke. When lumber demand dropped, for example, Horel had to lay off his valued Japanese employees to stave off bankruptcy.

Winnie (Horel Lautman) Watmough at the wheel of her Model A, c. 1946. SSIA

THE AMAZING WINNIE

Winnie Watmough, Chuck Horel's mother, had a legendary reputation on Salt Spring. She stood less than five feet tall and weighed under a hundred pounds. Nevertheless, even when pregnant with her first child in North Vancouver, Winnie often took one end of a cross-cut saw to help her first husband, logger Howard Horel, cut down cedar trees and cut shingle bolts. Patrick Reilly, who rented a cabin from Winnie in 1970, remembered that "she had arms on her like Popeye." Later, on Salt Spring in the twenties, Winnie drove logging trucks, working first with Howard and then with her second husband, Joe Lautman. When logging was slack, she washed dishes at Victoria's Douglas Hotel and later set up a laundry business for Victoria hotels. In the early thirties, she worked as a warden on Piers Island where Doukhobors were imprisoned.

Most loggers worked at every aspect of logging—falling, yarding, skidding or hauling, and booming the logs—though some would specialize. Launch and tugboat operators found work towing booms from Cusheon Cove to Victoria, Musgrave Landing to Genoa Bay, or Vesuvius Bay to Chemainus. Farmers such as Leon King worked as teamsters, hauling logs to the water, and people with specialized equipment contracted out their equipment and their own labour. Jack Bennett and his "Wee MacGregor" helped homesteaders cut firewood, while Ganges blacksmith Bill McAfee (not the Bill McAfee who ran a sawmill) made or mended much of the island's logging equipment.

Many islanders worked full- or part-time in logging, but companies also brought in workers. In addition to Scandinavians and East Indians, many Japanese worked in the industry, some for Japanese employers. According to Musgrave resident Walmus Newman, a Japanese camp close to Musgrave Landing in the 1930s had sixty men cutting pilings for the Japanese government.

Joe Nightingale and Jim Horel on springboards falling a tree. The bottle hanging from the tree held oil to lubricate the saw. SSIA

Emiek Sparrow and Newcombe Lee boom logs in front of the White Lodge (formerly the White House hotel), the site of today's Fulford Inn, c. 1914. SSIA

*Reid Bittancourt and son Lyndell cut a log into rounds with their "Wee MacGregor,"
c. 1931. Bittancourt Collection/SSIA*

THE SALT SPRING RANGER STATION

The extent of logging on the Gulf Islands in the 1940s prompted the
BC Forest Service to establish a ranger station on Salt Spring for forest fire protection. In addition to an office and launch headquarters
in Ganges, a forestry lookout man was assigned to spot forest fires
from the top of Mt. Bruce. Mike Gyves worked as a lookout man
during the summer, his daughter Val remembered, leaving her
mother to look after the cows. "He'd look down with his binoculars
and if a cow was in a field where it wasn't supposed to be, he'd
phone down and tell her. And she'd tell him to mind his own business."

Most logging shows or mills, many small and poorly financed, bought their supplies on credit at the island's two main stores, Mouat's and Patterson's. Mouat's also brokered for many outfits, buying their logs and reselling them to Vancouver Island mills.

Logging was dangerous work. The forces of nature could also cause problems: summer fires destroyed mills and stormy weather broke up log booms. And human error, like overloading the dilapidated dock in Cusheon Cove in 1926, greatly increased the industry's dangers and losses.

By the mid-1930s, Salt Spring's virgin timber had almost vanished. Small operators logged energetically in the forties and fifties, when logs fetched high prices, but large outfits felt that the island lacked sufficient timber.

Fred Hollings was one of the small operators. When he came to Salt Spring in 1941, after logging on Vancouver Island for twelve years, Hollings bought a quarter-section along Musgrave Road, where he logged from March to November, considering it too dangerous to log in heavy rain and snow.

The Hollings log boom was at the head of Fulford Harbour, near the family's home. Jean Hollings recalled that her husband built a combination bunkhouse-cookhouse at the top of Orchard Avenue, where she cooked many meals for the loggers. At his busiest, Hollings employed ten to twelve men.

Most loggers burned slash to clear logged areas, and Mt. Bruce, Mt. Sullivan, and Mt. Tuam seemed always shrouded in smoke. In

A spar tree being topped. Miles Smeeton wrote in A Change of Jungles: *"Up in the woods . . . they would select some particular tall tree as a spar tree and would then lop off its branches and top it. With a great block at the top and a donkey engine below they would then run a long wire cable away out to the area where the trees had been dropped and limbed by the fallers, shackle a chain round the butt and then winch it in to a stack below the tree, which was called 'the cold deck.' From there it would be loaded on to the logging trucks and taken down to the sea." SSIA*

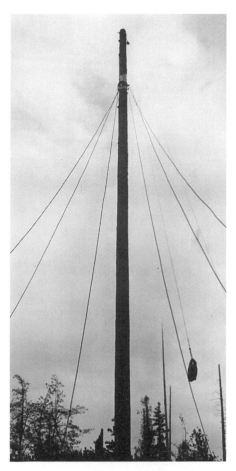

The spar tree ready for work. A donkey engine dragged logs more than 300 m to the tree using a cable-and-pulley system. SSIA

1943, fires actually burned out of control for some time, but no one died and the forest survived. Hollings believed in leaving the slash to enrich the soil naturally and even spread ashes from the family's woodstove as compost in the forest.

Hollings avoided bankruptcy by closely watching all costs—stumpage, road building, falling, yarding, hauling, and booming. He paid each logger $3.50 per day and received $13.50 per thousand board feet for his logs. At one time he made "probably only $10 per day for himself as the operator for $150 worth of logs." His daily earnings increased to $17 during the war, when the demand for wood was exceptionally high, but the labour shortage forced him to log with a skeleton crew. His logs, milled into railway ties at Bill McAfee's mill off Isabella Point Road, were sold primarily to Africa and England.[4]

John Bennett remembered that there were at least fifty-five log booms around the island in the forties and fifties. Every bay in the area now called Maracaibo contained a bag boom (logs held within chained boom sticks). Nine log dumps operated in Fulford Harbour, about five in Ganges Harbour, one on the Royal property on Beddis Road, and another at Burgoyne Bay.

In the early 1950s, forestry giant MacMillan Bloedel began amassing almost 5000 acres (2024 ha) on the island concentrated in three areas—on Mt. Tuam, above Sansum Narrows, and around Peter Arnell Park. By the 1980s, the timber on this land was ready to be logged, but islanders were hostile to logging. MacMillan Bloedel chose to sell the land to a consortium in 1987 for about $3.5 million. Ironically, many of the new buyers clearcut

Perhaps the last horse logger on the island, Cyril Beech used his team of Percherons to haul logs at Ganges Harbour. Courtesy Cyril Beech

the mature timber and then subdivided the land as "view lots."

Two other large companies—Weldwood and Texada Logging—bought land in the sixties. Weldwood bought 743 acres (300.7 ha) on Mt. Bruce from Canadian Collieries in 1964 and managed it as a tree farm. In 1990 Weldwood contracted a small Nanaimo company to cut the mature forest. The island's now strong anti-logging environmental movement loudly opposed the Weldwood decision, but cutting continued despite large demonstrations, passive resistance, and finally, destruction of some logging equipment. The loggers blamed the demonstrators; the environmentalists claimed that the company itself had damaged the equipment to discredit them. The mystery remained unsolved, but the experience embittered both loggers and environmentalists. Weldwood offered the land for sale in the early 1990s, and Texada Logging finally bought it in 1997, agreeing to sell it to the community for recreational-conservation use if funds were raised within a year.

Texada Logging carefully managed its more than 6000 acres (2428 ha) on

Mt. Tuam, Mt. Maxwell, and around Burgoyne Bay. Texada's chief forester in 1995, Mike Steeves, explained that the company planned to selectively cut one-third of its mature timber every twenty years. Cutting would be all but invisible as new growth replaced the trees cut.

Texada's large boom in Burgoyne Bay and its trucks on island roads were the main evidence of the company's logging. Its log-sorting operation on Burgoyne Bay, begun in 1977–78 and drastically reduced in 1992, employed about twenty people at its height and still employed two or three in the late nineties. Most Texada workers have come from off-island, although some islanders have benefited from part-time jobs and subcontracts.

A PRINCE COMES TO SALT SPRING

In 1958, Prince Thurn und Taxis of Bavaria, the head of one of Europe's wealthiest families, responded to an ad in a Munich newspaper offering BC real estate. Agent Frank Rainsford showed him Burgoyne Bay on a hot late-summer day, and Thurn und Taxis, who had already bought Texada Island land and the Texada Logging Company, fell in love with Salt Spring. He started buying land on the island in 1960 and eventually purchased 6000 acres (2428 ha) on the island, making Texada Logging the island's largest landowner. The prince's family still owned the company in the late nineties.

MINING—MUCH VENTURED, NOTHING MUCH GAINED

Sandstone was one of Salt Spring's few natural resources to turn a profit, though it came a distant second to logging. The Saltspring Island Stone Company, founded in 1859 by five partners on the north end of the island, was the earliest mining venture. In 1860, the partners left for the Cariboo gold rush, and we know nothing more of their company. However, we do know that stone from this quarry continued to be shipped to Victoria, Seattle, and San Francisco throughout the 1860s.[5]

For decades, sandstone was quarried elsewhere along the island's north-western shore. Sandstone from Estalon Bittancourt's quarry north of Booth Bay, which opened in 1886, reputedly went into the Esquimalt graving dock, the seawall of Victoria's Inner Harbour, and the San Francisco mint. Bittancourt split his sandstone from the bedrock with wedges, placed it on six-wheel carts, and winched it down a ramp onto scows. In 1913 the quarry still employed twenty-five East Indians, but these men never became part of the community. Like many other labourers brought to the island to work on specific jobs, they remained isolated by language and culture and left when their work was done.

Over the years, many people have tried, fruitlessly, to exploit Salt Spring's scant mineral resources. As early as 1853, Governor James Douglas hoped to base a salt industry on the north-end salt springs near Fernwood, but abandoned the idea when better salt was found near Nanaimo. In 1890, a Victoria group formed the Salt Spring Island Mining Company to develop mines in the south end, but found the deposits inadequate.

Abortive mining ventures marked 1896 too. Garnets were discovered on Joel Broadwell's property, but no mining resulted; a Mr. Bailey proposed drilling for oil on John Booth's property, but no drilling took place; a ton of quartz from the Ruckle farm near Cusheon Cove was crushed and tested in Tacoma, all to no end; and a test copper mine was dug on the same property nearer to Beaver Point, also to no avail. The year produced one short-lived success when coal was discovered in Vesuvius, and two or three tons were sold on Vancouver Island for 25 cents a bag. The optimistic miners then dug a shaft about 35 feet (11 m) into the bank, but again the venture amounted to nothing.

Vancouver Island's successful coal mines convinced some optimists that coal deposits might extend across the channel to Salt Spring. In 1900, some Vancouver prospectors drilled down 700 feet (212 m) looking for coal on Joel Broadwell's property and later on John Booth's Fernwood property near the salt springs. Neither site was promising.

Copper was soon sought on the face of Mt. Maxwell, said a *Colonist* story which read suspiciously like a mining company press release: "A.F. Gwin . . . has with him some fine specimens of ore, carrying gold and silver, as well as copper. These specimens were taken from the vein within five feet of the surface."[6]

THERE'S GOLD IN THEM THAR BIRDS!

In 1900, small amounts of gold were discovered in the gizzards of some ducks and geese that John Mollet had sent to market in Victoria. A mini-gold rush of optimistic prospectors arrived at what is now Ford Lake, but no one found any gold there.

Company after company invested money in this mine, but gave up in 1905. Meanwhile, another potential copper mine was reported at Broadwell's Mountain (today Channel Ridge) near Vesuvius Bay. This mine, and subsequent mining ventures, also came to nothing.

Salt Spring's most successful mining venture may have been the rhodonite mine on Musgrave Road. Rhodonite is a reddish translucent gemstone contained in black rock. Logger Fred Hollings discovered the outcrop of rhodonite on his property around 1950. The Hepburn family had been making jewellery from the rhodonite for some time, but Hollings acquired the mineral rights and started extracting it in 1954. The mine was just Hollings's hobby, but he sold tons of rhodonite-bearing rock to German, US, and Asian buyers. He also let people extract their own rock for a fee. The mine finally closed in the 1980s, and the Hollings family gave up the mineral rights. Today, a subdivision occupies the land that Fred Hollings logged and mined.

Many people hoped to strike it rich from Salt Spring's mineral resources, but most mining endeavours on the island cost more to develop than they earned. Nevertheless, given human nature, someone probably still dreams of making a fortune mining on Salt Spring.

LARGE-SCALE INDUSTRY IN WELBURY BAY

The volcanic ash *pozzuolana* was first used by the Romans to make mortar. The possibility of producing enough of it from the shale deposits in Salt Spring's Welbury Bay to challenge the cement market encouraged two successive companies to invest about $2 million between 1960 and 1963.

Alsam, the first investor, explored ways to make a lightweight aggregate for manufacturing concrete blocks and cement. The company invested about $650,000, but ran out of money before its plant went into production.

A second company, Holdfast Pozzolan, also investigated the use of shale to produce pozzolan. When plant manager Don Morrison learned of Welbury Bay's shale deposits, the company decided to build the plant nearby. Holdfast bought land and invested about $1.3 million in buildings and equipment, including a rotary kiln capable of reaching 1800°F to produce pozzolan from shale, a conveyor system from the plant to the water, and a 300-foot (91 m) wharf to accommodate large barges to take the pozzolan to market.

The pozzolan plant at Welbury Bay.
Courtesy Don Morrison

The Holdfast operation offered great promise of employment on Salt Spring. It hired at least thirty-five people to build the plant and twenty-four to staff it, all but one of whom were islanders. Holdfast ran three shifts twenty-four hours a day.

The plant went into production in June 1962, but the second Welbury Bay operation fared no better than the first. Holdfast halted operations in 1963.

13

Ferries and Roquefort Cheese

1919–1945

A TIME OF OPTIMISM

A period of optimism followed World War I. In 1919, the Gulf Islands Board of Trade formed to improve mail, freight, and passenger service to the islands. Seven years later, it was replaced by the Salt Spring Island Development Association, which had a more limited mandate: "to look after and promote the interests of Salt Spring Island." The 1921 census gave the population of all the southern Gulf Islands as 2437 people, with about 1000 on Salt Spring.

Ganges was increasingly the island's commercial centre. Mouat's store, at its hub, sold almost everything—groceries, clothes, hardware, stationery, hunting and fishing supplies, dry goods, animal feed, insurance, real estate. From 1913, the store had the island's Ford dealership and a gas pump. Mouat's also bought and resold logs, eggs, and farm produce and, in the mid-1920s, operated the island's only slaughterhouse, located on the old Mouat property on Tripp Road. Its butcher, Robert Wood, was Salt Spring's first.

In 1920, Richard Toynbee rented a garage from Mouat's and began work as a mechanic. Trained as a mechanical engineer, Toynbee had run a garage in Vancouver before coming to Salt Spring in 1910 with four of his brothers. Able to fix almost any kind of motor, he found ample work servicing the island's machinery, cars, and boats.

The Salt Spring Island Jam Factory began processing island fruit and berries in 1921, and the next year moved to a new building on Hereford Avenue. The company, a co-operative that never prospered, closed in 1929. Meanwhile, the Salt Spring Island Creamery hummed along, producing almost 3000 pounds (1361 kg) of butter weekly and making more than $50,000 in good years.

Bill Evans was one of the first barbers on the island in a new barbershop on the second floor of Mouat's store around 1923. A few years later, another barbershop opened in the Ganges Inn (Granny's Boarding House). Jim Akerman, who worked for the creamery and boarded at the inn, cut hair there part-time.

In 1925, Betty Turner opened a women's clothing store—the first in Ganges—built on pilings driven into the mud flats across from the Trading Company. (At that time, the parking lot north of the Ganges post office was a tidal inlet.) Later, Betty Turner's daughter, Norah, and her husband, Zenon Kropinski, managed the store.

Two small bakeries operated in the same location on Hereford Avenue, one run by the Baskerville family in 1927 and another, five years later, by Jack Anderson. In 1939, J. Henry McGill opened a much larger bakery, running it himself for the next twenty-one years. Two laundries opened in the early thirties: the Kelly and Gee laundry was short-lived, but the Nakamura laundry on Bittancourt Road lasted until 1937. Billie, the oldest Nakamura son, picked up and delivered the laundry by truck. Don Yuen, then the only

KEY DATES

1921 The first Fulford Community Hall opens.

1930 Gulf Islands Ferry Company begins operations.

1931 Salt Spring's population climbs to about 1200.
Royal Canadian Legion Branch 92 opens on Salt Spring.

1934 Beaver Point Hall is built.

1936 Arsonists destroy Fulford Community Hall and Beaver Point Hall.

1937 Electricity comes to the north end of the island.

1940 The Consolidated School opens; most island students now go to Ganges.

Downtown Ganges, from the Trading Company's wharf, c. 1920. From left: Mouat's store, Ganges Post Office in the back of Granny's Boarding House, Mr. Brayshaw's blacksmith shop, Gavin Mouat's real-estate and Ford car-sales office, and Dick Toynbee's Ganges Garage. SSIA

Dick Toynbee's Ganges Garage, c. 1942. The garage was built in 1916 by Mouat's store, on the site where the Bank of Montreal stood in the late nineties. Toynbee did machine-shop work and welding, as well as car repairs. SSIA

Chinese Canadian on-island, ran a market garden on Drake Road for years. Ivan Mouat remembered him delivering fruit and vegetables in baskets hung from a yoke around his neck. Later, he delivered by truck.

The long-lasting Salt Spring Island Land and Investment Company Limited began in 1928 in the Ganges Inn. It combined the insurance and real-estate division of Mouat Brothers, and the businesses of insurance agent Douglas Harris and real-estate agent Arthur Inglis. Company directors included Harris, Inglis, and Gilbert, William, and Gavin Mouat. Gavin Mouat eventually became the sole owner and renamed it Salt Spring Lands Limited. The company changed hands many times and eventually split into separate insurance and real estate companies.

As more people bought cars, tourism became important to the island's economy. In 1921, George and Florence Borradaile started renting out small cottages on their Ganges Hill property, first as Seabreeze Auto Court and then as Ganges Auto Camp. (The motel built there later took the original name.) Hew William and Margaret Pollok opened a resort in 1925 at the end of Bridgman Road. It was known first as Lyonesse, then as Beaver Point Auto Camp, and later as Solimar. This beautiful seafront resort, with two tennis courts and several boats, hosted regular regattas and the first Gulf Islands Tennis Tournament.

W.A. "Mac" McAfee in the doorway of his blacksmith shop (Gasoline Alley area), c. 1930. Children liked stopping here on their way to school. Photo by Jesse Bond, courtesy SSIA

In 1926, an ambitious scheme threatened to change the island forever. The Puget Sound Club's off-island promoters planned to invest almost $3 million in 10,000 south-end acres. The proposed club would have five hundred bungalows, two mountain lakes stocked with trout, 10,000 pheasants, a golf course, tennis courts, and bowling greens. Only members would enjoy the resort. The club didn't materialize, however.

New ferry service in 1930 between Fulford Harbour and Swartz Bay also boosted tourism. "McIntyre's Auto Road Guide of Salt Spring Island for 1932–33," a promotional pamphlet, listed ten places offering accommodation.[1]

Making better connections

Transportation and communication between the south and north ends of Salt Spring were still difficult, and the small communities functioned in relative isolation. Everyone complained about the inadequate services. Farmers had difficulty getting their products to market, doctors often couldn't reach their patients, and members of different island communities could communicate or visit only with considerable effort. The Musgrave community was by far the worst off, accessible as it was only by boat.

The island's roads improved quickly after Salt Spring acquired first a rock crusher (at the corner of the present Sky Valley Road and the Fulford-Ganges Road—"rock-crusher corner") and then the island's first Caterpillar tractor. Both were used to improve Creamery Hill and other sections of the Fulford-Ganges Road. The Caterpillar made it possible to fill gullies, thus eliminating the need for the bridges that crossed them.

In 1922, twenty-five men worked full-time on the roads, but many other islanders augmented their meagre farm income with road work. During the Depression the government also allowed landowners to pay their land taxes by doing road work. Out-of-work families were given a week's road work every month. As a result, many roads were built at this time.

Islanders also found their steamer service inadequate. In the 1920s, Canadian Pacific Railway (CPR) steamers sailed between Victoria or Sidney and various island ports. One of them also made a weekly stop at Ganges or Cusheon Cove on its trips between Vancouver and Victoria, and at both ports on a weekly sailing from Vancouver to the Gulf Islands.

The arrival of the CPR steamers was still an important event in the late thirties, as Bob Rush fondly remembered sixty years later:

> Boat days were special days. The dock and Mouat's store were a hive of activity. Crates of farm produce, butter, and livestock were on hand for shipment out. Mail, freight of all kinds, and visitors came off the boat. The first person to meet the boat was the postmaster, "Pop" Eaton, who grabbed the mail bags and hustled up to the post office to start sorting. Some people would wait around for their mail, or do their shopping or other things and then come back.[2]

"A LONG, DRAWN-OUT JOURNEY AND A ROTTEN AFFAIR"

Several entrepreneurs linked north-end residents with the CPR boats and Victoria. In 1924, Frank "Shorty" Crofton's jitney service took travellers from Ganges to Fulford Harbour in a Dodge touring car. In 1930, Harry Noon started the island's first taxi service using an open Model A Ford phaeton. During the Depression, passengers could take Wally Lasseter's launch from Fulford to Sidney, where they boarded first the train and later the bus to Victoria.

Jack Smith described the "effort and toil" of getting from Ganges to Victoria in the 1920s. Crofton charged $5 to $8 for a ride to Fulford, depending on road conditions and his mood. From Fulford, passengers travelled to Sidney in a crowded launch, often full of unpleasant gas fumes. The trip took up to two hours in rough weather. The final part of the journey to Victoria was made in the Flying Line, a long open-sided touring car that raced along at about 60 km/h, side curtains flapping in the wind. Passengers would arrive bitterly cold and hungry. "So it was a long, drawn-out journey and a rotten affair."

13

An aerial view of the Harbour House Hotel, early 1960s. By that time, a swimming pool had replaced one of the three tennis courts, but the land around the hotel was still largely undeveloped. Photo by A. Marshall Sharp. Courtesy Nora Sharp

– 224 –

"A FRIENDLY, CHUMMY HOTEL"

The Croftons' Harbour House Hotel expanded greatly in the 1920s. Additions included two tennis courts, a beer parlour managed by son Dermott Crofton, and a glassed-in dance pavilion (the Sun Room). Billy Eng, the hotel's long-time cook who joined the staff in 1926, regularly prepared tasty meals for fifty people, up to eighty for Christmas dinner. Billy didn't encourage guests in his kitchen; when too many drifted in, he would throw pepper on the hot stove, and they'd leave in a hurry. The Croftons produced most of the food themselves—garden vegetables, fruit from the hotel orchard, and chickens and lamb from Des Crofton's farm.

Guests stayed in the Croftons' home-hotel and in tents on the surrounding grounds (replaced by cabins around 1942). They came year after year from Victoria, Vancouver, Seattle, and other places accessible by boat and stayed all summer. The hotel's rates were low compared with other hotels—$14 a week for a tent and $18 for a room—all meals included! Some year-round guests got even better rates.

The hotel's entertainment included scavenger hunts, crab races on the hotel's billiard table, swimming from the hotel's pebble beach, and dances with local musicians. The dances attracted up to a hundred, including both hotel guests and locals, who paid 25 cents to attend. Doreen (Crofton) Morris remembered that people considered the Harbour House a family-oriented "friendly, chummy hotel," with blazing fires in the drawing-room and lounge, bridge every evening, and musical gatherings. It served as the island's social centre, Denise Crofton remembered, attracting people from all over the island.

In 1929, 90 percent of the island's population signed a petition requesting a ferry. J.H.S. Matson, owner of the Victoria *Colonist* and head of Vancouver Island Coach Lines, recognized a good opportunity and formed the Gulf Islands Ferry Company. The company bought and totally renovated the old *Island Princess*, put Captain George Maude in charge, and renamed the vessel the *Cy Peck* (after Lieutenant Colonel Cy Peck, VC, Salt Spring's MLA from 1924, who persuaded the government to subsidize the new ferry). On its inaugural trip, on September 28, 1930, the *Cy Peck* carried thirteen cars. The ferry was a great success, but, characteristically, islanders complained of the cost—25 cents per person, $1 per car! And since the ferry held at most twenty small cars, travellers had to arrive at least an hour before sailing. Still, Salt Spring now had daily service between Fulford Harbour and Swartz Bay on Vancouver Island.

The Cy Peck, *Salt Spring's first ferry, at the Beaver Point wharf in the 1930s. The Cy Peck sailed between Fulford and Swartz Bay, but took excursions from Beaver Point on weekends and on Wednesdays too in the summer. The little boat in the foreground belonged to Bob Patterson. SSIA*

Telephone service expanded rapidly during the 1920s. By 1924, the island had 106 telephones, and many lines carried more than the proposed six phones. The Dominion Government Telegraph and Telephone Company struggled to provide service from about eight in the morning to eleven at night except on Sunday, when the service extended from nine to six. Operators connected callers manually and relayed personal and emergency messages, birth announcements, and election results. Betty Stone and Doreen Morris, who worked in the telephone office in the mid-1920s, remembered their experiences fondly:

> STONE: There would be seven or eight on a party line. And at night, if there was anyone very ill, we had sort of three-way plugs. We'd plug them in with a doctor. Or if there was an emergency, they'd either wake Miss Aitkens, who was the agent, or myself, and we'd go and open the office for any emergencies, which there were once in a while. . . . And if there was a fire, you'd just phone up anybody that was around.

> MORRIS: And the questions you used to get. We'd phone the telephone operator and say, "Is the boat coming down the harbour? What time's the *Mary* coming in?" or "What is the time?" They were always very polite, you know. They'd give us the time. And if there was a fire—where was the fire? And Central would always tell us.[3]

By 1938, Salt Spring had 185 phones, but twenty-four-hour service came only after World War II.

COMMUNITY DEVELOPMENTS

Beaver Point, accessible mainly by water until the thirties, remained independent longer than most Salt Spring communities and retains its individuality today. The community revolved around the nearby wharf and, until they closed in 1951, the post office and store.

For years, the original families still owned most Beaver Point farms. At the end of Beaver Point Road, the Ruckleses—several generations of them—created their own small community. Henry had died in 1913, but his widow, Ella Anna, continued to live and work on the farm until her death in 1930. The Ruckles's oldest son, Alfred, lived with his wife, Helen, in a distinctive three-storey Victorian farmhouse he built with the help of Charles Beddis.

Alfred's half-brother, Daniel Henry Ruckle, and his wife, Polly, built a house nearby. Polly's brother, William Patterson, and his wife, Emily, lived in the store near the Beaver Point landing. In 1930, Henry Gordon Ruckle, Daniel Henry's oldest son, moved into the original Ruckle farmhouse with his new wife, Lotus (Fraser). Their two children, Gwen and Henry, were born soon after.

Farms farther south extended from the shoreline to Beaver Point Road. The Pappenburger, Monk, and Stevens families remained for many years. Leon King, who brought his wife Sophie to his family home, had his own logging camp, then worked as a fisherman, and finally built boats with Sophie. Leon's reputation as a fiddler made him welcome at Beaver Point social events.

In 1921, after arriving with his wife Frances Imogene and her five children, mining engineer John Cory Menhinick bought most of Theodore Trage's old farm. Frances's son Don Fraser took over the farm in the forties and developed the land along Menhinick Drive. Her daughter Lotus later married Henry Gordon Ruckle. Lotus and her daughter, Gwen, still lived on the Ruckle farm in the late nineties.

Among Beaver Point's best-known residents were Captain Macgregor Macintosh—who had lost his right arm during World War I—and his wife, Margaret. In 1931, Macintosh was the founding president of Salt Spring's Royal Canadian Legion Branch 92. He won a seat in the legislature as a Conservative and continued to serve as an MLA until 1941. He also served in World War II.

Beaver Point residents, most on large farms, were spread over a wide area. Other residents along Beaver Point Road included Charlie Monk, Alex and Elizabeth McLennan, Douglas McLennan in a separate house on the family property, Frank and Inez Pyatt, Bill and Winifred Stewart, Frank and Pearl Reynolds, Jim Akerman, Albert Emsley, Colonel Jasper and Dr. Margaret "Meta" Bryant, Arthur and Florence Hepburn, and their families. Even in the late nineties, the area still looked like a farming community.

The new Fulford ferry dramatically changed the Beaver Point community. Because of the ferry, CPR boats no longer stopped at Beaver Point, and the new ferry's freight rates from Fulford to Swartz Bay were considerably higher than the CPR rates. If farmers wanted to ship their produce to Vancouver, they now had to drive it to Ganges, which was the only island port with that service.

ROQUEFORT, ANYONE?

The Bryants—Colonel Jasper and Dr. Margaret ("Meta")—retired to Salt Spring following military service in India. From the 1920s, they kept goats and developed a prize-winning Roquefort-type cheese, which they aged in a cave on their property. The cheese was shipped to Spencer's, then Victoria's largest store.

The Bryants led a simple lifestyle. Their hilltop above Beaver Point Road lacked electricity, but they had their own generator and eventually a telephone. During the war, they saved gas by riding bicycles. Meta Bryant did locums and administered anaesthetic in the hospital through the late forties.

The Fulford area thrived with the changes, however. There were only four families in the area in 1926 when Robert and Anna McBride and their family moved from Vancouver to a big red farmhouse on the Fulford waterfront. (William Patterson later built his long-lived store on the site.) The Cudmores, who arrived in 1927, built their farmhouse on what is today Morningside Road, where Robbie and Bertha Daykin and Dave and Clara Maxwell also farmed. Alexander John and Maud (Lee) Mollet farmed north of the Fulford dock.

In 1928, Fred Cudmore opened Fulford's first commercial venture, an ice cream stall on the wharf—the ice cream came from Victoria every weekend—and soon built a general store on land purchased from McBride. Cudmore ran his store and was Fulford's postmaster from 1931 to 1944. His blacksmith brother, Arthur, built a garage across the road on the foundation of the McBride house, which had burned down years before. William Patterson expanded to Fulford in 1930, locating across from Cudmore.

With the new ferry and stores, Fulford looked like a village by 1930. It had also become a centre for the Fulford-Burgoyne community, which had

Beaver Point wharf, c. 1920. Captain Arthur Cecil Good established the Beaver Point General Store around 1911. He acquired a steamboat, the Newera, *to transport goods to and from Salt Spring. In 1915, William D. Patterson and his wife, Emily, took over the then-vacant store and began a Salt Spring institution. W.D. Patterson took over the post office at Beaver Point in 1918 and ran it until it closed in 1951. SSIA*

been drawn closer to Fulford Harbour with the construction of the Fulford Community Hall. This community included such long-standing island families as the Akermans, Gyveses, Shaws, Mollets, Lees, Horels, and Reids.

The Isabella Point community had its own school but no post office or store. Over the years, several English families settled here, including William and Caroline Hamilton, Arthur and Hilda Lacy, Albert and Mabel (Hamilton) Davis, Jack and Jessie Pierce, Tom and Alice Jackson, Captain Leopold ("Jock") and Betty Drummond, and their families. Nearby were the many families of Hawaiian ancestry (see chapter 7). Hawaiian and English children attended Isabella Point School together, but the two groups functioned as independent communities.

In 1926, Musgrave Landing was finally connected to the rest of the island when Ted Akerman constructed a rough road from Fulford. However, the community still depended largely on the twice-weekly CPR steamship service,

COMMUNITY SPIRIT AND COMMUNITY HALLS

In 1920, the South Salt Spring Island Women's Institute was established. Members recount that when the branch was formed, the men were so suspicious of their wives' involvement that more men than women attended the first meeting. That year the group undertook its first project, the construction of a badly needed community hall in Fulford. The Institute's directors—Emily Maxwell, Margaret Reid, Lucy Horel, Lily Mollet, and Betty Drummond—and chief fund-raiser Caroline Gyves organized card parties and dances, and canvassed to raise funds. The community volunteered labour and donated materials, and John Shaw, whose Roseneath farm stood opposite, donated the building site.

The 35' x 60' (11 x 18 m) Fulford Community Hall opened in the spring of 1921 and quickly housed activities such as fairs, dances, card parties, baby clinics, meetings, and exhibitions. Fire destroyed the hall only four years later, when a cleanup party overloaded the furnace with paper, and the overheated chimney ignited the roof. But the Women's Institute regrouped, and a new, even bigger hall opened at year's end. In 1936, this hall was also destroyed by fire, this time set by an arsonist. And once again a new, improved hall was built within a year through the generosity of community members.

Meanwhile, in 1934, Beaver Point residents built their own hall. Frank Pyatt donated land, and work bees built the 20' x 60' (6 x 18 m) structure with lumber, most of which was recycled from the defunct Cusheon Cove sawmill's bunkhouse. Only two years later, an arsonist burned the hall to the ground. The hall was quickly rebuilt and opened in 1937.

Jim Anderson and one of the Whims boys at Walker Hook, c. 1931. Jim Anderson moved to Isabella Point Road in the thirties. Anderson loved people to picnic on his beach, and his neighbours fondly remembered the tall, barefoot black man sweeping his beach to ready it for picnickers. In Salt Spring Island, *Bea Hamilton described Anderson's "park" as "a wheel of fortune, a 'beauty parlour,' little bunches of wild poppies and ferns placed in soup tins in little hollows in old tree trunks." SSIA*

which brought mail, feed, and livestock and took away wool, meat, and other farm products. Musgrave's post office had opened in 1923 with Walter Smith as postmaster. Mail was delivered to the Burgoyne wharf, where the Smiths picked it up. In 1926, Walter's brother Frank took over until the post office closed in 1957.

Perhaps only a dreamer and a strong individualist would homestead in the Musgrave area. But the Smiths and their neighbours worked hard to hack modest farms from dense bush. Arnold Smith's daughter, Marian Peters, remembered that the Musgrave farmers survived by eating fish and whatever they could grow, preserve, and can themselves. Walmus Newman, a longtime Musgrave resident, added that most families kept cows, chickens, and pigs for food, and horses for work. Only the Brantfords had enough pasture for dairy cows. Frank Smith kept goats and made Roquefort cheese, a whimsical achievement in this isolated setting. By the mid-1940s, of Musgrave's once-vibrant community, only the Smiths remained. Frank's goats ran wild all over the mountain. Miles Smeeton, who arrived in 1946, suggested in *A Change of Jungles* that the land couldn't sustain farming:

> They had come because there was land available for pre-emption, a quarter of a section of one hundred and sixty acres, free [a dollar an acre] to the man who would settle and show some improvement in his land. There was nothing to be made out of it, and all but three had left, leaving here and there hidden in the forest a small clearing full of bracken, one or two fruit trees gone wild, and shacks still with some utensils on the shelves. Most of them had had some trade or other and soon found that they could make better money in the towns.

Until the thirties, only about four families lived in Vesuvius village. Some of Estalon Bittancourt's children stayed in the Bittancourt homes near today's Vesuvius ferry terminal site. In 1918, Arthur and Nancy Inglis bought ten acres, put up cottages and tents, and took in tourists. A year later, Clarence Albert "Jock" and Phyllis Goodrich bought 65 acres (26 ha) between what are now Tantramar Drive and Quarry Drive. Jock, badly disabled in World War I, ran the usual mixed farming operation but emphasized dairy cattle. The Goodriches sold their milk around the bay and their cream to the Ganges Creamery. Their daughter Ruth and her husband, George Heinekey, continued the milk route for many years.

Vesuvius had no store at this time. People had their groceries delivered from Mouat's or the Trading Company, or from Woodward's food catalogue service in Vancouver. As Woodward's food had to be picked up at the Ganges dock, Mouat's was painfully aware of the competition. The Vesuvius School was located at Central, so children had to walk as far as 3 miles (5 km) to attend. The largest business at Vesuvius in the 1920s was Leo and Peggy Chaplin's poultry farm.

Many families who came to Salt Spring after World War I bought land with help from the federal Soldier Settlement Act of 1919. Australian-born Jack (John Edward) and Alice Bennett accompanied Jack's friend Jock Goodrich in 1919 and settled on Dukes Road with their daughter. Arthur and Amy Hedger, originally from England, came with their five children in

Vesuvius (Central) School in the 1930s. Courtesy Dick Toynbee

1922, and used a Soldier Settlement grant to buy the old Whims farm at the end of today's Hedger Road. Some longtime islanders came from other Gulf Islands. Captain Victor and Winnifred Best, originally from England, moved from Galiano Island with their five sons in 1920 and bought part of the old Tolson ranch just south of Ganges. In 1927, Harry and Margaret Simson and their three sons moved from Saturna Island, buying a 157-acre farm at Stone Cutters Bay. Jessie and Elizabeth Byron and their five sons fled the Depression in Saskatchewan in 1934, settling at the corner of today's North End and Epron roads. Americans bought some island land as recreational property—even at this time—including John and Mickey Kellogg of Illinois, who bought the 500-acre Clive Trench property near Musgrave Landing in 1938, and Anita Baldwin of California, who in 1934 bought much of the area known today as Maracaibo.

INCREASED SERVICES

Medical services increased on Salt Spring between the wars. Dr. H.E. Lawson opened a practice in 1923 in direct competition with Dr. Eva

Sutherland, who reputedly took umbrage. Two years later, Dr. Lawson replaced Dr. Sutherland as the health officer, moving into the small home and surgery that he built opposite Mahon Hall. Dr. Sutherland, who had become increasingly deaf, finally sold her practice to Dr. Raymond Rush in 1930.

The island had difficulty keeping a resident dentist. A Dr. Morgan stayed briefly in the late twenties, and a Dr. Verrinder worked from a trailer near Ganges wharf in the thirties. Other dentists visited from time to time to tend patients. A Vancouver dentist used to see patients on weekends in a cabin on the Harbour House hotel grounds, until the cabin burned down in 1934. Dental clinics occasionally came to the island to give dental care to the island's children.

Lady Minto Gulf Islands Hospital weathered one financial crisis after another. Donations from subscribers and fund-raising by the Women's Institute, IODE, Guild of Sunshine, and Girl Guides kept the hospital going, as subscriptions and government grants were insufficient. In 1927, the community started Pound Day to gather hospital groceries and supplies, placing boxes and lists of required items in stores. In 1930, the hospital was wired and equipped with an electric generator. A nurses' residence opened on a half-acre purchased from Dr. Lionel Beech's estate in 1935. Three years later, when about half of Salt Spring's residents subscribed, there was talk of replacing the inadequate hospital. Nurse Joane Millner remembered Lady Minto in the late 1940s:

> The hospital itself was a dear old building, but you had to be a workaholic to be able to cope with it. No elevators. Two bathrooms. You carried basins everywhere—and bedpans. One funny little room had to act as case room and operating theatre, and we had to do our sterilizing in a very ancient sterilizer that every time you thought you were going to be blown to kingdom come when you were operating it.[4]

Sue Mouat remembered that while a nurse might have only a couple of patients to tend to on a given night, she might also be assigned a job like painting the operating table.

The schools on the island were also ready for upgrading. In the early twenties, only the first two years of high school (Grades 9 and 10) were

The original Lady Minto Hospital, c. 1940. A new building replaced this one in 1958. This building served for a few years in the sixties as a dormitory for high school students from the outer Gulf Islands and in 1975 became the home of the Salt Spring Island Community Services Society. SSIA

taught in Jimmy Rogers's Ganges home, a former police building with two jail cells. Before then, Grade 8 was as far as students could go on Salt Spring. This situation continued until 1926, when a high school was established in a separate building that was also used to house poultry during fall fairs. Joe Garner, in *Never Fly Over an Eagle's Nest*, recorded a problem with this arrangement:

> On a warm Friday afternoon in May, a bad problem developed in our schoolroom. Close inspection revealed thousands of chicken fleas cavorting around on the boards. The class was dismissed. After discussion with Mr. [Archie] Robertson [the teacher], it was decided to treat the room with flea powder. We were all back at class as usual the next Monday morning. There was a lot of sneezing for a few days but that was the only annoying effect I can remember, except for a bit of itching from flea bites.

In its first year, the "chicken house school" had twenty-three students in Grades 9 and 10. Students paid $5 a month to attend and were responsible for their own books and transportation.

High education costs in 1938 forced the island to amalgamate five of its seven schools—Burgoyne Bay, Divide, Ganges, Vesuvius (Central), and Vesuvius North (at Fernwood). (Beaver Point School and Isabella Point School both functioned until 1951.) The construction of the new school became a community project. The government provided half of the required $30,000 and the community provided the rest through donations of labour and scarce cash. Volunteers were welcome, but the project also provided needed jobs. The new Consolidated School opened in 1940 and offered classes from Grades 1 to 12. The building housed Salt Spring Island Elementary School in the late nineties.

For two hundred islanders, perhaps the most exciting advance during this period happened in 1937. That year the Nanaimo Duncan Utility Company laid a cable from near Crofton to Parminter Point on the northwest side of Salt Spring and delivered electricity. (Manson Toynbee recalled that his family's electric bill was about $3 a month in the late 1930s.[5]) Power gave islanders all kinds of luxuries. One farmer at St. Mary Lake, for example, immediately bought himself a milking machine.

The fall fair on Rainbow Road with Mahon Hall on the right, c. 1920. Note that there were no school buildings on the site then. BCARS 75220

A BOOM TIME FOR PRIVATE SCHOOLS

Private schools flourished on Salt Spring during the 1920s and 1930s. Nora Halley's school operated until 1936, and Formby House School ran until around 1940. Meanwhile, several new schools had opened.

In the early 1920s, Mabel Ingham briefly ran a private girls' school where Hastings House stood in the late nineties. In 1927, a Mr. Benson opened Ganges Preparatory School for Boys, and Miss Nicholls' Gulf Island School for Girls opened in Leonard Tolson's former Ganges Private School building. The latter school offered sports and academic subjects to thirty students between seven and twelve and employed three or four teachers and a cook. A Miss Brindless ran another girls' school in the IODE room above the Salt Spring Island Trading Company.

Fulford's first and only private school was built in 1928 by Robert McBride, whose children had no school nearby. The school opened near the future ferry terminal site, with ten students and teacher Bertha (Trage) Daykin. However, McBride returned to Vancouver in 1931 after a paralyzing stroke, and the school soon closed.

In 1932, Ethel Moorehouse bought Jack Scovell's former property on Upper Ganges Road and opened a school in the guest cottage where Hugo Robertshaw had lived. After Moorehouse had a heart attack in 1936, her teenaged daughter Helen ran the school until the end of the year, when it closed.

Canadian Methodists and Congregationalists, and most Presbyterians, combined in 1925 to form the United Church of Canada. The following year, the church at Central was moved to a donated lot on Hereford Avenue and renamed Ganges United Church. Four years later the congregation built a manse just east of the church. Ganges now had two churches, but in 1938, St. Paul's (Anglican) Church on Dean Road burned to the ground. Two years later, Gavin Mouat donated land, and the Anglican community built St. George's Church at Park and Lower Ganges roads.

MAKING A LIVING FROM DEMON RUM

In 1916, official prohibition in BC closed the only legal sources of liquor—the pubs—and the island was not to have a liquor store until the fifties. Although bootleg spirits had long been readily available on Salt Spring, they were now essential for thirsty islanders. Suppliers were plentiful. John Pappenburger, Raffles Purdy, John Rogers, and others all sold potent cider. Doreen Morris remembered that Rogers also sold wine for 10 cents a jug or 50 cents a gallon. Old-timers remembered that, to avoid a personal transaction, Rogers left bottles of wine on a stump, and his customers would then take what they wanted and leave their money. Ken Goodrich said John Rogers "was to Salt Spring what Labatt's and Molson's were to the rest of the country.... No one [admittedly] bought anything from him, but everyone had some."

John Bennett tells a story of a day in 1938, when Rogers's dog barked at a man who came to buy wine. The customer complained to the police that the dog was dangerous, and a day or so later, they came to investigate and inevitably discovered the illicit booze. Several confiscated 40-gallon barrels of wine were emptied into Ganges Harbour, and Rogers had to appear in court. There he was reportedly surrounded by customers, including the judge, who sheepishly set a modest fine to preserve the island's supply of moonshine. However, Rogers never fully recovered from his unnerving brush with the law.

Reid Bittancourt's Winamac *was used to chase rumrunners along the BC coast in the thirties, but more often for utilitarian jobs like towing sheep to market. Bittancourt Collection/SSIA*

THINGS GO DOWNHILL QUICKLY

The Depression and war years dramatically slowed the island's development, as people struggled to feed, clothe, and house their families. Some left to find work. Others went out of their way to help each other, and according to John Bennett, nobody starved if they dug clams, shot deer, grew produce, or ate things that might seem unorthodox today:

> People lived off their garden and the bush—venison and the garden. Nobody went hungry. You ate some of the darndest things, but you didn't go hungry. . . . You'd butcher a sheep and you'd sell the meat to the store, which paid for two pairs of boots for the winter, and you were left with the heart, and the liver and the tongue and the head. And many's the night we sat down to supper with half of a sheep's head, which had been skinned out, the nose cut off, the eyes and the ears taken out. It was put in a big

pot and boiled up with rice, potatoes, carrots, and onions, and all the rest of it. . . . People wouldn't even look at it today. But it was good.[6]

Jobs were difficult to find. Longtime Cranberry resident Ted Brown remembered that his family sold milk and calves from their cow, and raised sheep for lambs, wool, and hides, which they sold to Mouat's. But this wasn't enough. They only managed to make ends meet by getting two or three days of relief work on the roads each month. (Those who got more work had to deduct their earnings from relief payments of about $11.50 per month.) People were also given seeds so they could grow their own produce.

Goods were cheap if you were lucky enough to have a job. In his autobiography, John Reid wrote that he earned about $2 a day:

This was sure a Depression: cigarettes 10 cents to 15 cents a package; gas was twenty-five cents a gallon; tea, coffee and butter was about twenty-five cents a pound; sugar was eight cents a pound; and a good pair of blue denims was ninety-five cents and the same for a good shirt. Woodward's in Vancouver sent out a ninety-five cent sheet every month and we sent our order there mostly.

LIFE CAN BE GOOD EVEN IF YOU'RE NOT RICH!

Relatively low expectations marked life in rural communities like Salt Spring during this period. Happiness depended less on money and possessions than on the things one did. Depression or not, farm families continued to enjoy their special island lifestyle, and even those families struggling to survive didn't feel poor. Chuck Horel, who grew up on Salt Spring between the wars, later said his family was probably desperately poor but didn't realize it.

And life wasn't all work. Islanders had their picnics, corn roasts on the beach, community hall dances, card playing, school concerts, and sports such as tennis and soccer. Val Reynolds remembered events at Beaver Point Hall:

You sort of made your own good times. And then out at Beaver Point at that time, they used to have square dances, old-time dances. And they used to have card parties now and then. Sometimes they'd have Halloween parties or Christmas parties. And always there were Christmas concerts in those years . . . in different schools or the halls for the different schools. Sometimes you'd go to half a dozen of them, one after the other.[7]

THE PARK THAT DISAPPEARED

In 1938, BC established Salt Spring's first provincial park—a 480-acre (194 ha) Class C park on Mt. Bruce—but removed its park status in 1955, when the government sold and subsequently logged some island Crown land. Mt. Maxwell Provincial Park, a 491-acre (199 ha) Class A park, was also created in 1938 and remains one of Salt Spring's prime tourist attractions.

The island had many private tennis courts, a few of which became clubs. In the 1920s, the North Salt Spring Tennis Club's season would begin in late May or June and last through September. Members would meet monthly for tennis teas. Two or three times during the summer they would play the Ganges club in a tournament—which the north-end farmers invariably lost.

Other sports remained popular, too, with rivalry between Fulford and Ganges as keen as ever. Many teams included males and females of all ages. Although players rarely had uniforms, there were certainly trophies for the winners. Bob Akerman, a keen all-around sportsman and an outstanding boxer, coached many boys in that sport. Blacksmith Bill McAfee was Akerman's counterpart in the Ganges sporting community, hosting countless sports-club meetings in his shop. Organized sport dwindled during World War II, since many young competitors left to enlist.

Movies were shown occasionally at Mahon and Fulford halls, but the island lacked a real movie theatre until 1939, when Victor Henn and his son Howard

The Rex Theatre. The section with the marquee no longer exists, but the original building housed the Core Inn in the late nineties. Courtesy Lillian (Henn) Muzychka

converted a house on McPhillips Avenue originally built by Ollie Garner into the Rex Theatre. They showed movies every Friday and Saturday night and Saturday afternoon. Old-timers remembered that the projector broke down during the first movie shown, *Bringing Up Baby*, starring Cary Grant. Adults paid 50 cents and children 25 cents to attend the 120-seat theatre. The Rex closed in the early sixties when Howard Henn's health declined.

ANOTHER WAR

World War II wreaked havoc on island life. Most islanders who enlisted joined the Canadian Scottish Regiment based in Victoria. (The Canadian Scottish grew out of the 16th Battalion, Canadian Expeditionary Force, created in 1914.) The regiment's first commanding officer in 1920 was Lieutenant Colonel Cy Peck, VC. In 1931, a new purely Salt Spring platoon (the 13th), commanded by Second Lieutenant Desmond Crofton, included thirty-eight island men. On duty, members of the 13th Platoon wore tartan

A picnic at Walker Hook, 1923. Courtesy Simone Chantelu

GOLF WAS A BARGAIN

In 1928, farmer Norman Wilson allowed the Salt Spring Golf and Country Club to use his sheep pastures as a golf course. Conditions remained primitive, with sheep sometimes taking the place of lawn-mowers. Wilson received only $30 to cut the greens and fairways from June to autumn 1928, which seemed a good deal for the club even if the sheep did help. Lionel Beddis received less than $25 to roll the golf course all season. The annual family membership in the golf club was initially $5. Green fees were 50 cents for Monday to Thursday mornings and $1 at other times. Members could work off their fees at the golf course. Barnsbury, the Wilson family home, was the clubhouse until it burned in 1959.

The May Queen and her attendants representing different island schools, c. 1930: (left to right) Nan Ruckle (Beaver Point), Mary Lacy (Isabella Point), Queen Mary Hague (Ganges), Victoria Thompson (Fulford-Burgoyne Valley), Ann Allan (Ganges), Jessie Nobbs (Cranberry Marsh). For decades, May 24 festivities were a big event in Fulford life. Courtesy Gwen and Lotus Ruckle

kilts, brass-buttoned tunics, spats, and web belts. Each soldier kept his uniform at home, but the platoon stored its arms and other equipment in Mahon Hall.

The home guard took the war seriously. The Red Cross trained people for a host of duties. Captain Victor Best, the island's veterinarian, took responsibility for identifying planes. There was also a Salt Spring detachment of the Pacific Coast Militia Rangers, a volunteer defence corps consisting mainly of men too young or too old to join the regular army.

Then there was the Air-Raid Precautions (ARP), whose members were always on the lookout for enemy fire that might pierce the island's defences. The ARP head was Arthur Elliott, a mechanic at Mouat's Garage, whose equipment consisted of two wheelbarrows with a pump in one and a siren in the other. The siren was made from an old cream separator and two cake pans, one with holes in it. When Elliott turned the separator handle, the siren made a loud noise. He enforced blackouts by pushing the siren wheelbarrow onto Ganges wharf each evening and sounding the siren.

When a Japanese attack finally seemed unlikely, Elliott decided that the island needed a fire department. A water-tank truck was created when Charlie Moore donated his old, black Buick, which hadn't run for some time, and Dick Toynbee used his welding torch to add a tank and a pump. Elliott then painted the car bright red, and it became Salt Spring's first fire truck. Getting a siren was much more difficult, however. Canadian government red tape blocked the importation of the siren ordered from the US. After lengthy correspondence, which required Elliott to fill out a multitude of forms and provide masses of additional, seemingly unrelated information, Elliott indulged his frustration with an ultimatum to the Ottawa mandarins in 1944. His letter ended:

> The volunteer brigade is as efficient as can be expected under the circumstances but the method of alarm at present is totally inadequate. It consists of an old motor horn of the press bulb type, implemented vocally by the fire chief. Unfortunately, due to the enforced drought brought about by the hasty and ill considered action of the present Beaurocracy [sic] in power, the vocal cords of the fire chief are unable longer to implement the bulb horn, although there is some hope that if this application is returned sufficiently often, he may find his voice again. It is feared, however, that should this happen, it will be more likely to coerce rather than suppress conflagrations.
>
> To finally sum up, WE NEED THE SIREN ASKED FOR, and would like to have it if it can be had, so please either pass this request or refuse it and let us know, but for God's sake don't go on writing any more damn fool letters, wasting time, paper and the taxpayer's money in idiotic requests for information which cannot have any practical bearing on the application.

Salt Spring got its siren, and Elliott received wide coverage in newspapers across the country, and even in *Time* magazine.

Nine islanders—J.C. Anderson, Sam J.L. Beddis, Fred Clemo, W.B. Drake, M.F. Headly, R.S.W. Hoole, S.J. Maxwell, W.A. Lee, and F.W.S. Turner—lost

No. 38 Company of the Pacific Coast Militia Rangers ready for emergencies.
Courtesy Dick Toynbee

their lives in World War II, and many others returned wounded. The war affected almost everyone in the community. Ida Crofton's description of her returned husband, Desmond, reflects the common experience:

> The change in him (not in appearance) is beyond description. The quick and ready smile gone, the clouded look of suffering he has seen.... Every man, woman and child should be made to visit military hospitals at least four times a year in every country in the world, and there couldn't possibly be any more wars. All these young athletic bodies broken or paralysed, the months and years of their young lives spent in these places, and this stricken look in their faces for some will never fade.[8]

All the years and all the changes notwithstanding, postwar Salt Spring was still a rural area of small, relatively intact communities connected by primitive but improving roads. Most islanders still struggled to earn a living, and their lives changed slowly over the years, like those in any small rural com-

A somewhat less sophisticated Ganges, 1940s. BCARS 75221

munity. Churchgoers attended local churches, children attended local schools, and shoppers patronized local stores. Ferry service to Vancouver Island was now regular, but islanders felt connections still left a lot to be desired. Electricity had come to the island, but only to parts of it. It didn't reach the Ruckles at Beaver Point, for example, until 1967.

The outlook and interests of the north and south ends remained as different as ever. John Bennett remembered, having grown up in the 1930s, that "Ganges was our headquarters. Got our mail and everything there. The boat came into Ganges. We hardly knew where Fulford was when we were kids." Bob Dodds, who grew up in Fulford, said, "See, in those days, there weren't cars and you didn't really know what was going on on the rest of the island. We knew what was going on at Fulford, but not in the north end. It was just too far." Two solitudes!

14

The Japanese Community

THE FIRST ARRIVALS

Few people of Japanese ancestry live on Salt Spring Island today, but in 1939, on the eve of World War II, seventy-seven Japanese Canadians lived on the island.[1] It's just about impossible to learn about these people, however. One reason for this is that during World War II the Canadian government forcibly moved these people to internment camps.

Their wartime experience was extremely painful to Japanese Canadians. Few ever returned to the BC coast. The Canadian government initially forbade them to return, but they had nothing to return to anyway. In 1943, government agents acting under the War Measures Act had seized and sold their houses and all their belongings. The lack of support from many former friends and neighbours, some of whom profited from their losses, added to the sorrow of Japanese Canadians. Only one Salt Spring family—the Murakamis—returned to the island and stayed, and the information in this short chapter came mainly from Kimiko Murakami and her daughter Mary Kitagawa.

The first Japanese known to have come to Canada settled in Victoria in 1877. Others, mostly single men, began arriving in BC in the 1890s. Like Chinese immigrants, they experienced much prejudice in Canada. When the Japanese tried to vote, they were not allowed to, and in 1895, British Columbia passed an amendment to the Provincial Elections Act that denied the vote to all Asians. (This right was not returned until 1949.) In 1907, the

KEY DATES

1877 The first Japanese to come to Canada settle in Victoria.

1895 Rev. Wilson records ten people of Japanese ancestry living on Salt Spring.

The Japanese are legally denied the right to vote in British Columbia elections.

1907 Japan agrees to limit emigration to Canada to 400 males per year.

1909 The Okano family moves to Salt Spring for the first time.

1928 Japanese emigration to Canada is now limited to 150 per year.

1942 All people of Japanese ancestry in BC are interned in the Interior and in other provinces.

1949 Freedom of movement and the franchise are returned to Japanese Canadians.

Canadian government persuaded Japan to limit the number of males emigrating to Canada to 400 per year, decreasing this to 150 in 1928. The Japanese were forbidden to buy Crown land, though they could buy land from private owners. Denied the franchise, they could not teach or work in any profession or the civil service. Almost the only jobs available to them were labouring jobs, as servants, or in primary industries such as fishing, logging, farming, and mining, for which the Japanese received much less pay than non-Japanese doing the same work.

The 1891 census does not list anybody of Japanese ancestry on Salt Spring. However, four years later, in his promotional booklet *Salt Spring Island*, Rev. E.F. Wilson wrote that there were ten. From time to time, Wilson also referred to Japanese residents in his news sheet, *Salt Spring Island Parish and Home*. In August 1896, he wrote:

> Several of the white residents and a large number of the Japs are off to the salmon fishing on the Fraser.

And, in October 1898:

> Our Japanese friend, Mr. Kinso, is busy these days converting our Douglas firs into props for Mexican mines, and piles for wharves

and bridges in China. There will be a succession of ships coming in to load, and quite a large number of hands, both white men and Japs are at work in the camp.

The 1901 census listed fifty-nine Japanese living on Salt Spring, often giving their occupations as fisherman, labourer, cook, or farmhand. Many of the Japanese on Salt Spring, having a reputation as excellent and inexpensive workers, earned a living doing "day work" on white settlers' farms and homesteads. Leonard Tolson made a typical appraisal of the quality and loyalty of Japanese workers:

> I employed Jap labour and learned to admire the Japs for their efficiency and faithfulness to their employers. (One of them, Yama, spent the night on the roof with a bucket of water because there was a forest fire nearby. We were away.)

Although both Japanese and Chinese workers provided important labour in the home, field, forest, and mill, few islanders welcomed them into the community, as a 1914 *Cowichan Leader* item suggested:

> Another influx of Orientals occurred this week. Twelve Chinamen are now located at Ganges and it is understood that another laundry will shortly be started. Bearing the future prosperity of the community in mind, it is doubtful if these are desirable acquisitions.

Omadan and his wife worked on the Ruckle farm around 1910 and lived in a small house on the farm.. Courtesy Gwen and Lotus Ruckle

Most of the Japanese on Salt Spring lived and worked in the north end, but there were some exceptions. Kyrle Symons, who taught at Beaver Point School in 1910, recalled in *That Amazing Institution* that J.H. Monk employed Japanese workers. Symons himself exchanged lessons for labour:

> They used to come to me at night, to learn to read from an infant's Reader; in return they used to cut and stack a fine lot of fire-wood for us every Sunday. They were deeply interested in the baby. I have snapshots of all these people and things, and very precious they are.

A Japanese settlement developed near Musgrave Landing (see chapter 12). In a reminiscence, Musgrave resident Walmus Newman located it just south of the Crown land greenbelt near the government float. Itinerant Japanese also cleared land for many south-end settlers in the 1880s and 1890s.

Salt Spring's best-known Japanese family is the Murakami family. Kimiko Murakami's parents, Kumanosuke and Riyo Okano, came to Canada in 1896, settling first in Steveston, a fishing port on the Fraser River that is now part of Richmond. The Okanos, both husband and wife, fished for their living and eventually owned a fleet of five fishing boats. In 1904, when Kimiko was born, the Okanos regularly visited Salt Spring beaches to cut firewood, and they had moved to Duck Bay (then Dock Bay) north of Vesuvius by around 1909. As a five-year-old, Kimiko often piloted the family's boat across the Strait of Georgia and through Porlier Pass to their home on Salt Spring. (All family members, including the children, contributed significantly to the family's enterprise.)

At this time, families of Japanese ancestry owned all of the five small houses in Duck Bay. One dwelling housed the Okanos, their three daughters, and a roomer named Mr. Negoro for a couple of years. The Okanos then moved to Nanaimo where Riyo Okano ran a candy store, and the family lived on a house barge. In 1910, Kimiko's two-year-old sister drowned after falling off a fishing boat. A year or two later, the family's house barge was destroyed by fire. To take their minds off these unhappy occurrences, the Okanos took a trip to Japan.

Kumanosuke Okano returned to Canada after six months. Riyo, due to give birth, stayed in Japan. After the baby was born, Riyo and the new baby returned to Canada, leaving Kimiko and her sister with their grandmother.

The two girls were distraught that their parents had abandoned them in this way. (In her nineties Kimiko had still not forgiven her mother for leaving her in Japan.) Finally, in March 1919, Kimiko and her sister rejoined their parents in Canada. The family spent time in Crofton before returning to Salt Spring the next year.

In December of that year, the Okanos sold three of their fishing boats to finance the purchase of their first 50 acres (20 ha) on Salt Spring. In time, the Okanos bought a total of 200 acres (80 ha), stretching from the end of Booth Bay east to Sharp Road and past Rainbow Road. Now they farmed more than they fished, giving up fishing completely around 1924. They grew tomatoes in an immense greenhouse, as Japanese farmers did on other Gulf Islands. The Okanos sold their raspberries, strawberries, and vegetables to A.P. Slades, produce distributors in Victoria. At first, the Okanos were the only residents on Sharp Road, but in time they had several neighbours.

Kimiko had a difficult time in school, having to learn English all over again after her stay in Japan. She went to Central School, where Mary Gyves (later Mary Brenton) was her teacher. She also remembered being the first female driver on Salt Spring in 1923, delivering eggs to Mouat's store in her parents' Model T truck and terrorizing everyone on the road.

The original Okano house. Courtesy Mary Kitagawa

The Okanos, like most islanders, ran a mixed farm. Here Kumanosuke Okano and his daughters, Sayoko and Kimiko (age nineteen, just before her marriage to Katsuyori Murakami), feed the chickens, c. 1923. Courtesy Mary Kitagawa

In 1925, Kimiko returned to Japan to celebrate her grandmother's eighty-eighth birthday. There she was introduced to Katsuyori Murakami, and relatives soon arranged their marriage. When the couple moved to Canada, Katsuyori entered as an "indentured immigrant" sponsored by Kimiko's parents, for whom he was to work for five years.

In 1932, the Murakamis bought 17 acres (7 ha) at the end of Sharp Road, adjacent to the Okanos' land. Katsuyori and Kimiko planted three acres in asparagus and another three in strawberries. Their produce was of such high quality that they often supplied the Empress Hotel in Victoria. They also kept five thousand chickens, selling the eggs to Mouat's store in Ganges, which then sold them to Victoria.

The 1930s were difficult for everyone, with so many people out of work and penniless. Kimiko remembered many people coming to beg food from the Okanos, who would give chickens and eggs to hungry neighbours. The Okanos were also generous in other ways. When the Salt Spring Consolidated School in Ganges was planned around 1940, both the Okanos and the Murakamis donated money, while other less affluent Japanese Canadians each donated a week of labour. Manson Toynbee remembered the Salt Spring Japanese as "community-minded people."

Other Japanese-Canadian families, like the Okanos, worked in various occupations and lived mainly in the north end. Several had come to Salt Spring before the Okanos bought land in 1919. A few, including Junichi Izumi and his two sons, lived and worked on Harry Bullock's estate. (Kimiko Murakami remembered Bullock as a kind man who befriended people of Japanese ancestry.) Nakazo and Hatsu Ito, who lived on North End Road near Fernwood, kept a thousand chickens to raise eggs to sell to Mouat's. The Shimojis lived in Vesuvius as early as 1912. The Tasakas fished out of Steveston every summer and, in the winter, returned to their Seaview Avenue property where Mr. Tasaka worked as a carpenter. (In summertime sixty years later, you could still see the Japanese vegetable called *fuki*, bog rhubarb, growing where the Tasakas planted it.) The Tasakas had twenty-five children, of whom eighteen survived. Eventually, they took their three youngest children back to Japan, where Mrs. Tasaka died at ninety-two.

Of those who came after the Murakamis, several bore the same name (Murakami is as common a name in Japanese as Smith is in English), but none were related to Katsuyori. Morihei Murakami, an expert boatbuilder, came around 1921. He married Sukino Okano, Kimiko's half-sister, and ran a tomato greenhouse on his property between Sharp and Canal roads. Tsunetaro Murakami made tofu on his 25 acres (10 ha) around what is now Wildwood Crescent. The Nakamuras, who lived on Bittancourt Road, ran a laundry business from their home before moving to Victoria in 1937. Torazo Iwasaki had a fishing boat and grew crops such as snow peas for the Japanese market in Vancouver. He lived with his wife, Fuku, and five children on 640 acres (259 ha) that he bought in the late 1930s, including 3 miles (5 km) of waterfront along today's Sunset Drive, from near Vesuvius to about Simson Road.

Members of the Mikado family return occasionally to visit old friends on Salt Spring. Masukichi Mikado left Hiroshima at seventeen in 1902 to work in Hawaii's sugar-cane fields, but moved to Chemainus three years later. In 1914, Masukichi returned to Japan to marry Tsutayo Okada. The couple returned to Chemainus the same year and then moved to Salt Spring, where Masukichi worked on Harry Bullock's farm. In 1936, the Mikados purchased their first Salt Spring land on Norton Road, where they built their home, ran a laundry business, and raised seven children. Bob Rush remembered being "raised" by Mary Mikado, who worked for Bob's parents. In 1942, the Canadian government interned the Mikado family in Alberta, where several sons were still living in the late nineties.

INTO THE DEPTHS OF HELL AND OUT AGAIN

Life for Japanese Canadians disintegrated after Japan bombed Pearl Harbor on December 7, 1941. Almost immediately after the bombing, the federal government declared war on Japan and seized some twelve hundred fishing boats owned by people of Japanese ancestry. At that time, people worried that Japanese Canadian fishermen would somehow convert their fishing fleet into a navy and take over BC.

A fearful British Columbia population demanded the evacuation of Japanese residents from the BC coast, and the government responded swiftly. On February 26, 1942, under the sweeping powers of the War Measures Act, the government began to expel "all persons of the Japanese racial origin" from a "protected area" within 100 miles (160 km) of the coast. In the Gulf Islands, as elsewhere, all people of Japanese ancestry were deprived of their land, their homes, and their personal possessions and interned in camps in BC's Interior or other parts of Canada. Some of those interned wrote a description of their evacuation:

> Japanese Canadians from along the coast were herded like cattle to a sorting compound at the Hastings Park livestock buildings in Vancouver where conditions were barbaric and degrading. Many families were separated as men were sent to work camps in the Rocky Mountains. Women and children were left to cope with these inhuman conditions and uncertainties. Men who opposed being separated from their families were sent to prisoner-of-war camps in Ontario. Internment centres were hurriedly created in the interior of BC. Hundreds of poorly built shacks became home to thousands of internees.[2]

The Japanese, allowed to take only what they could carry, left their houses, vehicles, and other possessions behind. Many of their empty houses were ransacked. The government auctioned their remaining possessions for a fraction of their worth. Salt Spring's Japanese Canadian community suffered the same fate—they lost everything.

Many people on Salt Spring felt unease and pain at the treatment their Japanese neighbours received. Manson Toynbee remembered the period:

Something that really touched me was after the entry of the Japanese into the war. First of all, there had been concerns that there could be damage done on the coast of B.C. And there had been the shelling of Vancouver Island. We had blackouts of course. There was the formation of the airplane spotters—the ARP. The Red Cross became active. We had the Pacific Coast Militia Rangers.

Then came the part that really did upset me—the expulsion, or I think it was called the "rehabilitation" or some such word, of the Japanese residents of the island. This bothered me for a number of reasons. For one thing, they had been hard-working, honest people. They supported island projects—the building of the new school, the building of St. George's Church. They were community-minded people....

And the thing that really hurt me most was that there weren't many islanders on hand to see them off when they went. I remember my father and I standing around the wharf in Ganges, and there wasn't much of a crowd. And I think really it was that a lot of people just were torn by this. Maybe they were afraid they'd break down, some of them if they were present.[3]

The departure of Japanese Canadians from Salt Spring in 1942. The man reaching out is Gavin Mouat. Courtesy Sam Mikado

A REAL—THOUGH UNWARRANTED—FEAR

Anyone who lived in British Columbia before World War II can testify that many people feared and resented Asians, especially the Japanese who had prospered in Canada. Their numbers had grown dramatically, too, with a birth rate double the provincial average. On Mayne Island, for example, one-third of the population was Japanese. Their prosperity was especially resented during the Depression when jobs were scarce.

The resentment and fear of Japanese Canadians was heightened by news media and politicians who made irresponsible statements. In 1922, Alan Webster Neil, MP for Comox-Alberni, told the House of Commons:

> Is it better to fight now when Japan controls only one-half of British Columbia or to leave the fighting until ten years hence when she will, by peaceful conquest, have absorbed the whole of British Columbia and have thousands of her trained troops scattered throughout British Columbia and the other provinces beyond the Rocky Mountains?

Even respected journalists like American Walter Lippmann, writing in the New York *Herald Tribune* in 1942, expressed similar feelings:

> The Pacific Coast is in immediate danger of a combined attack from within and without.... Since the outbreak of the Japanese war there has been no important sabotage on the Pacific Coast.... This is not, as some have liked to think, a sign that there is nothing to be feared. It is a sign that the blow is well organized and it is held back until it can be struck with maximum effect.

The Japanese shelling of the lighthouse at Estevan on June 20, 1942—a few months after the evacuation of Japanese Canadians from the BC coast began—seemed to confirm the government's fear of a Japanese invasion of the Pacific coast. Nevertheless, the only other hostile incident during the war was Japan's 1945 launching of incendiary balloons, some of which reached the BC coast. There was never any evidence of Japanese Canadian collusion with Japan during the war, despite the widespread public fear, and no Japanese Canadian was ever charged with treason.

Even after the war, Japanese Canadians were forbidden to return to the coast until the policy was rescinded in 1949. The government gave them an ultimatum: either move east of the Rockies or be deported to Japan. There were a few exceptions, though. The government permitted Victor and Evelyn Okano, Kimiko Murakami's brother and sister-in-law, to return to Salt Spring with their two children in 1948 for medical reasons. The senior Okanos, the Mikados, and Katsuyori Murakami's family had been sent to sugar beet farms in Alberta. In 1949, the Okanos opened a restaurant in Cardston, Alberta, but Murakami wanted to return to Salt Spring to tend the grave and memory of a son who had died at six months. Murakami also hoped to regain his property and, with it, his dream of years earlier. The Murakamis saved their money, and, over Kimiko's objections, returned to Salt Spring in 1954 and bought a property on Rainbow Road. Their arrival coincided with the departure to Victoria of Kimiko's brother and his family.

Other Japanese Canadians interned from Salt Spring in 1942 included Etsujiro Takebe, a bachelor, who returned around 1950 but died not long afterward in Lady Minto Hospital. The Numajiris, Hiranos, and Nakamuras ended up in Toronto. The Inouye and Mikado families stayed in Alberta where they had been interned. Morihei Murakami's family settled in Alberta and Saskatchewan. Tsunetaro Murakami returned to Japan, as did members of the Ohara family, although all but one Ohara son eventually returned to the Vancouver area. Torazo Iwasaki refused to accept his fate: he sued the government for the loss of his Salt Spring property. The court decided that he deserved more money, but Iwasaki disagreed with their valuation of his property and died a bitter man.

The Japanese were not welcomed back to the Gulf Islands, as Mayne Island's Marie Elliott reported:

> Many of the Mayne Island Japanese wished to regain their land or purchase from other owners. (The Soldier Settlement Board had bought Japanese properties and sold them to returning veterans.) But by that time a curious reluctance to allow the Japanese back had taken hold. No one wanted to be first to sell to them.[4]

When the Murakami family returned to Salt Spring, they were dismayed to find that the government had sold all their property and personal possessions. This was bad enough, but they also felt that islanders still discriminated against Japanese Canadians. Mary (Murakami) Kitagawa said that her sister Rose, one of the top graduates from Vancouver General Hospital, was told that she was unqualified to nurse at Lady Minto Hospital. Rose left the island, earned master's degrees from McGill and Boston universities, and eventually became vice-president of nursing at the University of BC Health Science Hospitals. Mary herself, with an education degree from the University of Toronto, reported that she was told that Japanese teachers were not wanted in the local schools. She too left the island and taught at Kitsilano Secondary School in Vancouver. The Murakamis' oldest daughter, Alice Tanaka, moved to California with her husband, Ted, and the youngest Murakami, Bruce, lived in Vancouver where he eventually owned two electronics stores. His brother, Richard, returned to Salt Spring in 1971, joining his mother and sister Violet at the family's new Rainbow Road home. Richard felt that islanders' residual prejudice had made it difficult to establish his autobody shop. With time, however, the Murakamis became successful, well-regarded members of the community.

The cemetery behind Central Hall has a Japanese Canadian section, which on the Murakamis' return to Salt Spring was overrun with brambles and strewn with garbage. All the grave markers had been destroyed or removed. Katsuyori Murakami began a labour of love, reconstructing the markers and positioning them beside the graves as he remembered them. The markers are unadorned, simply bearing each person's name—surname first in Japanese fashion. They commemorate a time when a small community of Japanese Canadians made their homes on Salt Spring.

When Kimiko Murakami died in July 1997, her passing was marked by a community celebration. More than 250 islanders filled Ganges United Church to overflowing to participate in the passing of a remarkable woman whose life reflected the Japanese experience on Salt Spring. Kimiko had been part of the fishing and farming community, had transcended the horrors of the internment period, and had once again become central to the community in which she spent most of her life. A wide cross-section of Salt Spring society sang "We'll Sing in the Sunshine," one of Kimiko's favourite songs, and the reception afterward became an old-timers' reunion signalling the end of an unhappy sequence in island history.

In this photo, Salt Spring Island photographer Barbara Woodley has captured the dignity and strength of character that many islanders remember most about Kimiko Murakami. Photo by Barbara Woodley.

15

Time for Each Other

1946–1960

SLOW GROWTH

Ganges was still a quiet little village in 1946, according to Joane Millner, who arrived that year. Centennial Park and the fire department were still to come. The land behind the fire hall did not exist; instead, a causeway joined the Trading Company to Mouat's. There were no banks or liquor store, and the stores had an old-fashioned air. The Trading Company sold everything across the counter, and clerks reached top shelves via tall ladders on wheels.

> Cats abounded in the Trading Company and they slept on the counters. Everybody loved them. There were barrels of this and barrels of that. When nobody was looking, you could put your hand in and help yourself to some coconut or whatever. It was a very easygoing, friendly place where everyone met and everyone knew each other. . . .

Life in Salt Spring Island's south end carried on blissfully ignorant of—or choosing to ignore—Ganges events. The south end remained rural as most people still lived on scattered farms. Few roads were paved and electricity was slow to arrive. Most development took place in the north end.

Island services continued to improve after the war. Residents formed the Fulford Harbour Waterworks District in 1945 and the North Salt Spring Island Waterworks District three years later to provide safe, adequate water. The latter company under chairman Gavin Mouat replaced the Ganges Water and Power Company started by John Charles Lang. It now supplied water to Vesuvius village as well as Ganges.

The volunteer fire department that had got its start under "chief warden" Arthur Elliott during the war became more established in 1946. Donald Goodman took over as "fire chief" of the now officially named Salt Spring Island Volunteer Fire Brigade. (Goodman served as chief until 1959.) A women's fire brigade operated in Vesuvius in 1953, but little information is available on it.

The community acquired a fine resource in 1949 when BC Parks created forty-acre Beaver Point Provincial Park from land originally donated by partners Henry Spikerman and Theodore Trage for Beaver Point School. The park, extending from Beaver Point Hall to what later became Ruckle Park, resulted from the hard lobbying of Donald Fraser, whose family owned the old Trage property.

After electrical service improved in 1950, the Salt Spring Island Board of Trade installed street lights in the main centres—six in Vesuvius, eighteen in Ganges, and six in Fulford—in 1952.

KEY DATES

1946 Salt Spring's population reaches 1755.

1948 The Salt Spring Island Chamber of Commerce begins operation.

1949 Beaver Point Provincial Park is created.

1950 Miles Acheson starts the *Spotlight*, Salt Spring's first news sheet since 1906.

1951 Salt Spring's population has increased to 1918.

1955 The *George S. Pearson* ferry begins service between Vesuvius and Crofton.

1958 A new building houses Lady Minto Gulf Islands Hospital.

1959 The island gains a public library.

1960 Woody Fisher starts the *Salt Spring Island Driftwood*.

Ganges, c. 1949. SSIA

Several new businesses opened in Ganges. In 1945, Alice Hougen opened her restaurant, the White Elephant, in rented space in Victor Henn's McPhillips Avenue home (the old Garner house), drawing on patrons of Henn's cinema next door. Then, from 1947 to 1963, the restaurant occupied the former Turner's Store on the waterfront. Its only Ganges competitor was the Log Cabin. In 1950, the Bank of Montreal opened near its current location and remained Salt Spring's only bank until 1969, when the Canadian Imperial Bank of Commerce opened a branch. By 1953, Ganges acquired further signs of civilization—a flower shop and the regular visits of an optometrist.

The Dominion Bureau of Statistics noted the 1951 population as 1918, but the Red Cross Disaster Service independently counted 3000 (not the first or last time that local population estimates have clashed with census figures). The island's news sheet, the *Spotlight*, estimated in December 1950 that the island had "approximately three hundred motor cars, telephones, and pigs." While services were generally far fewer than today, there was at least one exception—local bus service from Fulford to Ganges. In 1953, Pacific Western Airlines started twice-daily return flights from Ganges to Vancouver.

ONE OF LIFE'S NECESSITIES?

In 1951, five hundred Salt Spring voters petitioned the Liquor Control Board for a liquor store. Opponents immediately launched a counter-petition. Once again, islanders dramatically disagreed, and it was several years before Salt Spring had a liquor outlet.

Some—maybe most—islanders ran their businesses quite informally, as Jack Green, an employee of Salt Spring Lands Limited in 1954 suggests:

> At that time Salt Spring Lands operated out of the basement of the Ganges Inn. It was a mixed operation, handling insurance, real estate, subdivisions, log brokerage, trust funds, mortgages and financing, and, once in a while, auctions. In the same office were the North Salt Spring Waterworks and the Gulf Islands Ferry Company, both substantially Gavin Mouat projects. In the middle of it all Charlie Mellish had a desk where he repaired clocks and watches. If a tiny jewel flipped out of a watch that Charlie was working on, half the staff would crawl around with their noses to the floor until it was found.

Tourism expanded greatly at this time, especially in the north end. In 1947, Bevil and Marjorie Acland opened Acland's Resort on the Booth Bay property once belonging to Ernest and Mary Crofton. This resort became a Salt Spring landmark for years, changing little but its name—to the Booth Bay Resort—in 1961 when Thomas and Frances Portlock bought it. A restaurant—the Bay Window—started there in 1978 and stayed open under different owners even after the land was subdivided and the resort finally disappeared in the 1990s. Another newcomer was the St. Mary Lake Resort, which Capt. G.M.I. Blackburne opened in 1949.

DEVELOPMENT AT VESUVIUS

Most of Salt Spring's minimal development was carried out by Salt Spring Lands Limited. In 1944, Gavin Mouat bought the former Chaplin farm in Vesuvius and had it logged. In the fifties, he subdivided it. At about the same time, Emily Smith bought and subdivided the Inglis family's auto court property, which extended from Vesuvius beach to the old Goodrich farm. The subdivision was called Tantramar after the Tantramar Marsh in New Brunswick. These two Vesuvius subdivisions, selling mainly to people who wanted vacation or retirement property, started Vesuvius's long-standing cottage-country look. George Heinekey subdivided about 50 acres (20 ha) of the Goodrich farm about twenty years later, giving Vesuvius much of its late-nineties look by 1975.

Further tourist development required better connections to and on the island. In January 1951, the *Spotlight* commented on Salt Spring's economic future:

> Now this island has no natural resources, there are no mines, the soil is not very good, and there are few farms; the cost of freight prohibits it from ever being a manufacturing centre. Except for logging which will be over in a year or so, and sheep raising, there is no real industry except tourism. And tourism brings money not only to the island but also to the province and to the country itself. But for tourism, good roads are a necessity: they are also a necessity if people are to settle here.

DEVELOPMENTS IN TRANSPORTATION

Extensive road paving in the fifties transformed the island. For years, the lack of good roads had effectively separated the north and south ends. New roads built in the thirties brought people somewhat closer together, but the paved roads of the fifties made travel much easier and shrank the gap between Salt Spring's "two solitudes."

Until 1955 the island had only one ferry connection, the *Cy Peck* from Swartz Bay to Fulford Harbour, although the Canadian Pacific Railway (CPR) still provided its Princess service from Vancouver to the Gulf Islands. Joane Millner remembered the "sketchy" ferry service in 1946:

> We had the *Princess Mary* [the CPR boat] that came . . . [four] days a week, which took eight hours to go to Vancouver. The full service, dining-room service, with napkins, finger bowls, all the trimmings. For a dollar, you could have a stateroom. Or for five dollars, you could have the bridal suite. . . . Needless to say, we didn't leave the island very often. Our noses were to the grindstone, but it was a marvellous service as long as you had plenty of time.

When the ferries were in for repair, islanders had to rely on motorboats.

Long waits for the small *Cy Peck* were usual, as most people arrived early to ensure a place. Long weekends were particularly problematic. (Accountant Jack Green's "little Morris Minor 1000 was . . . sometimes promoted in the queue to fit a tail-end space.") Fortunately for those who spent many hours waiting at the ferry terminal, George and Mary Gervin took over the Fulford General Store in 1951 and reopened it as Mary Lee's Snack Shop. In 1955, Nancy Patterson bought the coffee shop, renaming it Nan's Coffee Bar. She successfully ran it—and a food concession on the Fulford ferry—for years. The restaurant has changed hands several times since then but was still a popular Fulford meeting place and respite for travellers in the late nineties.

In 1951, J.H.S. Matson sold the Gulf Islands Ferry Company, which operated the *Cy Peck*, to a group of island businessmen, including Gavin Mouat, Captain George Maude, Colonel Desmond Crofton, and Joseph Lautman. The new company had a provincial government contract worth $24,000 a

Fulford Harbour, c. 1960. The waterfront looked somewhat similar in the late nineties, except for the addition of the Fulford Marina and the ferry parking lot. The shelter to the right of the gasoline tanks (right) was the original Fulford fire hall. The ferry in the rear is the Cy Peck. *Photo by A. Marshall Sharp, courtesy Nora Sharp*

year, and the BC government set the ferry rates:

- car and driver—75 cents
- trucks of less than a half-ton load and up to fifteen feet—$1
- passengers, pigs, sheep, goats—25 cents
- cattle and horses—75 cents
- children under six—free

In 1952, the *Cy Peck* carried 56,864 passengers, 17,505 cars, and 3954 trucks. The company's directors explored ways of adding a new route between Vesuvius Bay and Crofton and finally bought the 126-foot *Fox Island*, which they renamed the *George S. Pearson*. The new ferry carried up

THE FERRY DEBATE CONTINUES

As early as 1945, a proposal to move the Fulford ferry terminal to Isabella Point—about half the distance from Swartz Bay, but exposed to storms and approached by steep roads—sparked the ongoing debate over Salt Spring ferry service. In the 1960s, the Salt Spring Island Chamber of Commerce proposed that Salt Spring become the hub of the Gulf Islands, with interisland and mainland connections via Long Harbour and Swartz Bay connections via Isabella Point. The Fulford community unhappily predicted its economic ruin and the idea was never adopted, although it continues to resurface from time to time.

to twenty-four cars and made six to eight trips between Crofton and Vesuvius every day in 1955, its first year.

An exodus from the island took place from 1952 to 1954 as property values declined. Former Islands Trust trustee John Stepaniuk remembered that "people were losing faith in the island. . . . The banks and other lenders were apprehensive because of the threat of the termination of transportation, the ending of intensive logging, and because farming was becoming a marginal operation."[1] The CPR cancelled Gulf Islands service from Vancouver, complicating islanders' lives. Sparky New of Galiano Island helped fill the gap by starting Gulf Islands Navigation Company service between Steveston and the Gulf Islands using the *Lady Rose* and later the *Island Princess*.

Improved ferry service boosted tourism, which in turn intensified the demand for boating facilities. Pete Frattinger built the Scott Point Marina (now an outstation of the Royal Vancouver Yacht Club) in 1957, and Warren Hastings and Ernest Watson opened the Ganges Boat Yard in 1960. The Ganges waterfront began to take on its late-nineties appearance.

Ganges, c. 1960. Log booms still occupied the harbour. In the right foreground are the Shell service station and the Trading Company. To their left, beyond the vacant lot, is the Log Cabin restaurant and behind it the telephone exchange building. The area around Mouat's was much smaller than it is today. The first landfill—where the Ganges fire hall now sits— had just been created on the right. Photo by A. Marshall Sharp, courtesy Nora Sharp

A COMMUNITY WITH A HEART

Salt Spring has a long tradition of caring for its residents. Traditionally, whenever one person or the whole community was in need, people pitched in to help. Many services grew from this ongoing community-building spirit.

Health care services on the island improved greatly after World War II. In 1945, Dr. Arnold Francis opened a nursing home in Reid Bittancourt's former store and ran it for twenty years. In the fifties, two dentists from Vancouver—Dr. William Touhey and Dr. J. Vance—each agreed to spend one to two weeks per month on the island. The Parents and Teachers Association arranged to have these dentists treat schoolchildren.

A PERSONAL LOW-COST HOUSING PROJECT

Energetic Winnie Watmough, working totally on her own, often helped less fortunate people. Although poor in her early years, she managed to make money from logging and the sale of her land. Around 1936 she decided to provide housing for old age pensioners on her property on Cusheon Lake Road. She began with two or three completely furnished cabins, which she rented for as little as $5 a month, but eventually had about twenty, many that she built herself. Winnie continued this until her death in 1975 at age seventy-nine.

Though embarrassingly outspoken, Winnie was well respected. For her work, she was featured on the CBC, written up by *Maclean's* magazine, and made a Citizen of the Year by the Salt Spring Island Chamber of Commerce.

Meanwhile, a new building to house Lady Minto Gulf Islands Hospital was long overdue. In 1949, Gavin Mouat donated land and Des and Ida Crofton donated a right of way. However, the estimated construction cost of $250,000 would have to come from property taxes, and tax hikes have always riled islanders. A long, acrimonious struggle swirled around Barbara Hastings, the hospital board's chairperson. After three referendums, a new twenty-five-bed hospital finally opened in 1958. The school board used the old hospital for several years as a dormitory for high school students from the outer Gulf Islands. In 1975, the Salt Spring Island Community Services Society took over the building.

Islanders often had to laugh at the informality of the health and funeral services in the fifties, as Jack Green remembered:

> Don Goodman, known as Goodie, was a busy man being the local
> undertaker, an orderly at … [Dr. Francis's nursing home] and
> operator of a service station. Some of the patients are said to have
> been a bit worried when he attended them in hospital. They
> weren't sure whether he was working as undertaker or orderly.
>
> A number of times, when I got on the ferry, I would be hailed
> from the hearse where Goodie and Doc Francis … would be sit-
> ting with their bottles on their laps. "What will it be, Jack.
> Embalming fluid or plasma?"

Islanders' generosity led to many improvements, such as the ambulance
service provided in 1960 by the Lions Club. Five dollars a year gave any family member ambulance service to Lady Minto Hospital and, if necessary, to
Duncan or Victoria hospitals. The BC Ambulance Service took over in 1974.
The Lady Minto Hospital Auxiliary Society, started in 1936, continued the
work of the Guild of Sunshine and other earlier hospital fund-raisers, sup-
plying many needs of both Lady Minto Hospital and Greenwoods extended
care facility.

In 1957, Salt Spring's Native Sons Society got a federal government grant
to build a museum—a library was a second choice—as a BC centennial project. Bob Akerman led volunteers in dismantling the Bryants' old log farmhouse off Beaver Point Road, carefully numbering each piece with chalk.
They laid a concrete pad and began reassembling the museum. As with many
Salt Spring projects, society members argued, this time with those who
wanted to build a new fire hall on the slab instead. Eventually, tired of the
bickering, the volunteers gave up the project. In the end, the school board
built offices on the pad and the museum was never built. The remaining
grant money went toward a library.

Salt Spring had only private libraries until 1958, when Mary Hawkins led
a group of twelve women who wanted to establish a library as a BC centennial project. They were successful, and the Centennial Library, staffed by volunteers, opened the next year in a room in Mouat's store with about thirteen
hundred books—mostly donated. In 1974, the library was renamed the
Mary Hawkins Memorial Library. To preserve the library's limited budget for
books, volunteers were still staffing the library in the late nineties despite
pressure from the BC government to hire professional librarians.

Friendly, informal ways marked Salt Spring's limited services in the fifties.

Telephone service remained personal, for example, even after BC Telephone took over and expanded the exchange. Ellen Bennett, who worked at the exchange on Hereford Avenue in the late 1950s and early 1960s, remembered:

> I always felt that the telephone operators were sort of the lifeline of the small community. We were secretaries to the doctors, the businessmen, the police,...the fire department. And when there was any emergency, wherever it was occurring, someone would just phone the operator and say "There's a fire" or "Get the police" or "I need a doctor in a hurry" and we just sent them. In the old days, the fire department was one fire chief and all the neighbours.... You just phoned in and screamed "Fire!" and half the time the operator knew who it was without identification, because you get very good ears for voices when you're a telephone operator.[2]

Ernest Harrison (right) was the first Black born on Salt Spring in 1867; a year later, Joe Akerman was the first white born on the island. This photograph was taken in 1950 when they were honoured by the provincial government. SSIA

People even called the operators when they wanted the time—which the operators knew because they were plugged into the outside world.

The system didn't always work, though, as Jack Green discovered: "One evening I was calling my wife from Victoria. Central told me that there was no point in putting the call through to my house, she'd just seen my wife going into the movie house across the street. Later I found that Shirley had

Dorothy (Elliott) Fanning and Elsy (Price) Perks work the switchboard, c. 1949.
BCARS 102324

been home the whole time." But another time, when Shirley found their nineteen-month-old son floating face down in their reservoir, Central reacted quickly to help save the boy's life, sending Donald Goodman and an ambulance with an inhalator. When the dial system finally replaced the switchboard in 1964, the community lost something precious—the personal attention of real people.

For John Stepaniuk, the fifties were a relaxed time of great community spirit, when "everybody was interested in everyone else" and worked—and played—co-operatively. Lloyd Reynolds, for example, would take his threshing machine, the only one on the island, from farm to farm. When newlyweds John and Mary Stepaniuk boarded the Fulford ferry, first mate Edward Lacy sent them to the bridge, and while Captain Maude served them sherry, the crew tied oil cans to their car.

Television changed the way islanders entertained themselves. People now had free entertainment at home, and even Mary Lee's Snack Shop in Fulford advertised its television for patrons. Jack Green felt that television reduced people's participation in community affairs. Television did create one new business, however, when Vic Okano opened his TV shop on Churchill Road.

The sleepy, island backwater was changing. John Stepaniuk, who came to the island in 1948, remembered this period nostalgically almost fifty years later:

> I miss seagulls, masses of seagulls in the harbour, the white crow that smashed her clams on the pavement. I miss Sampson and Whims with their teams of horses, milk cans and produce in the back, Mr. Furness with milk cans in his coupe, Bond with his vegetables, Palmer with his seeder and corn binder, Beech ploughing in spring with his team of greys, Miss Springford's garden, Mrs. Hastings taking her afternoon buggy ride, picking mushrooms after the first fall rain, the smell of land-clearing fires and fall wood cutting. Driving from Ganges to Fulford, progress was slowed several times by farmers and loggers blocking the narrow road while discussing the latest important issues. We had time for each other then.

GETTING THE WORD OUT

Since the first settlers arrived, Salt Spring has needed a source of news. At first the daily newspapers—Victoria's *British Colonist* (later the *Daily Colonist*) and *New Westminster Times*—carried Salt Spring news and ads. Soon the *Nanaimo Gazette* did likewise. Each paper relied on an islander to supply news, much as Jonathan Begg did in the early days when he was the island correspondent for the *British Colonist*. "News releases" invariably reflected the personal interests—and biases—of the correspondents.

Rev. E.F. Wilson published Salt Spring's own first news sheet— *Salt Spring Island Parish and Home* (later the *Salt Spring Island Church*

Monthly)—between 1895 and 1906. His short news entries reflected his bias toward the island's north end, where he and most of his social circle lived. Salt Spring news appeared in the *Cowichan Leader* from 1910 and then in the *Sidney and the Islands Review* (later the *Saanich Peninsula and Gulf Islands Review*). Both used island correspondents such as William Hamilton and Maggie (Mrs. A.J.) Smith.

Beginning in 1950, Miles Malcolm Acheson put out the mimeographed *Spotlight* for three years until his health deteriorated. Semi-retired Woody Fisher—he and his wife Barbara had come from Kansas in search of a relaxed lifestyle—started the mimeographed *Salt Spring Island Driftwood* in 1960. Ed Ketcham started the *Gulf Islander* on Galiano around the same time, and in 1966 the two papers merged as the *Gulf Islands Driftwood*. When Woody Fisher left the island, he sold the *Driftwood* to staffer Arlene Ward, who ran it for three years with her husband, Jim. Frank and Barbara Richards then bought it and ran it with family members including son Tony, who took over in 1979.

The *Driftwood* had competition for a few months in 1972 when a group of islanders started another tabloid. However, the *Sentinel*, published and edited by Alf Worthington, failed to attract much interest and quietly disappeared.

16

The Island Discovered

1961–1986

NEWCOMERS TRANSFORM SALT SPRING

S alt Spring Island's connections with the outside world improved dramatically in 1961, when the BC Ferry Corporation took over the Gulf Islands Ferry Company. Three years later, BC Ferries built a third Salt Spring ferry terminal at Long Harbour for ferries to the mainland and Vancouver Island, since the Canadian Pacific Railway (CPR) no longer provided that service.

Better connections and a stronger economy attracted new people to the Gulf Islands. City dwellers seeking vacation or retirement property were attracted by the relatively low prices of real estate, including small lots on or near the water.

Many other newcomers were seeking a change of lifestyle. Some wanted to bring up their children in what they considered a healthier community. Some left lucrative professional jobs, choosing a reduced income, fewer creature comforts, and a simpler life in a beautiful place. Many were willing to try menial, sometimes physically demanding jobs. Newcomers also included artists and craftspeople attracted by a congenial environment of like-minded people. Many were young people seeking to escape their parents' conventional lifestyles. They sought an unfettered life characterized by communal living, "creative" clothing, long hair, free love, religious cults, and the use of "soft" drugs like marijuana and LSD.

KEY DATES

1961 The BC Ferry Corporation buys the Gulf Islands Ferry Company.

1966 Salt Spring becomes part of the Capital Regional District.

1967 Artcraft, a summertime sale of Gulf Islands crafts, begins its first season.

1969 The BC government prohibits the subdivision of land under 10 acres (4 ha) in the Gulf Islands.

1972 The BC government buys the Ruckle farm for a new provincial park.

1973 The first Salt Spring Saturday farmers' market in Centennial Park takes place.

1974 The Islands Trust, with a "preserve and protect" mandate, is created to oversee land-use regulations on the Gulf Islands.

Salt Spring's first official community plan is adopted.

1975 Vesuvius Lodge burns to the ground.

1981 Eight partners buy the Mill Farm on Musgrave Road.

The Water Preservation Society is founded.

1986 The Ganges sewage treatment plant begins operation.

Many young American draft-dodgers, avoiding the Vietnam War, were among those who came to Salt Spring during the sixties. In some cases, whole families moved so that their sons would not be drafted. (Island activists Hank and Maggie Schubart and Ray and Virginia Newman were among them.) Gays and lesbians also found a relatively tolerant and receptive community.

Marc Holmes, a former Capital Regional District director and Islands Trust Salt Spring representative, described some of the changes that took place:

> Somewhere around the early sixties, Salt Spring left the age of innocence. Its quiet rural lifestyle and sleepy villages were forced struggling all the way into the modern twentieth-century pattern of living. Population increased, [there was] much building, crowding in some areas, traffic. Ferry line-ups became common. Fighting broke out between those who wanted to keep the island

the way it was and those determined to develop it for maximum monetary return.[1]

But for the early settlers' descendants—mostly hard-working farmers, loggers, and the few people providing services—life went on much as before, despite the changes. Islanders had rarely made much money, but as land values—and the cost of living—rose, many became land rich but cash poor. Increasingly, the children of long-term islanders either left the island or entered service industries. Chuck Horel, a logger's son, left for a while and then returned as a realtor and notary. Others took jobs on the ferries, in the building trades, and in growing areas such as tourism.

Interestingly, many newcomers shared the original settlers' outlook. They had sought a place where they could be themselves or "find themselves" without interference. And if they didn't fit into the existing island society, they formed their own social circles.

ISLAND ECONOMY GETS A BOOST

Services all over the island exploited the new market created by a growing population. Stores stocked the more sophisticated merchandise wanted by the new islanders. Vesuvius had a large store just south of the ferry terminal with gas pumps, a grease pit and limited automotive service, a major ramp down to floats, and clinker-built boats for rent. Roads like Sunset Drive were put in so that developers could sell lots in their new subdivisions and new owners could reach their properties. Many small cottages—for example, around Vesuvius Bay, on North Beach Road, and near Fulford Harbour—were built in the sixties.

All of a sudden, the demand for builders and tradespeople exceeded the limited supply. Boat-related activities and businesses grew, since many new property owners owned their own boats either for recreational purposes or to travel to and from the island. In 1962, the federal government installed a $185,000 boat basin and dock in Ganges. In time, marinas opened in both Ganges and Fulford to serve boaters.

Arts and crafts also contributed significantly to Salt Spring's economy during this period. Artists and craftspeople arrived from the sixties on, and many others learned their skills on Salt Spring. In 1967, Nita Brown, the island's night-school organizer, started the Gulf Islands Community Arts

United Church turned Legion Hall, c. 1958. By midtwentieth century, the Ganges United Church congregation had outgrown the small building that had been moved from Central to the north side of Hereford Avenue in 1926. Thanks to a property swap with the Canadian Legion, a new church was constructed in 1952 across the street. The Legion eventually sold the original church building, and it became a store. Photo by A. Marshall Sharp, courtesy of Nora Sharp

Council (CAC). The CAC organized Artcraft—a four- to five-month show and sale of handcrafted items—to sell its members' work. Crafts also eventually became the main focus of the Ganges Saturday farmers' market.

Almost every business on the island felt the gentle ripple passing through Salt Spring's economy. It was the beginning of a series of interconnected events that would completely change the island. New businesses provided still more jobs for islanders. In the past, islanders' children had had to work off-island or stay on the family farm. Now there were enough jobs not only for islanders but to attract workers from elsewhere. In 1964, Gulf Islands Secondary School opened to serve the expanding school population.

Ganges, c. 1967. Note the then-new secondary school in the centre of the photo, the old Consolidated School (now Salt Spring Elementary) in the foreground, Mahon Hall to the right, and below it a tennis court where a road and a parking lot were in the late nineties. Photo by A. Marshall Sharp, courtesy Nora Sharp

SURELY NOT A BRIDGE!

From time to time, people discuss connecting Salt Spring by bridge to Vancouver Island. In 1965, the *Salt Spring Island Driftwood* reported a proposal for a 1600-foot (488 m) bridge across Sansum Narrows from Burgoyne Bay. The approach was to be from the bottom of Lee's Hill. The bridge disputes have continued over the years. However, anti-bridgers won a significant battle in 1974 when their goal was included in the island's official community plan: "to remain an island unconnected to other land masses."

ALTERNATIVE COMMUNITIES

Many mid-sixties arrivals could not afford to buy or even rent property and squatted wherever they could. Some fixed up cabins—scattered across the island—that early homesteaders had long abandoned. Others lived in trailers or buses, or built shacks, often living communally in remote areas. A small community developed in the Musgrave area, where some people used cabins deserted during the Depression. Rugged, remote Musgrave has always been ideal for those wishing to live undisturbed by others.

In the seventies, the Bryants' deserted goat farm on Beaver Point Road also attracted squatters, mainly hippies, who settled into cabins they made from old barn lumber. At first, the community had a rough, wild atmosphere, but gradually people paired off and babies were born right there on Bryants' Mountain.

A few Salt Spring landowners offered low-priced rental accommodation, establishing small communities in the process. Brenda and Ernie Lowe, who had come to the island from California, bought Harry Bullock's old estate in 1961 and established Lakeridge Camp for Boys and Girls. Ernie Lowe continued building cabins for his summer camp after the Bullock mansion burned down in 1964, and started renting them in 1967. Eventually, ten cabins beside Bullock Lake rented to diverse people who formed their own community. Several musicians were attracted to this inexpensive, idyllic environment, including Chilliwack band members Bill Henderson, Claire Lawrence, and manager Clifford Jones.

Lakeridge had a jerry-built quality. Many cabins began to deteriorate even before they were finished. (One day an entire wall of the cabin beside the Hendersons fell out.) The exposed pipes delivering the cabins' water supply often froze in winter, and Lowe would be out thawing them with a propane torch and himself with the beer he kept in his pockets. Poor septic containment eventually contaminated the lake. At one point, everyone at Lakeridge developed trench mouth. Bill and May Henderson's rudimentary cabin had two small bedrooms and a living room with a kitchenette equipped with a 120-volt stove that provided electric shocks strong enough to throw May out of the house on one occasion. The Hendersons kept chickens, a Jersey cow tied to a tree, and a terraced garden roughly hewn out of the forest to produce much of their own food.

A community also grew at Cusheon Cove—another centre of low-cost

housing and an alternative lifestyle—on 90 acres (36 ha) owned by a benev-
olent Vancouver landowner. Between about 1972 and 1984, Rodney
Filtness, who in the nineties ran Rodrigo's restaurant in Fulford, took care of

THE MILL FARM DREAM

In 1981, eight people invested in a communal dream to buy Arnold
Smith's old 160-acre (65 ha) property on Musgrave Road, which
included about 65 acres (26 ha) of old-growth fir, the remains of the
original Smith farmhouse and the old mill, and freshwater springs.
Although the land was subdividable, the buyers planned private
homes on land shared in common.

Several partners built cabins, and a few lived on the site full-time.
By the early 1990s, however, with some additional owners, there
was discussion of changing the property's zoning to allow more
homes. Something went wrong, and in 1996, a minority of the owners requested a court order to sell the property. The Mill Farm was
listed for sale.

Its old-growth fir and proximity to adjacent Crown land on Mt.
Bruce gave the farm a special place in islanders' hearts, which made
it possible for the fledgling Salt Spring Island Conservancy to mobi-
lize support to persuade the provincial and regional governments to
buy the property and preserve it as a park. Eventually, the community—and generous off-island donors—contributed $150,000
toward the purchase price of $800,000, with the rest coming from
the Capital Regional District (CRD) and the Pacific Marine Heritage
Legacy Fund (a joint federal-provincial project to acquire Gulf
Islands parkland). The Mill Farm owners turned down a private
buyer's higher offer and, to protect the property from development,
accepted the government offer.

the land and buildings—a farmhouse, four small cabins, and a barn. Residents were able to fish, plant gardens, and live generally frugal lives. The cabins were mostly uninsulated, and residents had to haul fresh water from a nearby spring. The community broke up when the land was sold.

Newcomers were scattered around other areas too. Some rented the Maple Ridge cabins on Tripp Road on St. Mary Lake. Others lived in fisherman Harvey Hamilton's five cabins above Fulford Harbour. These early-1940s cabins have provided low-cost accommodation since their construction.

A pattern emerged. People seeking an alternative lifestyle with little or no income could live on Salt Spring if they were willing to live communally, give up many conventional comforts, recycle their clothes and other goods, and grow their own food. Linda Quiring, who later started Salt Spring Soapworks, remembered that people were squatting all over Salt Spring when she arrived in 1973. Most of them were forever broke and scrambling for money. Quiring remembered coming across a plastic-covered hole in the ground. Beside the hole, a telephone was rigged to a pole. The person living in the hole—for it was indeed someone's home—was a ferry worker "on call," who needed the phone to find out when to report for work.

Many newcomers embraced the widespread back-to-the-land movement of the seventies. Islanders organized a co-op to buy their food in bulk, buying food every two weeks from a Vancouver food co-op. Tom Gossett, who regularly made the trip in 1975, remembered the grains, nuts, and other mostly organic food being of "excellent quality."

Beaver Point Hall became the social hub of this alternative community. People reminisce nostalgically about the Beaver Point boogies—wild evenings with "magic mushrooms" handed out at the door, the sweet aroma of marijuana, and of course great music. Some of the island's many bands started here, including Sodbusters, El Bande Grande, Bogwater, Sea Biscuit, and Club Mongo.

Many of these newcomers passed through, but enough remained on the island to form a community. Eventually, many—some with families now—wanted to own their own land. To realize this dream, they often gave up buying anything but absolute essentials and determinedly sought work. Others opened their own businesses.

Many of the alternative beliefs and practices of the seventies, such as transcendental meditation, found their way to Salt Spring. One movement actually began on Salt Spring—the Sydney Banks Spiritual Foundation.

Scottish-born Sydney Banks, formerly a welder at Harmac Pulp Mill near Nanaimo, arrived in the early seventies and soon had a large following. He taught "higher awareness," advocating a spiritual path in harmony with then-popular books such as Herman Hesse's *Siddhartha*. One of Banks's first "disciples" was Linda Quiring, who wrote *Island of Knowledge* in 1975. In her book, Quiring quoted Banks:

> We are searching for true Self, the source of everything on earth. There are two ways of finding the secrets of the universe. One is by following the religious path to realize God. The other way is to realize true Self by finding out who you really are and what you really are, and what all of your games in life are which keep you in this illusionary state of believing that what you see is real. Now whether you find true Self or God, it doesn't matter. They are both the same. I prefer Self, but that's my trip.

The Sydney Banks Spiritual Foundation grew quickly, with hundreds of members joining chapters on Mayne Island and in Nanaimo, Courtenay, Victoria, and Vancouver. But in the late seventies, Banks advised his followers to get on with their lives and involve themselves in activities and work, thus ending his own movement.

One Salt Spring spiritual movement surviving in the late nineties was the Dharmasara Satsang Society, founded in Vancouver in 1974, with its aim to "foster the search by each person to find peace."[2] The society propounded Ashtanga Yoga taught by spiritual leader Baba Hari Dass, a monk who believed in silence. He answered questions on a small chalkboard. Many society members assumed new names that they felt better reflected their spiritual reality. In 1981, the society purchased 70 acres (28 ha) of Alan Blackburn's former farm and opened the Salt Spring Centre for the Creative and Healing Arts. Here it ran retreats and programs open to people of any religious belief.

Another survivor was the Kagyu Kunkhyab Chuling Vajrayana Buddhist Centre, which from 1975 offered programs and retreats introducing the beliefs and disciplines of Tibetan Buddhism. This centre, on 160 acres (65 ha) on Mt. Tuam—called Kunzang Dechen Osel Ling (Clear Light Park)—attracted Buddhists from around the world to retreats lasting from a few days to a few years.

An island subculture developed in the exciting sixties and seventies, drawing people from the mainland, Vancouver Island, and other Gulf Islands. Many were delving into the spiritual side of life, practising yoga, and focussing on life's fundamental questions. At the same time, they were learning survival skills like gardening and carpentry, and were supporting themselves by building houses, fishing, fixing cars, making crafts, and planting trees. In the process, they transformed the island.

Change was not always appreciated by longtime residents, and acts of vandalism included the burning of a teepee. But most old-timers tolerated the different cultures and changes on their island. And as with the earliest homesteaders, people with very different values and outlooks—whether their lives interconnected or not—shared the same little island in relative peace.

CONTROLS ON DEVELOPMENT

By the mid-sixties, islanders began to worry about controlling Salt Spring land development. Salt Spring had no community plan. The provincial government, which regulated land use, allowed lots as small as a third of an acre (0.13 ha). Surveyor Adrian Wolfe-Milner and realtor Chuck Horel were particularly concerned about a small-lot development on Old Scott Road, where the proposed lot size seemed too small for wells and the slope too steep for proper septic-disposal fields. Meanwhile, Horel and partner Rod Pringle, through their company H & P Holdings, were developing the Hundred Hills area along the Fulford-Ganges Road, Harrison Avenue along Booth Canal, and the old Beddis property along Wildwood Drive. Hart Bradley and Pete Frattinger were developing the Scott Point area.

In the late 1960s, two Gulf Islands subdivisions created 185 lots on tiny Mudge Island west of Gabriola Island and more than 1200 lots—Magic Lake Estates—on North Pender Island, which then had a total population of about seven hundred. Many people, fearing that the Gulf Islands would be carved into little pieces, persuaded the provincial government in 1969 to impose a temporary "ten-acre freeze" until local official community plans and zoning regulations were in place. (Gulf Islands land could not be divided into lots smaller than ten acres.) This measure slowed land development but didn't give islanders control over their own affairs, as the CRD still had planning jurisdiction.

The island's Chamber of Commerce formed the Salt Spring Island Community Planning Advisory Committee to ensure that islanders had input into the planning process. The committee, chaired by Adrian Wolfe-Milner and representing all areas of the island and a wide cross-section of islanders,[3] distributed a survey in early 1970 at its own expense. Almost half of the survey forms were returned, and the results were amazingly similar to surveys conducted twenty-five years later:

- 80 percent of the respondents liked the island the way it was and wanted it to remain that way

- 95 percent favoured planning; 74 percent supported zoning

- 93 percent wanted parts of the island kept as open and undeveloped land

- 87 percent favoured controls in sixteen subject areas—with a high of 97 percent favouring controls on garbage dumping and a low of 79 percent supporting controls on quarrying

- 84 percent wanted controls on the location and use of house trailers

- 82 percent favoured a building code and building inspection

- 79 percent wanted logging permitted but under strict control

- 79 percent wanted more beach accesses

- 68 percent wanted more parks

- 62 percent wanted local government

- 58 percent supported increased services even if this meant higher taxes; only 21 percent favoured reducing services to keep taxes down

Islanders expressed most concern about pollution, sewers, and subdivisions. Most wanted future growth to be concentrated in Ganges, Fulford, and Vesuvius. A minority wanted to improve transportation on and off the island, although hiking trails, local bus service, wider roads, and bicycle paths also had strong support.

Later in 1970, the CRD proposed a zoning plan for Salt Spring that would restrict business and industry to Ganges, Fulford, and Vesuvius, zoning the

Ganges, c. 1959. The area around Mouat's in Ganges was originally much smaller than it is today. The Ganges firehall now stands on the first piece of land recovered from the sea in 1960. Photo by A. Marshall Sharp, courtesy Nora Sharp

Ganges, c. 1965. A second addition of land created Centennial Park in 1964 (shown around the cenotaph). In this photo, the area behind the firehall that was filled about five years later still contains log booms. Photo by A. Marshall Sharp, courtesy Nora Sharp

Ganges, c. 1970. Land was reclaimed in 1969-70 after a partnership of Toynbees and Mouats had purchased Mouat's store but realized parking was insufficient for a growing business. They received government permission to fill in an extensive area behind the fire-hall, later buying the land from the provincial government for its market value minus the cost of the fill. Note the beginning of the Harbour Building next to Mouat's store. An extensive parking area was also built on this new land. Photo by A. Marshall Sharp, courtesy Nora Sharp

rest of the island "rural." Any commercial or industrial uses outside those areas would be deemed "non-conforming" and allowed to continue but forbidden to expand. This led to heated, well-attended meetings. The CRD eventually backed down and, in 1974, adopted the first Salt Spring official community plan, based on the results of the community survey. However, the CRD still had the responsibility for interpreting and implementing the plan. The same year, a local zoning by-law committee drafted a Salt Spring subdivision and development design by-law, which also specified land-use zones. The CRD rejected this and wrote its own subdivision by-law for the island.

Governing Salt Spring

In the late nineties, Salt Spring was unincorporated and had no municipal government. Instead, two provincial government bodies—the Capital Regional District (CRD) and the Islands Trust—regulated most of its affairs.

In 1966, BC introduced regional districts to manage land-use regulation, municipal-type works and services, and regional hospital districts, among other things. Salt Spring became an electoral area within the CRD the next year and elected Doug Cavaye as the island's first regional director. In 1970, the provincial building code was adopted for the island, to take effect the following year. Up to this time, builders had required only an electrical permit.

In 1974, the BC government created the Islands Trust with a mandate "to preserve and protect the Trust area and its unique amenities and environment for the benefit of the residents of the Trust area and of the Province generally." (The Gulf Islands formed virtually the only area in Canada protected by statute.) At first, the Trust had only an advisory role and veto power over the regional district's plans, but in 1978, the Trust gained responsibility for community planning and land-use by-laws. In 1990, the Trust was made an autonomous local government, with land-use planning and regulatory authority.

Here's how the Islands Trust worked in the late nineties. Salt Spring and the other twelve major islands each elected two representatives to the Trust Council, which made broad policy and budget decisions affecting all the islands. Each island also had a local Trust committee consisting of its two elected trustees plus a third trustee from the Trust's four-person executive committee, which was elected by all of the trustees. Local Trust committees were responsible for developing, adopting, and administering official community plans and for zoning and subdivision by-laws.

All government functions outside Islands Trust jurisdiction were handled by the CRD, provincial bodies such as BC Hydro or the Ministry of Social Services, or the RCMP. CRD responsibilities included building inspection, fire protection, local parks and recreation, liquid- and solid-waste disposal, recycling, and animal control. Roads were handled by the Ministry of Transportation and Highways. Subdivision approval was the responsibility of a Ministry of Transportation and Highways applications approval officer.

Strata development, a tool for optimizing land use, was permitted by BC's Bare Lands Strata Title Act in 1976. Stratas combine private ownership of a home and lot with joint ownership of a larger body of shared land. As in condominiums, members pay fees to cover garbage collection, landscaping, utilities, security, road maintenance, and so on. Three large Salt Spring strata developments began in the eighties, all in particularly lovely settings: Maracaibo Estates, Reginald Hill, and Musgrave Landing. Their exclusivity and cost restricted them to relatively affluent buyers. Several multifamily condominium-type developments were also allowed in higher-density Ganges.

Subdivisions, stratas, and condominiums dramatically increased Salt Spring's population. For example, the large north-end Channel Ridge development, approved and begun in 1985 amidst great controversy, covers more than 1400 upland acres (567 ha). It was planned to eventually include a total of 577 residences, including 302 units in a 90-acre (36 ha) village zoned to include 75,000 square feet (6968 m^2) of commercial space—a little more than half the retail space in Ganges. The plan also set aside 272 acres (110 ha) as a watershed preservation area, 15 acres (6 ha) for a school and a park, 30 acres (12 ha) as public parkland, and 200 acres (81 ha) for the use of Channel Ridge owners.

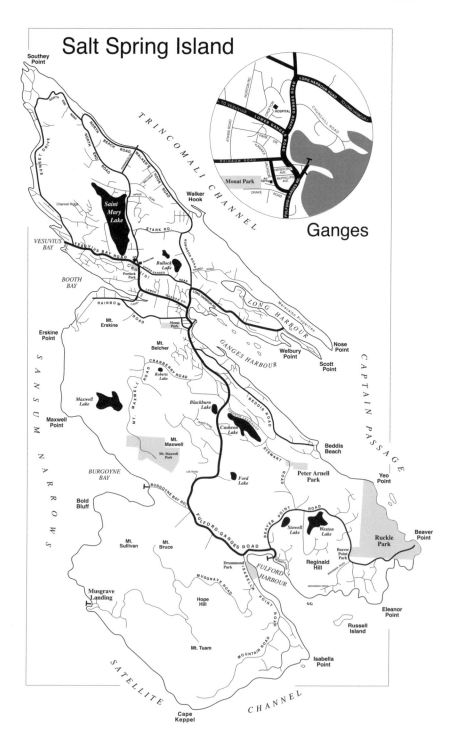

Salt Spring Island

Ganges

THE GREAT SEWER DEBATE

Salt Spring's most controversial and divisive issue since the incorporation battle of the late-nineteenth century was the twenty-year Ganges sewer debate. Sewage disposal became a problem in the early sixties. The biggest offenders were the hospital, whose drainage field didn't work (the ground couldn't absorb sewage, which in wet weather ran off as surface water to create a health hazard on neighbouring property), and the Consolidated School, which discharged sewage directly into Ganges Harbour. Some waterfront shops did likewise, while others stored sewage in tanks and trucked it to a disposal site on a nearby farm. Lack of a sewer system severely limited Ganges development.

Chamber of Commerce president Chuck Horel proposed a sewage system to serve Ganges—from Ganges Hill to Crofton Road—as early as 1966, suggesting that Ganges incorporate as a village to pay the estimated $400,000 cost. This proposal was defeated in a referendum.

What kind of system was best? Who would benefit? And who would pay? These were the main concerns.

A controversial sewer system built for the Maliview subdivision in 1970 discharged treated waste into the ocean. Environmentalists, rejecting this approach for Ganges, formed the Sewer Alternatives Committee and eventually advocated a coal-filtration system with ground disposal of the effluent. However, Ganges lacked sufficient surrounding land for septic-disposal systems, and while some Ganges merchants wanted to continue storing sewage for later removal, many users felt that this was already too cumbersome and expensive (with an annual cost of about $120,000). And the sewage volume—like the village—was increasing dramatically.

Mouat's Trading Company appeared to be in a position to gain the most from a sewer, which would allow village development to continue around the store, partly on Mouat's own land. Phil and Yvette Valcourt—owners of Valcourt Centre shopping mall in Upper Ganges—would likely gain the most from the sewer's rejection, as development would then take place on and around their land. The issue was further clouded in the eighties when Yvette Valcourt's election as CRD director seemed to put her in a conflict-of-interest situation.

Mouat's had originally proposed building a sewage system for its own use, but the provincial government would only approve a system for all of

Ganges. People within the sewer area would have to cover the costs, with some federal and provincial government grants for installation.

Islanders took sides, dissension rapidly escalated, tempers mounted, and open hostility erupted. Even in the late nineties, some people claimed that the smell in Ganges before the installation of the sewage-treatment plant had been unbearable, while others remembered no smell. Sewer proponents said that a discharge-after-treatment system with an outfall far out in the harbour would be a definite improvement over the existing practice of discharging sewage directly into the ocean near shore. (Islanders hotly debated the question of how far offshore the waste should be discharged.) Opponents claimed that the sewage plant would increase development and thus the amount of sewage discharge, treated or not, into the ocean.

Perhaps the most serious question behind the debate was whether further development of Ganges—and thus the whole island—should be allowed. To develop or not to develop has always been a favourite topic for debate on Salt Spring. Some old-timers were already having trouble with the changes to the island's mix of people and the resulting land development and construction. Ironically, many of the newcomers also opposed any further changes to the island they'd chosen as their home.

"There goes the neighbourhood!"

Reprinted with permission of Adrian Raeside and the Gulf Islands Driftwood.

Soon political parties and candidates took sides. Numerous studies, undertaken at great expense, helped decision-makers determine the choice of sewer system. Debate and acrimony rose. In 1980, when the province's Pollution Control Branch ordered construction of the sewer, the Sewer Alternatives Committee claimed in court that the branch was acting beyond its mandate. The court overruled the branch, but the provincial government ultimately authorized the sewer's construction, which would use the farthest suggested outfall, almost 3 miles (5 km) from the head of Ganges Harbour. Opponents continued to argue in the late nineties that imposing this decision had disenfranchised the community.

Tempers flared anew as construction began. In 1981, an anchored barge loaded with plastic sewer pipes was set on fire and the pipes destroyed, reportedly a loss of $250,000. Later the same year, someone set a second fire and shot and killed the barge watchman's dog.

By the time the sewer system was finally completed in 1986, Salt Spring's official population had almost tripled (to 6164) since discussion had begun twenty years earlier. And the total cost of the sewer, including extensive legal costs and many studies, had grown to about $5 million, almost thirteen times the original estimate. Large federal and provincial grants and a twenty-year bond issue financed the project.

The Ganges sewer system was rated in the late nineties among the top three in BC. Nevertheless, the sewer debate—combining such diverse issues as health, development, and the environment—remained contentious.

Islanders wishing to preserve Salt Spring as it was on their arrival are often accused of wanting to "raise the drawbridge" to prevent others from sharing their paradise. Some people saw the Ganges sewer system as opening the floodgate for development. Others felt that development would have happened anyway. In any case, the development that took place after the installation of the sewer system changed the island irrevocably.

PARKS FOR EVERYONE

A number of small but important parks created in the sixties and seventies provided space for island events and recreational activities. In 1961, 50-acre (20 ha) Mouat Provincial Park near Ganges became the island's only drive-in campground. (Mouat Provincial Park was converted to a local park in 1995, when BC Parks transferred some of its smaller holdings to local authorities.)

WATER, WATER EVERYWHERE

The availability of fresh water has always been crucial in the Gulf Islands, with shallow water tables and few freshwater lakes, although Salt Spring is better endowed than other Gulf Islands. In 1980, Tom Gossett, Mike Larmour, Sid Filkow, and others campaigned to protect Maxwell Lake, the island's purest water source. The next year, they founded the Water Preservation Society to preserve potable water at its source and to strengthen islanders' awareness of this precious resource. In the early nineties, the society had gas motors banned from St. Mary Lake, which supplies much of Salt Spring's drinking water. By the late nineties, the society held 20 acres (8 ha) of land around Lake Maxwell to protect that water source and had been assured of another 272 acres (110 ha) in Channel Ridge. The society also helped increase islanders' interest in environmental preservation.

Three years later, planning for Centennial Park in Ganges began. The Ganges boat basin and federal government dock had just been created, and the dredged fill created new land for the park. John Stepaniuk remembered levelling the clamshells that were part of the fill and bringing topsoil from his own property. Many island families donated money for memorial trees. With government grants and much community support and financing, the park opened in 1967 and quickly became a popular meeting place and the home of such island institutions as the Saturday farmers' market, which started in 1973.

Fulford gained a park in 1971 to commemorate BC's entry into Confederation, when Captain Leopold ("Jock") and Betty Drummond donated land for a children's playground. Drummond Park quickly became a place for community celebrations in the south end.

The crown jewel of Salt Spring's parks was acquired in 1972 when the BC government announced that it had purchased the 1200-acre (486 ha) Ruckle farm at Beaver Point for $750,000. The land became Salt Spring's largest provincial park in 1974—and one of the loveliest in the province. The Ruckle family, wanting the land maintained for public use, had accepted a price well below its value and favourable terms: family members were allowed to remain in their homes for the rest of their lives. Ruckle Park, with more than 6 km of shoreline, is an environmental microcosm of the Gulf Islands.

Portlock Park, the island's main recreational area, was developed at Central in 1974. The Lions Club bought the 10-acre (4 ha) park, named after club president Tom Portlock, and spent $91,000 developing it. Over the years, the club added tennis courts, a swimming pool, a soccer field, base-ball diamonds, a children's playground, and a quarter-mile (0.4 km) track.

FIRE! FIRE!

Fire, including arson, destroyed many of Salt Spring's heritage buildings during the sixties, seventies and early eighties: Harry Bullock's house (then owned by Ernie Lowe) in 1964, the old Harbour House Hotel in 1972, and the Vesuvius Lodge in 1975. Forest fires also took their toll. A fire on Mt. Tuam in 1961 destroyed 1185 acres (480 ha) and cost $13,650 to put out. A 1981 fire burned out of control on Mt. Maxwell for two weeks while water bombers, helicopters, and one hundred volunteers fought it.

Salt Spring hired its first professional fire chief in 1969. The main firehall was located in Ganges. A second firehall in Fulford, originally on Morningside Drive near the ferry terminal, was relocated in 1981 near Fulford Hall. A third firehall was built at Central in 1994. By the late nineties, the fire department had three paid members as well as many volunteers. With improved roads and better-equipped and trained firefighters, the island's buildings and forests stood a better chance of surviving into the twenty-first century.

17

Salt Spring in Transition

1986–1998

MORE AFFLUENT IMMIGRANTS

Many newcomers arrived in the eighties and nineties, especially recently retired couples seeking their place in the sun. Attracted to Salt Spring Island's beauty, climate, recreational possibilities, amenities, and services, retirees accounted for about one in five people on the island by 1991. The retirees especially valued Salt Spring's health care services, including good doctors, an ambulance service, and Lady Minto Hospital. Proximity to Vancouver and Vancouver Island for shopping, entertainment, and medical care also appealed.

By 1996, the island's official population had reached 9247, more than four times higher than thirty years earlier. But that figure is misleading. When Canada Post reorganized postal service on the island in 1995, it estimated that it was serving about 12,000 people.

Proximity to larger centres—particularly Vancouver, Victoria, and Nanaimo—encouraged others to move to the island too. By the late nineties, many people who lived on Salt Spring worked off-island, commuting to their workplaces daily or weekly. (Interestingly, for years, people living on Vancouver Island have also commuted to work on Salt Spring.) Professionals and entrepreneurs whose work was portable thanks to daily courier service and electronic communications—faxes, e-mail, the Internet—found that

Population Growth, 1961–1996

Year	Population	Increase	Percent Increase
1961	2100 (est.)		
1966	2238	138	6.6
1971	3163	925	41.3
1976	4410	1247	39.4
1981	5443	1033	23.4
1986	6164	721	13.2
1991	7871	1707	27.7
1996	9247	1376	17.5

SOURCE: Dominion Bureau of Statistics, Statistics Canada, and BC Statistics

they could live on Salt Spring without endangering their livelihoods.

Recent arrivals were often more affluent and more interested in creature comforts than their forerunners of the sixties and seventies. Their needs and wants, supported by savings and pensions, boosted the local economy and intensified the demand for goods and services. Their arrival led to a proliferation of services, rapidly escalating property values, and a building boom. Land prices increased dramatically from pre-1960 prices of a hundred dollars an acre for farm or nonwaterfront "bushland," as former Capital Regional District (CRD) director Marc Holmes recalled:

KEY DATES

1986 Salt Spring's Festival of the Arts has its first season.
The Salt Spring Hysterical Society gives its first performance.
1987 A chapter of the Raging Grannies forms on Salt Spring.
1989 Islanders make plans to build ArtSpring, an arts centre for the island.
1996 The Core Inn youth centre opens.
Salt Spring's official population reaches 9247.
1998 The Islands Trust approves Salt Spring's second official community plan.

One hundred acres of Fulford Harbour seafront, where the Reginald Hill strata-title development is now, were offered to Jean and me for $34,000 when we came here. We turned it down as we thought the land was too steep to be of value. Today [1986], there are about twenty-four lots with an average price of at least $75,000 each. [These lots had quadrupled in price by the late nineties.] The pioneer Lassiter family was just developing Roland Road when we came here and offered seafront lots for $3,000 and view lots for $2,750.[1]

The island changed. It even *looked* different, with new condos, strata developments, and homes. Salt Spring has always offered its citizens more than a nonisland community of comparable size, but the new services and amenities were sophisticated and diverse. Trendy 1990s Ganges with its specialized shops, gourmet food markets, cafés, and restaurants—even a sushi bar—was charming to some, but abhorrent to others who preferred "the good old days."

By the early 1990s, Salt Spring had two museums: the Bittancourt Heritage House Museum on the Farmers' Institute's grounds and Bob Akerman's private museum (shown here) just north of Fulford Hall. Courtesy Bob Akerman

Church on the move: In 1993, a new Anglican Church opened in Ganges. All Saints by the Sea grew out of St. George's, which was moved across the street and used as the kernel of a handsome new building, constructed with about 25,000 hours of volunteer labour, an endeavour worthy of pioneer days. Courtesy Al Robertson

The most significant changes were to the island's psyche. Newcomers brought new ideas and often new values that clashed dramatically with the strong working-class ethic of a farming community. They questioned traditional political values and institutions. Many involved themselves in local affairs and local government, and were articulate about their values and causes.

FINDING A JOB

Employment was relatively varied and plentiful by the nineties. In 1991, people ran home-based businesses in about one of five Salt Spring homes (almost twice the city rate) and 17 percent of islanders were self-employed (the provincial average was only 7 percent). Many of these businesses were in the tourist industry (e.g., bed and breakfasts, arts and crafts studios) and in the building trades.

Economic Activity in 1991:

General Categories	Number Employed	Percent
Retail and service industries	1500	44
Public service sector (e.g., health care, education, government, BC Ferries, BC Hydro)	1000	26
Industrial and trades sector	1100	30
	3600	100

Specific Activities		
Tourism	1200 (seasonal)	
Construction	430	12
Transportation and storage	200	5.6
Manufacturing	110	3
Resources (agriculture, fishing, forestry)	340	10

SOURCE: Islands Trust, "Salt Spring Island: Snapshot of Today—Choices for Tomorrow."

Islanders found new ways and rediscovered old ways to earn a living. One of the rediscoveries was the portable sawmill. Photo by Derrick Lundy

DO ISLANDS NEED THE COAST GUARD?

The Canadian Coast Guard established its Ganges station in 1980 in a trailer shared with the fisheries officer at Centennial Park dock. In the late nineties it moved to a small building on the government wharf behind Mouat's Mall. At that time, in a highly controversial effort to economize, the government was threatening to eliminate the Ganges station.

The tourist industry has grown steadily. In 1993, the Chamber of Commerce estimated that 200,000 tourists visited each summer, briefly doubling the island's population. In 1998, the *Salt Spring Island Directory* (the island's telephone book) listed almost thirty restaurants, more than sixty bed-and-breakfast establishments, two motels, two inns, two hotels (including upscale Hastings House), three kayaking companies, and three marinas. The Salt Spring Island Chamber of Commerce claimed, perhaps optimistically, that tourism in 1995 contributed as much as $12 million to the island's economy and twelve hundred full- and part-time jobs.

Arts and crafts continued to flourish on the island. Signs for craftspeople and artists—potters, painters, stained-glass and basket makers, woodworkers, quilters, paper makers, and others—dotted island roads. By the late nineties, arts and crafts were one of Salt Spring's main tourist attractions. Although the most successful artisans also sold in nearby Victoria, Vancouver, and throughout North America, the Saturday market remained the single, most important venue for most artists' and craftsworkers' products on Salt Spring.

As house and property costs escalated, many people expressed concern that low-income islanders, especially service-sector workers, would be

Farmers' markets flourished in Ganges from the fifties, but the modern Saturday market dated only from 1973. The Saturday market, with its eclectic mix of crafts, produce, and take-out food, became a "must-do" for tourists and an important source of income for many islanders. Photo by Derrick Lundy

unable to afford to live on Salt Spring, and that the island would become an enclave of the wealthy. One thing became clear—Salt Spring would not be Salt Spring without a diversity of lifestyles.

A CARING COMMUNITY

Salt Spring has always responded energetically to residents' needs. When people suffer, the community rallies round, as it did with the founding of the Core Inn youth centre and the Salt Spring Transition House.

In 1993, a rash of car thefts and joy rides by teenagers culminated in an accident that killed two teens and badly injured two others. After the tragedy sparked community discussion of how to help troubled youth, a youth centre was proposed. Social worker Bev Unger and teen-youth worker Trish Nobile campaigned to raise $250,000 to purchase the old Garner house on

MAKE IT, BAKE IT, OR GROW IT

A typically bitter island controversy arose over the Saturday market in Centennial Park. Since its venue was a public park, the Salt Spring Parks and Recreation Commission was responsible for managing it. Soon vendors had trouble finding spots in the popular market, and local vendors complained that off-islanders were squeezing them out. Parked cars were creating a midtown traffic bottleneck, and local merchants felt that the market competed unfairly, since market vendors paid no property taxes. Some people questioned whether a market was an appropriate use for a public park.

After several attempts to move the market to a less congested site, a 1982 referendum found that islanders wanted the market in the park, but they wanted it to sell only home-produced goods. In 1990, another survey also recommended that vendors be required to buy a permit to sell in the market. Two years later, the market introduced a "make it, bake it, or grow it" policy that also gave priority to Gulf Islands vendors. The farmer-flea market had become a farmer-crafts market.

Some longtime vendors, now prevented from selling wares that were not produced on-island, set up a competing market beside the Harbour House Hotel. Off the beaten track, it dwindled and closed after a few seasons. The issue of who could sell in the Centennial Park market still simmered in 1996, but the crowds and vendor surveys suggested that most people had accepted the new market.

McPhillips Avenue. Islanders were generous, and one anonymous donor gave $125,000. In 1995, the Core Inn—commemorating the two youths who had died, Ilan Corin Nelson and Kiowna Corin Lalonde—opened "to provide activities and programs designed to satisfy the social, emotional, and

Taylor, Neacol, and Jarrod Booth. In 1986, Jarrod Booth was diagnosed with brain cancer. Three years later, family friend Brian Harding began encouraging islanders to send Jarrod Christmas cards to cheer him up. The media soon got wind of it and the campaign snowballed. That Christmas, Jarrod received about 200,000 cards from around the world. At the beginning of 1990, the Booth family travelled to England where this feat was entered into the Guinness Book of Records. Sadly, Jarrod died before the end of the year. Photo by Derrick Lundy

physical needs of youth." The Core Inn appeared to be one way to counter what seemed like many infractions committed by teens in the 1990s.

The establishment of Salt Spring Transition House was another community response to a critical need. The house opened in 1995 to provide crisis support and a temporary haven for women and their children in abusive or otherwise dangerous situations. After a single anonymous benefactor donated a house, the community provided furnishings and funds.

Mike Gluss and Bob Simons continued a tradition of providing communal, low-cost housing in 1989, when they bought Yawaca, an 11.5-acre (4.6 ha) former YWCA camp at Beaver Point. Its eleven buildings—a farmhouse, barn-workshop, dining hall, and eight cabins—had plumbing and water but were filthy and needed repairs. Gluss and Simons fixed up the "Y camp" and quickly attracted tenants. In 1998, under different ownership, it was still providing low-income accommodation.

By the late nineties, most island community services, however funded, came under the Salt Spring Island Community Services Society's umbrella. From 1975, the society occupied the Community Centre on the Fulford-Ganges Road, the original Lady Minto Hospital. Near the turn of the century, it ran a wide variety of services, including adult counselling services, services for youth and the developmentally challenged, and a food bank.

When an arsonist caused severe damage to historic Burgoyne United Church in 1997, many people offered help. The church received a new organ, a new roof, and a complete renovation from a caring community. Photo by Derrick Lundy

An army of volunteers and service clubs also contributed much to the community. The Lions Club built Pioneer Village, which offered low-cost housing for seniors, with the help of government grants on land donated by Ida Crofton. Croftonbrook—run by the Lions Club, the Legion, and the Rotary Club—provided the same service. The Rotary Club financed the helicopter pad at Lady Minto Hospital, and service clubs have bought equipment for both the hospital and Greenwoods extended-care facility. These are just a few examples of islanders' generous gifts of time and money to help the elderly, the sick, the disabled, and others in need.

Many islanders have also worked to make the world a better place through church groups and internationally active organizations such as Ten Days for Global Justice and the Voice of Women for Peace. Islanders have sponsored refugees and volunteered their resources and skills to other countries. Many significant projects and movements have originated in the Gulf Islands.

The Salt Spring Nuclear Disarmament Group ran a peace information centre on the island in the early eighties and undertook numerous campaigns to support world peace. Pedal for Peace, which originated on Galiano Island, sent rotating groups of twenty-five people cycling to Ottawa to promote peace. The national Peace Petition Caravan Campaign, started on Salt Spring in 1984, sought to make Canada a nuclear-free zone. Its east and west coast delegations, which included islanders Louise Beijk, Arthur and Louise Rumsey, and Mary Williamson, met in Ottawa to present then prime minister Brian Mulroney with upward of 400,000 signatures they had collected while crossing the country.

The Ometepe Gulf Islands Friendship Association (OGIFA), started in 1988 by Ron Pither of Mayne Island and George Harris of Galiano, was formed to provide fresh water on Ometepe Island in Lake Nicaragua. OGIFA was launched on Salt Spring in 1989. Chaired by Marg Simons, the group raised money for enough equipment and training to improve the Ometepe water-distribution system. In the late nineties, OGIFA continued to raise money for new water projects.

A RECREATIONAL AND CULTURAL SMORGASBORD

Salt Spring's almost infinite recreational and cultural pursuits—team and individual sports, church and community celebrations, a plethora of cultural and interest groups, dances, crafts, and more—continued into the nineties. While the highlight of Fulford life from the 1920s—the annual May Day celebration—was in decline in the sixties and ended in 1970, it was replaced by many new festival-cum-fund-raisers. Pirates' Day started in the sixties, Sea Capers in the seventies, Fulford Day in the eighties. The annual fall fair, resurrected in 1976, continued to offer something for everyone, and islanders constantly dream up new celebrations—like the Erotic Festival in 1995, which was still taking place three years later.

Sportive islanders continued their mostly outdoor activities—kayaking, hiking, sailing, biking, swimming, playing tennis and golf. Many team sports—soccer, baseball, lacrosse, hockey—involved both adults and youth. (Some islanders yearned for an indoor swimming pool and others for an ice rink, but the political and financial support for such facilities were never available.)

Other activities satisfied a cultural need—theatre, music, art—or appealed to an interest—crafts, dance, a skill such as photography. On any given day in 1998, different islanders might have enjoyed yoga, a duplicate bridge

THE RAGING GRANNIES

Visitors to Salt Spring's Saturday market in the late nineties might have encountered a group of singers dressed in fanciful hats and outfits. This group of older women—known as the Raging Grannies—was trying, through satirical songs and skits, to increase awareness of issues that included peace, the environment, social justice, pornography, pollution, clearcut logging, and First Nations' rights. In the words of the Grannies, in *The Raging Grannies Songbook*, they were "enraged about the state of the Earth we are leaving for our precious grandchildren,...the system that has allowed this to happen and the institutions that perpetuate the atrocities against our planet." The Salt Spring chapter, founded in 1987, was Canada's second.

The Raging Grannies spreading the word. From left to right: Barb Hicks, Beth Arris, Lou Rumsey, Virginia Newman, Marg Simons, Sue Bradford, and Mary Williamson. Photo by Derrick Lundy

A contingent of the Island Paddlers participate in the June 1995 Salt Spring Sea Capers festival. Events like a boat-building contest, a "walk on water" competition, concerts, picnics, treasure hunts, and a tug-of-war have amused tourists as well as islanders since the festival began in 1978. Photo by Derrick Lundy

tournament, a lunchtime concert, tai chi, a woodworking class, or a track-and-field meet, to name but a few. Of the island's many clubs, the Salt Spring Trail and Nature Club—founded in 1973 by a mix of old-timers such as Ruby Alton and Lassie Dodds and then newcomers such as Mary Silvander, Doris Anderson, Jean Holmes, and Loes Holland—may be the largest.

For years, Salt Spring has attracted talented people in the arts. Artists Robert Bateman and Carol Evans, architect Hank Schubart, poets Phyllis Webb and Brian Brett, actors Stuart Margolin and Scott Hyland, filmmakers Mort Ransen and Ann Wheeler, broadcaster Arthur Black, and musicians Valdy, Ray and Virginia Newman, Bill Henderson, Shari Ulrich, and Randy Bachman—the list could go on and on—all were drawn to the island's natural beauty and eclectic atmosphere. The island has also spawned many theatre groups, choirs (in the late nineties perhaps one hundred islanders participated in the two largest choirs, Tuned Air and Salt Spring Singers) and musical groups of all kinds—classical, jazz, rock, new age, you name it. And from July 1986, Salt Spring's Festival of the Arts has annually sponsored high-quality performances in literature, theatre, music, and dance, enthusiastically attended by both islanders and visitors.

The Salt Spring Painters Guild holds a special place in the hearts of many islanders, mainly because of its association with Allan W. Edwards of the Federation of Canadian Artists. In 1980, Edwards began giving summer art seminars, then annual classes for the Salt Spring School of Art,

A BIT OF A GIGGLE

In 1986, a group of islanders began discovering the meaning of life—at least Salt Spring life—through humour. The immensely popular Salt Spring Hysterical Society began as a monthly amateur standup comedy night, sponsored by one of Salt Spring's theatre groups—Off-Centre Stage—in the old Valcourt Centre theatre in Upper Ganges. Its success convinced members that they had enough material to put together a show. When they were choosing a name, a member of Salt Spring's Historical Society expressed distaste at possible confusion between "hysterical" and "historical." The choice was obvious. It had to be the Hysterical Society!

Hysterical Society members Arvid Chalmers, Anne Lyon, and Sid Filkow in an early skit. Photo by Derrick Lundy

Original Hysterical Society members were Arvid Chalmers, Reid Collins, Sid Filkow, Anne Lyon, Mike Hayes, James Wilkinson, Mary Williamson, and Shilo Zylbergold. In its second year, the group performed in the Salt Spring Festival of the Arts and became a regular feature of the festival for years. The group was so good that it was also in demand on many of the other Gulf Islands, as well as on Vancouver Island.

which continued through the eighties. The Painters Guild operated an art gallery above the Ganges post office for several years, and Edwards also funded and encouraged the Salt Spring Festival of the Arts.

Many other galleries have showcased the island's artists and craftspeople, and its pubs and community halls have provided venues for the island's musicians, but—though people talked about one for years—the island always lacked a real theatre. From around 1970, an "activity centre" added to Salt Spring Elementary School functioned as the island's chief performance venue. In the late nineties, others included Mahon Hall, Beaver Point Hall, spaces in the United and Anglican churches, and a specially designed area of the new Gulf Islands Secondary School.

The first rumble of something more grandiose came in 1985, when Salt Spring architect Neil Morie presented plans for a 25,000-square-foot (2323 m²) Islands Arts Centre as part of his thesis for his architectural degree. In 1989, teacher Lawrie Neish, actor April Curtis, and architect Bob Hassell began planning ArtSpring, a more modest 12,000-square-foot (1112 m²) arts centre, including a 264-seat theatre and a visual- and creative-arts wing. After much fund-raising and volunteer effort, construction began in 1991. The building reached the lockup stage four years and $1.4 million later, but couldn't be finished without further funds. In 1998, the ArtSpring board launched a "Funding to the Finish" campaign which raised the money needed to complete the building.

PLANNING FOR THE FUTURE

A quickly growing community on highly desirable real estate needs some planning and controls. The creation of the Islands Trust in the seventies reflected government agreement that limits were necessary to preserve the Gulf Islands' particular charm and ambience. Back in 1970, then MLA David Anderson had even suggested establishing a Gulf Islands national park with progressive expropriation of land, lifetime tenure for property owners, and no provision for the land's sale or transfer. Land title would revert to the Crown when the property owners died. Since then, others have suggested similar schemes to conserve the Gulf Islands' special environment and beauty.

When the first official community plan took effect in 1974, islanders expected to re-examine and revise it every five years or so. However, it was 1989 before the community planning association undertook a major review of the community plan goals, and some of its recommendations were reflected in new by-laws. By 1994, many islanders felt that the original plan couldn't deal with some of the new issues and challenges facing the community. The trustees started the review process by advertising in the *Driftwood*, circulating print material describing the process and issues, organizing feedback sessions on various topics, and convening focus groups to advise the Islands Trust on revisions to the official community plan.

In April 1996, a first draft of the new official community plan was circulated for response. Islanders' reaction was swift and ferocious. "Too much and too restrictive," many critics felt. The trustees wondered whether they'd tried to include too much, too soon. A second draft of the plan, much reduced from the detailed first draft, appeared in October just before the local elections. (Neither trustee stood for re-election.) Now environmentalists felt that the revised plan was much too weak. After additional changes, the new trustees approved the second official community plan in 1998. This plan embodied the same premise as its predecessor—that no zoning changes should increase the island's potential overall population density allowed for under existing zoning.

The Islands Trust calculated that Salt Spring's population under existing zoning could potentially reach more than 26,000 residents:

> If all of the subdivisions permitted under current zoning occur, and if every lot is fully developed, there could be as many as 7,650 dwelling units (including multi-family units) and 3,605 seasonal cottages on the island. At the current occupancy rate of 2.36 people per dwelling, this would translate into a population of approximately 18,050. If seasonal cottages were actually constructed on all of these lots, and a similar occupancy rate were assumed, it is conceivable that the population could climb as high as 26,600.[2]

That would be almost three times Salt Spring's official 1996 population. Would the island then have enough people? Too many? If the island did reach "buildout," would there be pressure to create even more building lots to allow even more people to live there? Should more lots be created anyway to keep real estate prices down, thus encouraging low-income residents and preventing the island from becoming an exclusive haven for the rich? And if such uncontrolled growth proceeded, would the island's "rural and unspoiled character, natural beauty and views"—the first goal of the 1974 official community plan—be preserved? Or might ferry costs increase so much that pressure for homes and land would become a nonissue?

Salt Spring's Hysterical Society offered one unequivocal answer in their song "Please Don't Come":

> *Chorus*:
> If you love the islands,
> Please don't come, please don't come, please don't come.
> If you love the islands, please don't come.
> There's no more room for anyone.
> You can come for a visit or pass on through,
> Spend all your money like the tourists do.
> But if you're thinkin' about settling down,
> Do it off, not on the island.
>
> *Chorus*
>
> You've got a yellow kayak and a mountain bike,
> A job in the city that you just don't like.
> You come here searching for the meaning of life.
> You'll find it off, not on the island.
>
> *Chorus*
>
> We change our names and our houses too.
> Long-term couples are very few.
> You got a relationship important to you,
> Keep it off, not on the island.
>
> *Chorus*
>
> We're a bunch of goofers[3] wearing rubber boots.
> We don't much like those men in suits.
> You got lots of money and are quiet too.
> Keep it off, not on the island.
>
> *Chorus*[4]

"537–653": VIVE LA DIFFÉRENCE

The residents of the south end proudly embrace a rural look. They also proudly recite their "653" telephone exchange, assigned to Fulford in 1970. Shilo Zylbergold of the Salt Spring Hysterical Society—a south-ender himself—wrote a song about a damsel from the south end on the loose in the 537-exchange north:

> *Chorus*
> And her hair said 537,
> And her clothes said 537,
> And her lips said 537, but
> Her gumboots said 653.
>
> With a house built on skids,
> Three dogs and four kids,
> A staircase that creaked
> And a skylight that leaked
> And a truck in the ditch
> And head lice that itched.
> Her gumboots said 653.

In 1997, Ganges (the north end) was sufficiently large to warrant a third telephone exchange—538.

THE ISLAND AT THE END OF THE MILLENNIUM

The island's south end did not look dramatically different in the late nineties from the way it looked fifty years earlier, except for paved roads and increased traffic. Farms and small acreages still occupied the Fulford-Burgoyne Valley, and the "wild" spaces of Mt. Bruce, Mt. Tuam, and Hope

Hill were almost as unpopulated as when they were collectively called Musgrave Mountain. Although the rate of population growth in the mid-nineties was higher in the south end, possibly because it contained the most undeveloped land, more than 75 percent of the island's population lived on the north end of the island.[5]

Ganges in the late nineties showed the effects of greater population density and residential and commercial development. The few basic, utilitarian buildings of 1950s "downtown Ganges" had been replaced by numerous more sophisticated shops, many of them built in shopping-centre clusters and connected by walkways. Some village roads were curbed, and some sidewalks existed. Coffee shops and outdoor cafés multiplied, and several condominium developments were built. Salt Spring's business community—particularly shop owners and those associated with tourism—were enthusiastic about these developments, but some old-timers—unimpressed by the town's updated look—regularly complained about the traffic, the difficulty of finding a parking spot, and the faster pace.

Perhaps the great changes to the island are epitomized in the $15-million Gulf Islands Secondary School opened in 1995. Although built with a great deal of community involvement, it bears little resemblance to the modest Consolidated School constructed debt-free in 1938 through the community's donations of labour, money, and supplies. The cost of maintaining and staffing the new high school in the late nineties added to the school district's huge annual deficits, which in 1998 approached a million dollars.

Despite the island's late-nineties hustle and bustle, a few things remained virtually unchanged. There were still no traffic lights on the island in 1998. Almost everyone continued to complain about the island's rate of growth and about BC Ferries' service and cost. And almost every proposed change drew an outcry from some islanders. Salt Spring residents continued to be independent, strong-willed, outspoken, and "factious," as Rev. Wilson described the people he met on the island more than one hundred years earlier.

Contrary and inconsistent as Salt Spring history—and perhaps islanders themselves—may appear, there have always been some constants. The same polarizing issues keep resurfacing—ferries and transportation in general, development and growth, jobs, economic and cultural diversity, incorporation and greater control by islanders of the island's destiny, water and the protection of water sources. The island's contrariness and inconsistency have caused some to move on in disgust, but for many others they are its essence.

And if the number of the island's newcomers and visitors counts for anything, Salt Spring's eclectic nature must be one of its main attractions.

When all is said, the sheer beauty of the place remains—the picturesque bays and coves, the expansive views over a usually placid sea, the rugged mountains and lush valleys, the beaches dotted with sea creatures and driftwood, the twisted splendour of the arbutus and Garry oak trees, and the springtime meadows resplendent with wild flowers. No wonder the island has attracted so many interesting, creative, and idiosyncratic residents.

Courtesy Derrick Lundy.

Notes

Abbreviations:
BCA—British Columbia Archives
SSIA—Salt Spring Island Archives

In addition to the items listed in the bibliography, the following newspapers were important sources of information for this book: *Sidney and Islands Review* (later the *Saanich Peninsula and Gulf Islands Review*), *Cowichan Leader*, and *Gulf Islands Driftwood*. Much information was also obtained from the author's personal interviews and the oral history collections of the Salt Spring Island Archives. Source notes have been provided mainly for quotations; readers who wish further information on sources can refer to the manuscript of this book deposited in the Salt Spring Island Archives.

Introduction

1. Margaret (Shaw) Walter, *Early Days Among the Gulf Islands of British Columbia*, pp. 16, 20; Tsartlip elder Earl Claxton, Sr., comments on MS; and Dave Elliott, Sr., *Saltwater People*, p. 31.

2. Cited in A.F. Flucke, "Early Days on Saltspring Island," p. 161.

1: In the Beginning: Aboriginal Salt Spring

Much of the information in this chapter was derived from *Coast Salish Essays* and *Coast Salish and Western Washington Indians* by Wayne Suttles, *The Salish Indians of Vancouver Island* by Diamond Jenness, and *Saltwater People* by Dave Elliott, Sr. All of the quotations by Dave Elliott, Sr., are from *Saltwater People*.

1. At time of writing the Hul'qumi'num Treaty Group (including the Cowichan, Penelakut, and Lyackson peoples) had a land claim on all the Gulf Islands.

2. Wayne Suttles, *Coast Salish and Western Washington Indians I*, p. 26.

3. Dave Johnstone, "Long Harbour," p. 1.

4. David Lewis Rozen, "Place-Names of the Island Halkomelem Indian People," p. 108.

5. Roberta L. Bagshaw, ed., *No Better Land*, p. 223.

6. Roberta L. Hall and James C. Haggarty, "Human Skeletal Remains and Associated Cultural Material from the Hill Site," p. 101.

7. Robert E. McKechnie, *Strong Medicine*, p. 76.

8. Cited in Ruth Kirk, *Wisdom of the Elders*, p. 33.

9. Bea Hamilton, *Salt Spring Island*, pp. 163–64.

2: Land for Five Shillings

Much of the information provided in this chapter was derived from A.F. Flucke, "Early Days on Saltspring Island," pp. 166–70.

1. Ruth Wells Sandwell, "Reading the Land," p. 250.

2. Letter from Jonathan Begg to William and Margret Chisholm, March 10, 1860; copy in SSIA.

3: Eking Out a Living, 1859–1872

The main sources for the information and quotations in this chapter are Roberta L. Bagshaw, ed., *No Better Land*, pp. 222–32; A.F. Flucke, "Early Days on Salt Spring Island"; Marie Wallace, "Notes made by Marie Albertina Stark (afterwards Mrs. Wallace) from the recollections of her mother, Sylvia Stark"; Margaret (Shaw) Walter, *Early Days Among the Gulf Islands of British Columbia*; interview with Mary (Gyves) Brenton and Caroline Gyves, May 5, 1977, tape 9A in SSIA; A.S. Deaville, *The Colonial Postal Systems: Vancouver Island, 1849–71*, from p. 321.

1. Vesuvius Bay and Central were often used interchangeably; for example, the Vesuvius School was actually at Central. To avoid confusion, this community is referred to as Vesuvius-Central. Similarly, the valley extending from Burgoyne Bay in the west to Fulford Harbour in the east is called the Fulford-Burgoyne Valley or simply the valley.

2. *Daily Colonist*, July 5, 1931, p. 10.

3. Letter from Jonathan Begg to William and Margret Chisholm, March 10, 1860; copy in SSIA.

4. Letter from Jonathan Begg to William and Margret Chisholm, March 19, 1860; copy in SSIA.

5. Mathew MacFie, *Vancouver Island and British Columbia*, p. 186.

6. *Daily Chronicle* (Victoria), February 28, 1866; cited in Ruth Wells Sandwell, "Reading the Land," p. 88.

7. Margaret (Shaw) Walter, *Early Days Among the Gulf Islands of British Columbia*, p. 25.

8. *British Colonist*, September 19 and 27, 1862; cited in Jean Barman, *The West Beyond the West*, p. 90.

9. Margaret (Shaw) Walter, *Early Days Among the Gulf Islands of British Columbia*, p. 32.

10. This date is suggested in Crawford Kilian, *Go Do Some Great Thing*, p. 109. Some doubt exists about when Jones actually started teaching, however, with some writers suggesting 1863 or 1864.

4: The Black Community

Much of the information in this chapter was derived from Crawford Kilian, *Go Do Some Great Thing*; Marie Wallace, "Notes made by Marie Albertina Stark (afterwards Mrs. Wallace) from the recollections of her mother, Sylvia Stark"; Charles C. Irby, "The Black Settlers on Saltspring Island, Canada, in the Nineteenth Century"; and James William Pilton, "Negro Settlement in British Columbia, 1858–1871."

1. Mifflin W. Gibbs, *Shadow and Light*, p. 63.

2. Cited in A.F. Flucke, "Early Days on Saltspring Island," p. 190.

3. Charles C. Irby, "The Black Settlers on Saltspring Island, Canada, in the Nineteenth Century," p. 40. Irby based this information on a communication from Peggy C. Walker, who in turn took her figures from Rev. Ebenezer Robson's diary.

4. BC Department of Education, First Annual Report of the Superintendent of Education for the year ending July 31, 1872.

5. James William Pilton, "Negro Settlement in British Columbia, 1858–1871," p. 146.

6. Will included in probate file no. 1754, British Columbia Supreme Court (Victoria), Probates 1859–1974, GR 1304, BCA; cited in Ruth Wells Sandwell, "Reading the Land," p. 327.

7. Letter signed by John A. Caldwell, March 6, 1947.

5: Government, Law, and Disorder

Much of the information in this chapter has been derived from A.F. Flucke's article "Early Days on Saltspring Island" and letters from Jonathan Begg to William and Margret Chisholm, March 10, 1860 and June 3, 1860.

1. Cited in Crawford Kilian, *Go Do Some Great Thing*, p. 107.

2. Cited in A.F. Flucke, "Early Days on Saltspring Island," p. 182.

3. Charles Robson (commander of the *Forward*), letter of proceedings to Sir Thomas Maitland (rear admiral and commander in chief), May 20, 1861, encl. in Maitland to Sec. of the Admiralty, May 24, 1861, Admiralty Papers, P.R.O. 1/5761, Y165; copy in SSIA.

4. Captain John T. Walbran, *British Columbia Coast Names*, p. 186.

5. Robson to Maitland; cited in Barry M. Gough, *Gunboat Frontier*, p. 136.

6. For a complete description of this event, see Gulf Islands Branch, BC Historical Association, *A Gulf Islands Patchwork*, p. 61.

7. Captain John T. Walbran, *British Columbia Coast Names*, pp. 298–99. Some of the details of these events have been corrected from Walbran's account by research conducted by Chris Arnett for his upcoming book, "The Terror of the Coast."

6: A Troubled Adolescence, 1873–1883

The discussion of Salt Spring's incorporation is based on A.F. Flucke, "Early Days on Saltspring Island," pp. 195–202.

1. John P. Booth to William Smithe, January 26, 1883; cited in Flucke, p. 199.

2. Ruth Wells Sandwell, "Reading the Land," pp. 90, 250.

3. Ashdown Henry Green, "1874 diary of Ashdown Henry Green," regarding the survey of Salt Spring Island," BCA, ADD MSS. 437, entry for September 28. This 1874 diary is the source of all of the other quotations from Green.

7: The Hawaiian Community

Much of the information in this chapter is derived from Jean Barman, "New Land, New Lives" and "The Worth of an Everyday Woman: Maria Mahoi and Her Two Families," and Tom Koppel, *Kanaka*.

1. Talk by Michael Halloran to the Victoria Cemetery Society at St. Paul's churchyard, Salt Spring Island, April 20, 1997.

2. Jean Barman, "The Worth of an Everyday Woman," p. 24.

3. Jean Barman, "New Land, New Lives," p. 20.

8: Connections and Communities, 1884–1899

Among the main sources for this chapter are Rev. E.F. Wilson's *Salt Spring Island, British Columbia, 1895*; his unpublished memoir "Our Life on Salt Spring Island, BC"; and his monthly newsletter *Salt Spring Island Parish and Home* (later *Salt Spring Island Church Monthly*). All of the quotations by Leonard Tolson are from his unpublished memoir "To Nora, Margaret, Edith, and Others" and are reprinted with permission. Much of the information on the Pappenburgers was provided by Shirley Morrison from her own research.

1. Rev. E.F. Wilson, *Salt Spring Island, British Columbia, 1895*, pp. 24–25.
2. Lukin Johnston, *Beyond the Rockies*, pp. 22–23.
3. The Hamiltons had a total of thirteen children, three of whom died in infancy.
4. Research report on island post offices by William E. Topping, Fellow, Royal Philatelic Society, London, in SSIA.
5. Letter from Mary Inglin to Dr. Jean Barman, February 10, 1988; copy in SSIA.
6. E.R. Cartwright, *A Late Summer*, p. 10.
7. Rev. E.F. Wilson, "Our Life on Salt Spring Island, B.C.," pp. 143–45.
8. Bea Hamilton, *Salt Spring Island*, p. 115.

9: Into the Twentieth Century, 1900–1918

1. E.R. Cartwright, *A Late Summer*, pp. 13–14.
2. Leonard Tolson, "To Nora, Margaret, Edith, and Others." Reprinted with permission.
3. Joe Garner, *Never Fly Over an Eagle's Nest*, p. 135.
4. Derek Reimer, ed., *The Gulf Islands*, p. 12.
5. Bea Hamilton, *Salt Spring Island*, pp. 146–47.
6. Rev. E.F. Wilson, "Our Lives on Salt Spring Island," April 2, 1911 (p. 36).
7. Peter Cartwright, "A Short History of the North Salt Spring Waterworks District."

10: Farming the Hard Way

Much information for this chapter comes from Mort Stratton's well-researched, unpublished history of agriculture on Salt Spring written for the Salt Spring Island Historical Society (copy in SSIA).

1. Rev. E.F. Wilson, *Salt Spring Island Parish and Home*, October 1900.
2. Cited in Ruth Wells Sandwell, "Reading the Land," p. 112.
3. Rev. E.F. Wilson, *Salt Spring Island, British Columbia, 1895*, p. 16.
4. Miles Smeeton, *A Change of Jungles*, p. 169.
5. Islands Trust, "Salt Spring Island: Snapshot of Today—Choices for Tomorrow," a discussion paper for review and comment, February 1995, p. 23.

11: The Squire of Salt Spring

Much of the information in this chapter was derived from interviews with Donald Goodman, Malcolm Bond, Denise Crofton, Irene Palmer, and Mary Stepaniuk.

1. From Donald Goodman tape, Salt Spring Senior Citizens Project. Interviewed by Mary Williamson, November 2, 1977.

2. Bullock's great-grandfather, Rev. Charles Penry Bullock, was vicar of St. Paul's, Portland Square, and Charles's brother, another Harry Bullock, was a wealthy shipowner. Bullock's father, George Martin Bullock, was vicar of Chalfont St. Peter, Buckinghamshire. His mother, Cordelia Wright, came from a family probably higher on the English social scale than the Bullocks, since the Wrights were gentlemen farmers—esquires of the Grange, Chalfont St. Peter. One ancestor was alderman of London and lord mayor of London for a year.

3. The boys included Jesse Bond, Earl Moore, Spenser Walker, Harold Warburton, George Belford, Donald Goodman, Ralph Ricketts, Bill Currie, Scotty Allen, Fred Clemo, Alf Hougen, Chuck Hougen, Jack Judd, and George Judd.

4. Letter dated December 16, 1896, Bristol, to Alice Collins from H.W. Bullock; copy in SSIA.

5. Derek Reimer, ed., *The Gulf Islanders*, pp. 18–19.

6. From Tony Farr interview with Mary Inglin, tape 19, SSIA.

7. Derek Reimer, ed., *The Gulf Islanders*, p. 19.

8. Conversation with Denise and John Crofton, February 18, 1997.

9. Interview with Dr. Raymond Rush by Tony Farr, September 28, 1984, tape 53, SSIA.

10. Telephone conversation with Anne Mouat, May 8, 1997.

11. From Tony Farr interview with Mary Inglin; tape 19, SSIA.

12. Derek Reimer, ed., *The Gulf Islanders*, p. 19.

12: Logging, Mining, and Red Ink

This chapter owes much to the fine research of Sue Mouat and Bob Rush, as well as information provided in telephone interviews by Hank Doerksen and Fred Doneghy, both of whom worked on Salt Spring for the forest service in the 1950s.

1. Ken Bernsohn, *Cutting Up the North*, p. 11.

2. Ken Bernsohn, *Cutting Up the North*, pp. 24 and 28.

3. Joe Garner, "Logging on Salt Spring Was Vital to the Island."

4. Interview with Fred Hollings; tape in SSIA.

5. Ruth Wells Sandwell, "Reading the Land," p. 98.

6. *Colonist*, July 28, 1901.

13: Ferries and Roquefort Cheese, 1919–1945

1. Inglis's Auto Camp at Vesuvius Bay, the Vesuvius Lodge run by Kay Frampton, Rainbow Beach Camp run by Arthur Raymond Layard, George and Florence Borradaile's Ganges Auto Camp, Isabella Emsley's Stowe Lake Park, The White Lodge at the head of Fulford Harbour run by Mrs. H.C. Cullington, Beaver Point Auto Camp, Ganges House (also known as Ganges Inn and Granny's Boarding House) run by Jane Mouat, The Maple Inn in Ganges run by Jimmy and Kitty Rogers, and the Harbour House Hotel. Another resort, Bluegates, on Weston Lake, then run by Margaret and Captain Macgregor Macintosh, was purchased by Tom and Kay Butt in 1940 and renamed Weston Lake Cottages.

2. Reminiscence of Bob Rush on the ninetieth anniversary of Mouat's store.

3. Interview with Doreen Morris; tape 13, SSIA.

4. Interview with Joane Millner, March 2, 1984; tape 24, SSIA.

5. Manson Toynbee, address to Salt Spring Island Historical Society, February 9, 1993; tape in SSIA.

6. Ruth Sandwell's interview with Evelyn Lee and John Bennett, August 27, 1990; (tape 83:1), SSIA.

7. Ruth Sandwell's interview with Celia Valentine Reynolds, July 31, 1990 (tape 73), SSIA.

8. From a letter by Ida Crofton to her sister in London, quoted in a presentation to the Salt Spring Historical Society by John Crofton and Ivan Mouat on November 14, 1995.

14: The Japanese Community

This chapter owes much to Kimiko Murakami and Mary Kitagawa, who provided a great deal of material and reviewed the chapter several times for accuracy.

1. Mary Kitagawa's records from the reminiscences of her mother, Kimiko Murakami.

2. Japanese Canadian Citizens Association, *Bilingual Human Rights Guide for Japanese Canadians*, p. 8.

3. Manson Toynbee, address to Salt Spring Island Historical Society, February 9, 1993; SSIA.

4. Marie Elliott, "The Japanese of Mayne Island," p. 182.

15: Time for Each Other, 1946–1960

The quotations by Joan Millner were taken from her interview with Tony Farr in 1984, while the quotations attributed to Jack Green were taken from his reminiscence entitled "A Few Drops From Old Salt Spring."

1. Interview with John Stepaniuk, May 12, 1997.

2. Tony Farr interview with Ellen Bennett, January 6, 1984; tape 23, SSIA.

16: The Island Discovered, 1961–1986

1. Marc Holmes, "Salt Spring Island, 1940–1980," address to Salt Spring Island Historical Society, February 11, 1986; tape 41, SSIA.

2. Information provided by the Salt Spring Centre.

3. The committee members included Ruby Alton, Betty Baker, Juanita Brown, Louise Foulis, Tom Harcus, Robert Holloman, Major Gordon Matthews, Rod Pringle, Hank Schubart, Gladys Slingsby, Andrew Stevens, Alfred Temmel, Adrian Wolfe-Milner, Jack Wood, and Dr. S. Wood.

17: Salt Spring in Transition, 1986–1998

1. Marc Holmes, "Salt Spring Island, 1940–1980," address to Salt Spring Island Historical Society, February 11, 1986; tape 41, SSIA.

2. Islands Trust, "Salt Spring Island: Snapshot of Today—Choices for Tomorrow," p. 11. This was written before the transfer of some land into the Forest Land Reserve reduced density potential by about 400 dwelling units.

3. In 1997, developer Brian Hauff obtained building permits to build his Salt Spring Island Village Resort on Bullock Lake. Most islanders seemed to agree that the proposed 123 units plus a 20,000-square-foot conference centre and lodge was too much density on only 35 acres (14 ha) and was inconsistent with the level of development elsewhere on the island. When Hauff called islanders "a bunch of goofers," many people took the label as a badge of honour, and proudly began wearing "I'm a Goofer" T-shirts.

4. Music and chorus by Reid Collins; lyrics for verses by Mike Hayes and Arvid Chalmers. Reprinted with permission.

5. Islands Trust, "Salt Spring Island: Snapshot of Today—Choices for Tomorrow," p. 9.

Selected Bibliography

Abbreviations:
BCARS—British Columbia Archives and Records Service
SSIA—Salt Spring Island Archives

Books and Pamphlets

Adachi, Ken. *The Enemy That Never Was: The History of the Japanese Canadians.* Toronto: McClelland & Stewart, 1976.

Akrigg, G.P.V. and Helen. *British Columbia Chronicle, 1847–1871: Gold and Colonists.* Vancouver: Discovery Press, 1977.

————. *1001 British Columbia Place Names.* 3rd rev. ed. Vancouver: Discovery Press, 1973.

Arnett, Chris. *The Terror of the Coast: Land Alienation and Colonial War on the East Coast of Vancouver Island and the Gulf Islands, 1849–1863.* Vancouver: Talon Books, forthcoming.

Bagshaw, Roberta L., ed. *No Better Land: The 1860 Diaries of the Anglican Colonial Bishop, George Hills.* Victoria: Sono Nis Press, 1996.

Barman, Jean. *The West Beyond the West: A History of British Columbia.* Rev. ed. Toronto: University of Toronto Press, 1996.

Bernsohn, Ken. *Cutting Up the North: The History of the Forest Industry in the Northern Interior.* Vancouver: Hancock House, c. 1980.

Cartwright, E.R. *A Late Summer: The Memoirs of E.R. Cartwright.* London: Caravel Press, 1964.

Cunningham, Margaret. *Upon a Certain Island: The First Hundred Years of Anglican Ministry on Salt Spring Island, 1885–1985* (pamphlet).

Deaville, A.S. *The Colonial Postal Systems: Vancouver Island, 1849–71.* Victoria: King's Printer, 1928.

Dunae, Patrick A. *Gentlemen Emigrants: From the British Public Schools to the Canadian Frontier.* Vancouver: Douglas & McIntyre, 1981.

Elliott, Sr., Dave. *Saltwater People: A Resource Book for the Saanich Native Studies Program.* Edited by Janet Poth. Saanich, BC: Native Education, School District 63 (Saanich), 1983, 1990.

Elliott, Marie. "The Japanese of Mayne Island." In Gulf Islands Branch, BC Historical Federation, *More Tales From the Outer Gulf Islands.* Pender Island, BC: Gulf Islands Branch, BC Historical Federation, 1993.

Fladmark, Knut R. *British Columbia Prehistory.* Ottawa: National Museums of Canada, 1986.

Garner, Joe. *Never Fly Over an Eagle's Nest.* Nanaimo, BC: Cinnabar Press, 1980, 1982.

————. *Never Drop Your Rope.* Nanaimo, BC: Cinnabar Press, 1988.

Gibbs, Mifflin Wistar. *Shadow and Light: An Autobiography.* New York: Arno Press and the New York Times, 1968 (originally published in Washington, DC, in 1902).

Gough, Barry M. *Gunboat Frontier: British Maritime Authority and Northwest Coast Indians, 1846–1890.* Vancouver: University of British Columbia Press, 1984.

Gulf Islands Branch, BC Historical Association. *A Gulf Islands Patchwork: Some Early Events on the Islands of Galiano, Mayne, Saturna, North and South Pender.* Sidney, BC: Peninsula Printing Co., 1961.

Gulf Islands Branch, BC Historical Federation. *More Tales From the Outer Gulf Islands*. Pender Island, BC: Gulf Islands Branch, BC Historical Federation, 1993.

Hacking, Norman R., and Lamb, W. Kaye. *The Princess Story*. Vancouver: Mitchell Press, 1974.

Hamilton, Bea. *Salt Spring Island*. Vancouver: Mitchell Press, 1969.

Hearn, George, and David Wilkie. *The Cordwood Limited: A History of the Victoria and Sidney Railway*. Victoria, BC: The British Columbia Railway Historical Association, 1966.

Hill, Beth and Ray. *Indian Petroglyphs of the Pacific Northwest*. Saanichton, BC: Hancock House Publishers, 1974.

Hill, Beth; Sue Mouat, Margaret Cunningham; and Lillian Horsdal. *Times Past: Salt Spring Island Houses and History Before the Turn of the Century*. May 1983.

Hill-Tout, Charles. *The Salish People*, vols. I–IV. Ed. Ralph Maud. Vancouver: Talonbooks, 1979.

Japanese Canadian Citizens Association (Human Rights Committee). *Bilingual Human Rights Guide for Japanese Canadians*. Vancouver: JCCA, 1995.

Johnston, Lukin. *Beyond the Rockies: Three Thousand Miles by Trail and Canoe Through Little-known British Columbia*. London and Toronto: J.M. Dent & Sons, 1929.

Kilian, Crawford. *Go Do Some Great Thing: The Black Pioneers of British Columbia*. Vancouver: Douglas & McIntyre, 1978. Pages 101-15 deal with Blacks on Salt Spring Island.

Kirk, Ruth. *Wisdom of the Elders: Native Traditions on the Northwest Coast*. Vancouver: Douglas and McIntyre/British Columbia Provincial Museum, 1986.

Koppel, Tom. *Kanaka: The Untold Story of Hawaiian Pioneers in British Columbia and the Pacific Northwest*. Vancouver/Toronto: Whitecap Books, 1995.

MacFie, Matthew. *Vancouver Island and British Columbia: Their History, Resources, and Prospects*. London: Longman, Green, 1865; Toronto: Coles (reprint), 1972.

McKechnie, Robert E. *Strong Medicine*. Vancouver: J.J. Douglas, 1972.

McLaren, Jean, and Heidi Brown, eds. *The Raging Grannies Songbook*. Gabriola Island BC: New Society Publishers, 1993.

Murray, Peter. *Homesteads and Snug Harbours: The Gulf Islands*. Ganges, BC: Horsdal and Schubart, 1991.

Norcross, H. Blanche, ed. *Nanaimo Retrospective: The First Century*. Nanaimo, BC: Nanaimo Historical Society, 1978.

Ormsby, Margaret. *British Columbia: A History*. Toronto: Macmillan, 1958.

Ovanin, Thomas K. *Island Heritage Buildings: A Selection of Heritage Buildings in the Islands Trust Area*. Victoria: Queen's Printer, 1984.

Pedlow, Ken. *Ruckle Provincial Park: A Documentary History*. Victoria, BC: Heritage Conservation Branch, Ministry of Provincial Secretary and Government Services, 1984.

Quiring, Linda. *Island of Knowledge*. Ganges, BC: Sydney Banks Spiritual Foundation, 1975.

Reimer, Derek, ed. *The Gulf Islanders*. Victoria: Aural History, Provincial Archives of British Columbia, 1976.

Roberts, Eric A. *Salt Spring Saga: An Exciting Story of Pioneer Days*. Ganges: Driftwood, 1962.

Smeeton, Miles. *A Change of Jungles*. London: Rupert Hart-Davis, 1962.

Stevens, Homer, and Rolf Knight. *Homer Stevens: A Life in Fishing*. Madeira Park, BC: Harbour Publishing, 1992.

Suttles, Wayne P. *Coast Salish Essays*. Vancouver: Talon Books/Seattle and Washington: University of Washington Press, 1987.

————. *Coast Salish and Western Washington Indians I: The Economic Life of the Coast Salish of Haro and Rosario Straits*. New York/London: Garland Publishing, 1974.

Symons, Kyrle C. *That Amazing Institution: The Story of St. Michael's School, Victoria, BC, from 1910–1948*. Victoria: St. Michael's School, 1949.

Toynbee, Richard Mouat. *Snapshots of Early Salt Spring and Other Favoured Islands*. Ganges, BC: Mouat's Trading Co. Ltd., 1978.

Turner, Robert D. *The Pacific Princesses*. Victoria: Sono Nis Press, 1977.

Underhill, Stuart. *The Iron Church*. Victoria, BC: Braemar Books, 1984.

Walbran, Capt. John T. *British Columbia Coast Names: Their Origin and History*. Ottawa: Government Printing Bureau, 1909; facsimile paperback edition: Toronto/Vancouver: Douglas & McIntyre, 1977.

Walter, Margaret (Shaw). *Early Days Among the Gulf Islands of British Columbia*. 2nd ed. Hebden Printing Co. Ltd., n.d.

Wilson, Rev. E.F. *Salt Spring Island, British Columbia, 1895*. BC Facsimile reproduction by Salt Spring Island Historical Society.

_____. *Salt Spring Island Parish and Home*. Photocopy. SSIA.

_____. *Salt Spring Island Church Monthly*. Photocopy. SSIA.

Articles

Acheson, S., et al. "Report of the Archaeological Survey of the Southwestern Gulf of Georgia," November 1, 1975 (Archaeological Sites Advisory Board of British Columbia, 1975).

Barman, Jean. "New Land, New Lives: Hawaiian Settlement in British Columbia." *The Hawaiian Journal of History* 29 (1995), pp. 1–32.

_____. "William Naukana." *Dictionary of Canadian Biography*, vol. XIII, pp. 761–62. Toronto: University of Toronto Press, 1994.

Borradaile, John. "Henry Wright Bullock: Saltspring's Unforgettable Character." *Times Colonist*, Dec. 16, 1984.

Cassidy, Stephen; Michael Cranny; and Philip Murton. "Report of the Gulf Island Archaeological Survey," September 1, 1974 (Archaeological Sites Advisory Board of British Columbia, 1974).

Crofton, John. "The Rise and Sad Demise of Salt Spring's Lodge of Hope." *BC Historical News* 26:3 (Summer 1993), pp. 30–32.

_____. "Salt Spring Island and the Canadian Scottish Regiment." *BC Historical News*, vol. 23, no. 4 (Fall 1990), pp. 12–14.

Davidson, Mary. "Burgoyne United Church." *BC Historical News*, vol. 22, no. 3 (Summer 1989), pp. 11–14.

Douglas, Gilean. "Cariboo Doctor." *Daily Colonist*, Sept. 14, 1975.

"Driftwood Was Brain-Child of Woody Fisher." *Gulf Islands Driftwood*, Mar. 20, 1985.

Farr, Tony. "Harry Bullock, Pioneer Photographer." *BC Historical News*, Fall 1996, pp. 22–24.

Flucke, A.F. "Early Days on Saltspring Island." *British Columbia Historical Quarterly*, vol. XV, nos. 3 and 4 (July–Oct. 1951), pp. 161–201.

Garner, Joe. "Logging on Salt Spring Was Vital to the Island." *Gulf Islands Driftwood*, Feb. 27, 1991.

Hamilton, Bea. "The Builders Undismayed." *Daily Colonist*, August 14, 1960.

_____. "Little St. Paul's at Fulford: Pioneer Church of Gulf Island." *Daily Colonist*, Jan. 24, 1960.

Hill, Beth. "Drama at Bittancourt Boathouse." *Pacific Yachting*, May 1997, pp. 70–77.

Horsdal, Lilian. "Farmer Bond of Salt Spring." *Daily Colonist*, June 17, 1978.

_____. "Hepburns of Salt Spring." *Daily Colonist*, Mar. 11, 1973.

Irby, Charles C. "The Black Settlers on Saltspring Island, Canada, in the Nineteenth Century." Association of Pacific Coast Geographers, *Yearbook*, vol. 36, pp. 35–44. Corvallis, OR: Oregon State University Press, 1974.

Johnstone, David. "Long Harbour." *The Midden* XX.3 (June 1988): 1.

Paterson, T.W. "Fighting Coplands Fell From Grace." *Times Colonist*, Nov. 18, 1990.

Richards, Frank. "The Newspaper Wasn't Always Driftwood." *Gulf Islands Driftwood*, Feb. 27, 1991.

Richards, Valerie. "Fulford Hall Has Served Community 60 Years." *Gulf Islands Driftwood*, Nov. 19, 1980.

Roberts, G.W. "DfRu 4: The Hill Site: Archaeological Sites Advisory Board Salvage Excavation," March 1973.

Sharp, Brenda G. "Caldwells of Salt Spring." *Victoria Daily Colonist*, March 24, 1968.

Sjuberg, Gail. "Fulford Hall: Celebrating 75 Years." *Gulf Islands Driftwood*, June 26, 1996.

Stratton, Morton. "The Bittancourts and the Nortons: Early Salt Spring Home Builders." *Gulf Islands Driftwood*, May 27, 1981.

————. "Mahon Brothers Left Community Hall." *Gulf Islands Driftwood*, June 10, 1981.

Watmough, Charles and Winnie. "Trials on an Early Salt Spring Island Homestead." *Times Colonist*, May 15, 1988.

White, Sharon. "Fame of Island Company Spread Around Globe." *Gulf Islands Driftwood*, February 5, 1986.

————. "Salt Spring's Earlier Days Not Always Placid." *Gulf Islands Driftwood*, January 29, 1986.

Worthington, Elsie. "They Played the Game." *Daily Colonist*, Nov. 10, 1963.

Wright, Tom. "Ups and Downs in the Life of Jonathan Begg, 1860–1861." *The Gulf Islands Guardian*, Fall 1993, pp. 22–25.

————. "A Salt Spring Scalawag." *The Gulf Islands Guardian*, vol. 5, no. 4 (Summer 1996), pp. 25–28.

————. "A Voice From the Past." *The Gulf Islands Guardian*, Spring 1993, pp. 28–31.

Unpublished Material

Aitken, Alexander. "Diary" (April 14, 1891–May 25, 1892). SSIA.

Akerman, Bob. "Pioneer Life in Salt Spring." Address tp Salt Spring Island Historical Society, February 13, 1990.

Barman, Jean. "The Worth of an Everyday Woman: Maria Mahoi and Her Two Families." Unpublished article. SSIA.

Beddis, John. "Diary" (Jan. 1–June 30, 1890). SSIA.

Begg, Jonathan. Letters to William and Margaret Chisholm, March 10, March 19, and June 3, 1860. Copies in SSIA.

Caldwell, John A. Letter dated March 6, 1947. SSIA.

Cartwright, Peter. "A Short History of the North Salt Spring Waterworks District." Unpublished MS, 1977. SSIA.

Crofton, John. "The Croftons of Salt Spring Island." Address to Salt Spring Island Historical Society, November 12, 1985.

Davidson, Mary. "The McLennans on Salt Spring." Address to Salt Spring Island Historical Society, January 9, 1990.

Green, Ashdown Henry. "1874 Diary of Ashdown Henry Green regarding the survey of Salt Spring Island." BCARS. ADD MSS. 437.

Green, Jack A. "A Few Drops From Old Salt Spring." MS. SSIA.

Guthrie, Nonnie. "Acland's (Booth Bay) Resort." Address to Salt Spring Island Historical Society, February 7, 1986.

Hall, Roberta L., and James C. Haggarty, "Human Skeletal Remains and Associated Cultural Material from the Hill Site, DfRu 4, Saltspring Island, British Columbia." Jerome S. Cybulski, ed., *Contributions to Physical Anthropology, 1978–1980*, National Museum of Man Series, Archaeological Survey of Canada, Paper No. 106. Ottawa: National Museums of Canada, 1981.

Holmes, Marc. "Salt Spring Island, 1940–1980." Address to Salt Spring Island Historical Society, February 11, 1986.

Hope of Salt Spring, Lodge Number 7. "Minutes." SSIA.

Horel, Charles. "Our Tribal History." A family history in the form of a letter. SSIA.

Islands Trust. "Salt Spring Island: Snapshot of Today—Choices for Tomorrow." Discussion paper for review and comment, Feb. 1995.

Jenness, Diamond. "The Saanich Indians of Vancouver Island." MS. Archives of Ethnology Division, Museum of Civilization, Ottawa.

Lang, John Charles. "Log Book" (1914). SSIA.

Mouat, W.M. "Ganges Inn." MS. (1958). SSIA.

Newman, Walmus. "Reminiscence of Walmus Newman, recorded by May Taylor." SSIA.

Pilton, James William, "Negro Settlement in British Columbia, 1858–1871," Master's thesis, University of British Columbia, September 1951.

Reid, John Dunlop. "Autobiography of John Dunlop Reid," MS, p. 19. SSIA.

Robson, Rev. Ebenezer. "Diaries." MS. BCARS.

Rozen, David Lewis. "Place-Names of the Island Halkomelem Indian People." M.A. thesis, Faculty of Graduate Studies (Department of Anthropology and Sociology), University of British Columbia, July 1985.

Ruckle, Gwen. "The Ruckle Family." Address to Salt Spring Island Historical Society, March 13, 1984.

"Salt Spring: Island in the Gulf," a radio program by Jan Williams for CBC series entitled "Between Ourselves" (1965). Tape in SSIA.

Sampson, Rocky. "A Brief History of the Sampson Family of Salt Spring Island, BC." SSIA.

Sandwell, Ruth Wells. "Reading the Land: Rural Discourse and the Practice of Settlement, Salt Spring Island, British Columbia, 1859–1891." Ph.D. diss., Simon Fraser University, 1997.

Sandwell, Ruth, and John Lutz. "Who Killed William Robinson? Race, Justice and Settling the Land." Website (http://web.uvic.ca/history-robinson).

Shambaugh, Alice Purvis. "Migration and Memories: A History of the Purvis Family." MS. SSIA.

Tolson, Leonard. "To Nora, Margaret, Edith, and Others" (a personal reminiscence), unpublished MS. SSIA.

Toynbee, Manson. Address to Salt Spring Island Historical Society, February 9, 1993. Tape. SSIA.

Wark, Robyn. "Tourism Growth Management: Issues and Opportunities for Salt Spring Island." Report. Burnaby, BC: Centre for Tourism Policy and Research, School of Resource Management, Simon Fraser University, Dec. 1994.

Wilson, Rev. E.F. "Our Life on Salt Spring Island, BC." Unpublished diary of Rev. E.F. Wilson. SSIA.

Wallace, Marie. "Notes made by Marie Albertina Stark (afterwards Mrs. Wallace) from the recollections of her mother, Sylvia Stark, who was born a slave in Clay County, Missouri, and settled on Salt Spring Island with her husband, Louis Stark, and family in the year 1860, as homesteaders," BC Archives, ADD MS 91. SSIA.

Interviews

Interviews, both those already recorded and stored in the Salt Spring Island Archives and those conducted by the author especially for this book, were an invaluable source of oral history. The following interviews from the archives were particularly helpful:

- The CBC Imbert Orchard Collection—August 23, 1972: Desmond Gerald Crofton; October 1965: Ina and Bea Hamilton and Mabel Davis; Beryl (Scott) Weatherell; Len A. Bittancourt; Margaret (Purdy) Cunningham; David and Clara Maxwell; Sophie (Purser) King

- Salt Spring Senior Citizens Project (interviewers: Amber Hindle, Mary Williamson, Margaret Simons, and others)-Myrtle Holloman, April 18, 1977; Bob Akerman, April 28,

1977; Ruth (Goodrich) Heinekey and Iris (Goodrich) Pattison, April 28, 1977; Emily Patterson, April 29, 1977; Mary Brenton and Caroline Gyves, May 5, 1977; Lotus Ruckle, June 17, 1977; Elizabeth Sampson, 1977; Donald Goodman, November 2, 1977; Doreen (Crofton) Morris and Betty Stone, 1977

- Andrew Stevens, January 1982
- Tony Farr Collection (interviewers: Tony Farr and others)—Gladys King, n.d.; Dr. Raymond Rush, September 28, 1984; Mary Inglin, n.d.; Ted Brown, April 13, 1982; Daisy (Lang) Cartwright, July 10, 1982
- Salt Spring Island Historical Society Collection (interviewers: Tony Farr and others)— Ellen Bennett, January 6, 1984; Joan Millner, March 2, 1984; Jack Smith, February 1, 1986; Charles Horel, January 17, 1986; Dorothy James, January 24, 1986; Gertrude Lang, Freda Thompson, and Daisy Cartwright, October 15, 1975; Margaret Price, March 25, 1985; Dr. Raymond Rush, September 28, 1984
- Salt Spring Island Oral History Project/Sound Archives (interviewer: Ruth Sandwell)— Gordon Cudmore, July 3, 1990; Margaret Cunningham, July 5, 1990; Kimiko Murikami and Alice Tanaka, July 11, 1990; Paul Layard, July 19, 1990; Bob Patterson, July 24, 1990; Daisy Gear, July 25, 1990; Valentine Reynolds, July 31, 1990; Bob, Dorothy, and Lassie Dodds, August 8, 1990; Daphne Bradley, August 9, 1990; Robert Hele, August 14, 1990; Ivan Mouat, August 16, 1990; Ted Brown, August 21, 1990; Dorothy James, August 22, 1990; Evelyn Lee and John Bennett, August 27, 1990; Denise Crofton and Doreen Morris, August 28, 1990; Donald Goodman, September 19, 1990; Charles Horel, August 24, 1990

The following people were interviewed by the author in person or on the telephone: Bob Akerman, December 15, 1996, and September 5, 1997; Ruby Alton, July 15, 1997; Joan Angus, August 27, 1997; Robbie Beddis, August 3, 1997; Cyril and Dorothy Beech, July 1, 1997; John and Ellen Bennett, April 8 and September 11, 1997; Paul Boatman, August 1997; Malcolm Bond, May 1, 1997; Eric Booth, September 29, 1997; Sharon Brawn, March 10, 1997; Juanita Brown, September 24, 1997; Arvid Chalmers, August 20, 1997; Simone Chantelu, October 8, 1997; Denise Crofton, February 18 and May 12, 1997; John Crofton, February 12 and 18, 1997; Migs Edwards, August 20, 1997; Donald Goodman, May 5, 18, and 22, 1997; Ken Goodrich, July 22, 1997; Tom Gossett, September 26 and October 17, 1997; Tamar Griggs, June 8, 1997; Val Gyves, July 15, 1997; Bill Henderson, July 27, 1997; Florence Hepburn, July 22, 1997; Barb Hicks, August 15, 1997; Ray Hill, September 18, 1997; Michael Hobbs, 1997; Jean Hollings, July 2, 1997; Marc and Jean Holmes, July 8 and October 1, 1997; Chuck and Natalie Horel, 1997; Chuck and Alice Hougen, August 3, 1997; Joan Ingram, February 6, 1997; Dan Jason, August 20, 1997; Mary Kitagawa, December 17, 1996; Edward and Molly Lacy, July 13, 1997; Pat and Marguerite Lee, May 18, 1997; Ron and Evelyn Lee, July 3, 1997; Robert McBride, August 31, 1997; Sam and Bob Mikado, April 14, 1998; Mary Mollet, September 1, 1997; Helen Moorhouse, July 10, 1997; Neil Morie, August 20, 1997; Don Morrison, July 4, 1997; Shirley Morrison, February 8, 1997; Kimiko Murakami, December 17, 1996; Irene Palmer, May 16, 1997; Bob Patterson, April 23, 1997; Iris Pattison, July 22, 1997; Elsy Perks, August 3, 1997; Marian Peters, September 25, 1997; Linda Quiring, August 1 and August 20, 1997; Frank Rainsford, September 11, 1997; Patrick Reilly, July 22, 1997; Bernie Reynolds, August 3, 1997; Oscar Riley, September 5, 1997; Gwen and Lotus Ruckle, April 25 and August 20, 1997; Louise and Arthur Rumsey, October 17, 1997; Maggie and Hank Schubart, September 22, 1997; Wilfrid Seymour, August 3, 1997; Bob Simons, August 20, 1997; Marg Simons, September 1997; David Simson, March 10, 1997; Sheila (Halley) Smith, August 3, 1997; John Stepaniuk, May 12, 1997; Bob and Peggy Tolson, February 7, 1997; Dick Toynbee, July 10, 1997; Tom Toynbee, July 14, 1997; Jessie (Nobbs) Wagg, August 3, 1997; Louise Wolfe-Milner, July 9, 1997, Tom Wright, July 31, 1997.

Index

Shaw family, 230
Shepherd, Horace John, 111
Shepherd family, 93
Shimoji family, 255
Ship's Anchor Inn, 194
Ship's Inn, 194
Shoal harbour, 22
Sidney, 40, 68, 165, 223
Sidney and Islands Review, 150, 153, 276 (*see also* *Saanich Peninsula and Gulf Islands Review*)
Sidney Trading Company, 107
Silvander, Mary, 310
Simons, Bob, 306; Marg, 308, 309
Simson, Harry, 234; Margaret, 234
Singer, F.M., Lumber Company, 202, 205, 206
Sir James Douglas, 98
Slades, A.P., 253
Slingsby, Gladys, 324
Smedley, Fred, 130
Smeeton, Beryl, 183; Miles, 155, 183, 211, 233
Smith, Arnold, 155–56, 157, 232, 283; Emily, 266; Frank, 155–56, 178, 232–33; Jack, 223; Maggie (Mrs. A.J.), 276; Marian (*see* Peters, Marian); Walter, 155–56, 232
Smith family, 178, 232, 233
Smithe, Premier William, 89
Solimar, 221 (*see also* Beaver Point Auto Camp; Lyonesse)
Songhees people, 16, 101, 113
Sooke people, 16
South Salt Spring Island Women's Institute, 231, 235
Southey Point, 38, 55, 202
Southgate, J.J., 70, 71
Sparrow, Babington, 125; Emiek, 106, 209; James, 106; John, 38–39, 67, 95, 114, 125
Sparrow family, 93
Speed, Thomas Frank, 147
Spikerman, Henry, 41, 86, 90, 91, 263
Spikerman family, 93
sports (*see* recreation)
Spotlight, 263, 264, 266, 276
Spotts, Fielding, 59, 69
Springford, Miss, 275
Stark, Louis, 43, 44, 45–46, 50, 53, 58, 59, 60, 63–67, 68, 130, 174; Louise, 67, 68; Sylvia, 42, 44, 45, 53, 57–58, 59, 60, 63–67, 68, 75; Willis, 53, 66, 67, 68, 157, 171
steamer service, 41–43, 98, 112, 114, 115, 139–42, 158, 174 (*see also* transportation)
Steeves, Mike, 214
Stepaniuk, John, 269, 274, 275, 296; Mary, 274

Stephens, James, 39; Samuel Francis, 39
Stevens, Andrew Alexander, 324; Anne, 120, 136, 139, 186, 228; Emma (King), 113, 228; Eva (Jenkins), 120, 228; Henry, 120, 126, 157, 228; John, 13, 113, 228; Walter, 120, 228
Stevens Boarding House, 113, 119, 120, 121, 124, 131, 139, 186
Stewart, Bill, 228; Winifred, 228
Stewart's Lake (*see* Weston Lake)
Stone, Betty, 227
Stone Cutters Bay, 234
Storer, C.P., 166
Stowe Lake (*see* Stowell Lake)
Stowe Lake Park, 323
Stowell Lake, 13
Stuart Island, 22
Sullivan, Mt., 211
Sutherland, Dr. Eva, 234–35
Suttles, Wayne, 18, 22
Sydney Banks Spiritual Foundation, 284–85
Symons, Kyrle, 158, 252

Tahouney family, 111
Takebe, Etsujiro, 259
Tanaka, Alice (Murakami), 260; Ted, 260
Tantramar, 266
Tasaka family, 255
Taylor, Charles, 150
Tegurviei, Mary (*see* King, Mary)
telephone service, 113, 144, 158, 206, 226–27, 273–74, 315
Temmel, Alfred, 324
Texada Island, 214
Texada Logging, 213–14
Thompson, Victoria, 245
Thompson River gold rush, 27, 28
Thurn und Taxis, Prince, 202, 214
Tides Inn, 194
Tolson, Charles W., 129, 130, 136, 138, 234; Evelyn Grace (Wilson), 129, 130, 136, 234; John, 129; Leonard, 117, 120, 126, 129–30, 131, 136, 138, 142, 152, 157, 162, 234, 238, 251
Touhey, Dr. William, 270
tourism, 221–22, 265–66, 303, 323
Toynbee, Albert, 156, 158; Charles, 156, 157, 158; Jessie (Mouat), 126, 149, 163; Manson, 198, 237, 254, 256; Richard, 156, 218, 220, 246
Toynbee family, 289
Trading Company (*see* Salt Spring Island Trading Company)